S0-AFX-846

THE TROUBLE WITH BOYS

The trouble with boys

A WISE AND SYMPATHETIC GUIDE TO THE RISKY BUSINESS OF RAISING SONS

ANGELA PHILLIPS

BasicBooks
A Division of HarperCollinsPublishers

Copyright © 1994 by Angela Phillips.
Published by BasicBooks,
A Division of HarperCollins*Publishers,* Inc.

First published in the United Kingdom in 1993 by Pandora,
An imprint of HarperCollins*Publishers.*

All rights reserved. Printed in the United States of America. No part of
this book may be reproduced in any manner whatsoever without written
permission except in the case of brief quotations embodied in critical
articles and reviews. For information, address BasicBooks, 10 East 53rd
Street, New York, NY 10022-5299.

Designed by Ellen Levine

LIBRARY OF CONGRESS CATALOGING-IN-PUBLICATION DATA
Phillips, Angela.
    The trouble with boys : a wise and sympathetic guide to the risky
business of raising sons / Angela Phillips.
        p. cm.
    Includes bibliographical references and index.
    ISBN 0–465–08734–5 (cloth)
    ISBN 0–465–08735–3 (paper)
    1. Boys. 2. Masculinity. 3. Parenting. 4. Mothers and sons.
5. Fathers and sons. I. Title.
HQ775.P55 1994
649'.132—dc20   94–12656
                                                                    CIP

95 96 97 98 ❖/RRD 9 8 7 6 5 4 3 2 1

CONTENTS

I
THE TROUBLE WITH POWER
*How the need for power in the world imposes its agenda on the
ways boys and men behave*

II
WHATEVER HAPPENED TO MY SWEET BABY?
*The development of boys from birth through the eyes of
parents and other caregivers; the unseen messages that
society uses to tell a boy how to be a man*

III
ALL MEN OF WOMAN BORN
The relationship between mothers and sons

IV
FATHERS AND SONS
How fathers (whether they are present, absent, inadequate, or involved) influence the development of their sons

V
THE POWER OF PEERS
The voices of boys themselves, and of their teachers, on what it feels like to grow up male

ACKNOWLEDGMENTS

There are hundreds of people whose lives thread through the pages of this book. Some took the trouble to talk at length or fill in questionnaires. Others have added wisdom, insight, or anecdote from casual conversations over a kitchen table or a glass of wine. Where their names have been published elsewhere, I have used them. Otherwise I have used pseudonyms, as I promised to do. I am grateful to all of them and hope that they feel that this book represents their feelings and experiences fairly. The discussions I have had with them have all added to my understanding of what it means to grow up male in our society.

There are others also whose help has been absolutely invaluable. Jane Hawksley, Sheila Ernst, and Lynne Segal read early drafts and gave advice and criticism. Charlie Lewis put me on to the academic studies that allowed me to ground my ideas in soundly based research. The work of Mavis Hetherington and Eleanor Maccoby's teams has provided real food for thought, and I hope that I have not taken too many liberties in interpreting their work.

I am grateful, too, to John Gosler for the endless chats and cups of coffee, which make isolated freelance work tolerable, and to

John and Charlie for timely intervention with my ailing computer, and to Michelle Kass for being endlessly enthusiastic about the idea and execution of *The Trouble with Boys,* and to all those wonderful friends who are part of the "village" in which I bring up my children. Last, but most of all, my thanks to my children for being the people they are.

FOREWORD
Robert Coles

We become the particular men and women we are as a consequence of many events and experiences. We are born here, not there, and now, not then; we have a particular woman and man as mother and father, who have handed us ourselves and, through their words and actions, their ideas and ideals, our assumptions and values, our notions of how we ought to look, dress, talk, and behave. This is pure common sense, and yet how hard it can be for us to let the obvious take hold in our minds, so eager can we be to yield our minds to one or another ascendant if not imperial ideology. It is the virtue of this book, published at a time when men and women in the industrial West are struggling to figure out their respective fates and possibilities, that complexity is not shortchanged, that a discussion on "the trouble with boys" isn't permitted to become a harangue or a polemic. Rather, we readers are asked to meet a substantial number of psychologists and sociologists and, very important, plenty of ordinary men and women and children, whose collective voices, written and spoken, tell us, yet again, that human beings are capable of a broad diversity in their appetites, preferences, habits, and inclinations.

Not that the author, a sensitive and sensible English journalist, doesn't address us with a strong point of view. She writes as one convinced that all too many boys grow up to be cold and callous husbands and fathers because they have learned that this is what men should be if they are to be considered by others, by themselves, as true men. She writes with the conviction, in her own words, that the trouble with boys is that all too commonly "the only picture available [to them of what they should be like as grownups] is that of a brute"—and so the brutishness of all too many of us. Yet she also writes as one who appreciates the many forces and pressures at work in shaping sexual identity; and she does not want to ignore the emotional and behavioral differences between boys and girls that continue to puzzle us as we try to sort out nature and nurture, or the importance of history itself as it bears on culture and even biology.

In the midst of a thoughtful discussion of what makes for a "good enough father," the reader is told that "this book is about the current uncertainty in the construction of masculinity"—a nice summary both of a central theme and a challenge: how to live amid obvious perplexity, not to mention the clear shifts in opinion and belief that have taken place in recent years. Unsurprisingly, we are exhorted to change our notion of the desirable, to hope for a different kind of boyhood, to encourage boys to become more openhearted, warm-spirited, gentle, thoughtful of others. The author knows, of course, that not all girls achieve such a goal, even as some boys are already as kindly and empathic as any contemporary parent or psychiatrist might wish them to be. She is addressing a matter that both invites and resists generalizations: the differences that distinguish us because of our sexuality. We are, each of us, individuals for whom gender is but one of many significant aspects of our existence—class, race, nationality, and other significant forces are all at work on a child's growing sense of what is possible or desirable.

At several points in her discussion of how today's men struggle for new personal outlooks and directions, the author mentions Robert Bly, whose cries and songs are familiar to us on this side of the Atlantic. She looks with favorable understanding on his efforts, but I must say I find her line of argument, and too, her manner of presentation, far more instructive, much more becoming. She avoids the shrillness and self-congratulation that can accompany a certain critique of the macho personality as it exerts (still) its influence on so many of us men, who have learned to strut, to pound our fists on platforms and kitchen tables, and alas, to direct them with so much pitiable and abhorrent vehemence at wives and girlfriends, and even children. The vulnerability, pitiable and inexorable, that informs such outbursts of self-insistence, the uncertainty and fear that fuel the "brutishness" the author mentions, in no way serve as excuses, but ought to be comprehended by us as we try to encourage in ourselves and in our children a different way of seeing things, a different way of being.

How well, in that regard, I remember my work (as a hospital resident in child psychiatry) with a bully of a boy, ten years old, who was intimidating his neighborhood friends and his classmates. He started in on me right away, asked me repeatedly why I was spending my time with children, why I wasn't as "tough" as his father (who had abandoned his family, and saw this boy infrequently!). It took us a long time to figure out together what the lad meant by "tough" and, more important, what he feared would happen if he didn't become "tough," if he stopped his relentless pursuit of the bullying stance. Ultimately he and I would have to consider the most basic of questions, one perhaps as much spiritual as psychological: What are we meant to be, what kind of person, and why? One day, my young patient asked me what I had wanted to be when I was his age. Though he had a professional choice in mind, I tried to share with him another perspective, that of my mother, who had told me her idea of what truly mattered: to respect others, to reach out to them with consideration—"a lifetime job," she had declared. I am not saying that my mom's advice took instantly with the young fellow, but I sure remember being glad that she had been the mother she was, that she had given me such advice. And as I read this lively, engaging, and suggestive book, I kept recalling my mother with growing gratitude: in her bones she had a sense of what Angela Phillips and the various witnesses she summons are trying to share with us.

THE TROUBLE WITH BOYS

Introduction

What are little girls made of?
Sugar and spice, and everything nice;
That's what little girls are made of.

What are little boys made of?
Snips and snails, and puppy-dogs' tails;
That's what little boys are made of.

This is a book about boys and how they grow up to be men. It is at the same time an attempt to work out why, in the twenty years in which women have done so much to change themselves, men have changed so little. These themes are inextricably woven together because it is women who give birth to the boys who still grow up expecting to hold the power at home and at work. It is our sons who turn their anger against their communities, just as much as it is our sons who grow up to make and enforce the rules.

This is also a book about love, puzzlement, and, for many mothers, anguish, for those are the things they feel as they watch their sons grow up. Some see their sons almost as creatures from a different planet, and watching this extraterrestrial being come to terms with the experience of living on this planet can be very painful. One of the things that struck me so forcefully as the mother of a son is that growing up male is hard, very hard. Men may still grow up to inherit the earth but they give up a great deal on the way.

I began to see that, for many boys, the process of attaining manhood is a process of desensitization, in which the openness of the small child shrinks further and further into the shell of the man. It is a process from which most mothers feel helpless to protect their sons because it is the means by which their sons separate from them; to hold them back serves only to prolong the agony. They look at the world outside and they feel afraid of what it will do, and yet they know that their sons must go out there.

Fathers could do a great deal to help their sons through this process. They feel far less puzzled because they see their sons doing the things they did when they were young. Why is it that they do so little to help throw light on the subject? Is it because they are rarely there and don't believe the mother's stories of conflict? Or maybe to think about it brings back too painfully their memories of their own struggles to become men. Perhaps it is their own buried experience they are hiding from.

For better or worse, it is against these two poles of influence— the mother and the father, the parent to be "like" and the parent to be "unlike"—that every child must define himself or herself. If there is no mother, or no father, the child will invent one, for every child needs a history through which to create a future. As child psychiatrist Sebastian Kraemer once told me: "Every child has a father in his head."

It is popularly assumed that, by her greater presence, the mother holds the greater power in child rearing. To some extent, and at some times, that is true, but even through his absence a father presents a power that goes largely unchallenged. It is this power (both in two-parent and one-parent families), though she may be unable to name it, that every mother confronts. He is her own father as well as her children's father. His shadow floats beside her. He is the "other": the bearer of pizza at the end of a bad day, the provider of goodies on weekend access visits, or the threat of violence that hangs over her life. He is the alternative against which she will be judged.

A father who is available will have a direct influence on the child who wants to grow up "like Dad" though if Dad is violent, or emotionally absent, it will not be a benign influence. The father who is not there is like a television superhero. He is insubstantial, changeable, and short on words. The more insubstantial this figure seems, the more the child must fill in for himself, and it is that "filling" that is provided by the rest of society: school, the media, and other adults and children. It is that social context that will provide the box of colors from which each child will fill in the blank parts of his or her drawing of life.

Over the last twenty years the social context in which the average girl grows up, in a Western industrialized country, has changed dramatically. No longer will she see women as merely the bearers and carers. In the United States and the United Kingdom, over 70 percent of mothers go out to work. A girl may look at her mother's life and ask herself why it is that, in spite of the fact that both her parents earn money, her mother still does most of the housework. Or she may believe that, in order to be truly female, she must take on this double burden. Either way, she is most unlikely to see a future for herself as simply a house-wife or homemaker.

For boys the situation has not changed in the same way. The men they see around them are not radically different from the men their fathers would have seen. They still expect to hold authority in the family; they still expect to be the main earners and to deter-mine how the family economy will be managed; they still do little housework and spend far less time with their children than their wives do. One study found that, even when both parents work full-time, the mother spends three times as long in sole charge of her children (Brannen and Moss, 1991).

The fact that women are changing has had very little concrete effect, so far, on the behavior of men. It is the changes in the world of work that are having a great impact. As industrial processes are transformed by technology, men are less likely than ever before to be able to live by the sweat of their brows and the strength of their backs. Our industrial heartlands have become wastelands breeding vandals instead of engineers.

Twenty-five years ago a boy living in northeast England would have left school and gone straight into an apprenticeship in one of the massive engineering factories flanking the Tyne River. He would have learned a trade from an older man, who would teach not only his skills but also his way of looking at the world. His transition into work would be a rite of passage into manhood, his first paycheck his initiation ceremony.

He would become part of a tradition with its roots in the labor movement. The union would be his religion, collective organization his creed, the boss and the ruling class his enemy. He would drink in an attitude with his nightly beer, an attitude that says the workingman is king in his own domain.

Today the factories of the Tyne have vanished. The solidly built houses on its banks have been vandalized. People who have lived all their lives in these terraces have fled out of fear for their safety. They have fled from the young men who, as evening draws in, would as soon throw a brick through your car window as say hello.

For these young men there are no apprenticeships, no jobs, and the only rite of passage is that of the first blood drawn. No initiation but that which happens with a girl up against some back-alley wall. There is no union for men without a job, and collective action has been replaced by the creed of consumerism—a creed that positively excludes all those without the cash to buy into it. The enemy is no longer the boss but other men, men who are different: blacks, Jews, queers, men who support a different football team, men from a different neighborhood.

These young men still drink in an attitude with their beers: it says that, by fair means or foul, man must remain king of his own domain. But often there is no domain. A man without a wage has no value in a family system in which wage earning is a man's only function. A woman alone with a baby has the right to social support. Why should she exchange that (meager) financial independence for a life of equal poverty in which the family economy is controlled by someone else?

The romantic answer would be "for love" but research indicates that, contrary to all our myths, women are the less romantic sex, brought up, as we shall see later, to have brightly colored dreams of romance and a down-to-earth expectation that their dreams will not be fulfilled. For them, men are separate, different, and they have been brought up to find emotional solace in a network of relationships with other women and with their children. While women might dream of Prince Charming, they will manage on their own, thank you very much, until he comes along.

It is men, far more than women, who believe in finding the perfect princess, the woman of their own to replace the mother who loved them wholeheartedly and without criticism. This search, admittedly, leads many men out of relationships as fast as it gets them in, because few women want to play mother to their partners and fewer women are prepared to tolerate the violence with which so many men seek to enforce their right to be king in their own home. A 1993 survey found that only 37 percent of men questioned did not see violence as an option to be used against their partners (Mooney).

Women who are more self-sufficient are less likely to put up with abuse and more likely to make demands within a relationship, and this growing confidence has as much to do with the boom in single-parent families as does male fecklessness. Although women are economically disadvantaged by divorce, and considerably less likely to remarry, according to the marriage research organization One Plus One, men suffer psychologically far more when a major relationship breaks down.

I recently heard a middle-aged West Indian man remark bitterly: "A woman only want a man to get a baby. When baby come she don't need a man no more." Social scientist William Julius Wilson traced the so-called decline of the black American family and found that, far from being rooted in slavery, it is rooted far more recently in the soaring joblessness among black American men.

Tracing the number of employed black or white men per every 100 women of the same color and age he finds that, back in the 1950s and early 1960s, black men were no more likely to be unemployed than their white counterparts, and black women seeking a partner had an equally high chance of landing one with job prospects as a white woman. By the mid-1980s only 45 black women out of 100 had any chance of pairing up with an employed black male in his early twenties. By the age of thirty the chances had improved only marginally. At this life stage, there are between 80 and 90 employed white men for every 100 white women.

Without a job what is a man? How does a boy become one? The process taking place along the Tyne and among black American men is repeated wherever heavy "men's work" is disappearing: in Hull, where fishing has been in decline for twenty years and the only available work is packing imported frozen fish; in Scotland, where the shipyards have declined to almost nothing; in Ohio, where the steel industry has been "rationalized"; and all over the former Soviet Union, where heavy, unmodernized industries have given way overnight under the impact of democratization.

In these areas male unemployment remains stubbornly high. Young men raised with the expectation of "men's work," with commensurate wages, are not prepared to stand in lines packing fish. That work can be left to women (working shifts in order to accommodate the child-care responsibilities) or to men from recently arrived immigrant groups who have not yet absorbed the dominant male ideology of their adopted country. A "real man" would rather do nothing than earn a "woman's wage." Increasingly, a "real man" has no place anywhere—either at work or at home. Is it surprising that his domain has become the street? Better to be king of the road in a stolen car than not to be a man. Small wonder, then, that researchers at Southampton University found a strong link between increasing unemployment and a rising male suicide rate.

Those men whose class and education have carved out another route to masculinity have not been spared the uncertainties assailing those from working-class communities. A middle-class man must also find a way of defining his difference, marking out his masculinity, his specialness. He too needs the security of a role in which he is clearly defined as the leader, the top dog in a partnership with women. For him, income and the status symbols that go with it are all-important: the company car, the car phone, the air of continual busyness.

However, there is a problem. A man who sits all day in an office has no obvious right to demand care and consideration from a female partner who is also sitting all day in an office. The work men now do is not radically different from that which women do. How can men be expected to be treated as special, as men have done before, when the things that they are doing are not really special at all?

A new ploy has emerged to provide the necessary difference. Very special and important "man's work" requires them to stay away from home for ever increasing hours. This way men cut themselves off from women, because a woman cannot work such long hours—she has to care for the children. Brannen and Moss's *Managing Mothers* found that men almost always work longer hours than their wives, and the longer a wife's hours, the longer her partner's would be. In marking out this separation, men are taking themselves ever further from their children, leaving their sons more and more to imagine, and less actually to see, when they invent their own futures.

The efforts of men to maintain the status quo are beginning to show signs of strain. In spite of the lack of practical change in the balance of power in the world and the family, there is undoubtedly a growing air of anxiety. In their effort to change themselves, women have started to shift the basis of the world in which men, and masculinity, have managed to survive for so long unchanged.

Some men, feeling what they believe to be the rug being pulled out from under them, are frightened and angry; they will try to hang on to the rug, they will try to shake off the women who are tripping them up, and, in their rage, they will hit out at women individually and collectively.

We will get more men like George Hennard, who wrote, before killing fourteen women in a Texas cafeteria: "Please give me the satisfaction of some day laughing in the face of all those, mostly white, treacherous female vipers who tried to destroy me and my family." We will get more writers like Neil Lyndon, who turns his own confusion against women and the feminism that "divided my generation, effectively disempowering and disenfranchising its members."

Both these men, in their different ways, are clutching the rug of male power as it moves beneath them. They are afraid of a future in which men will have to play a different part. They are too afraid to see that the way forward for men lies in going along with change, not in fiercely defending the status quo. Like boys frozen in an eternal adolescence, they will oppose change proposed by women, just as they defied their mothers in order to define themselves as not-women.

Men won't change just because women wish it. Nor can they change simply by willing it themselves. The process that created masculinity also formed society as we understand it and, in turn, society forms new men in the same image. Significant change cannot come without an understanding of that mold of gender, class, and culture that turns a boy into a man.

This book is not a recipe for better boys; it is an attempt to start untying the knot of masculinity and looking for the road signs that may help parents, and others concerned with young people, to mark out a new road for boys to follow, one that will allow them to recognize that they don't need to be better than girls in order to be men and that masculinity can be just as variable as femininity has become.

I

THE
TROUBLE
WITH POWER

1

Boys in Trouble

What is it about men that creates, in one group, the thirst for power and, in another, the thirst for destruction? Why is it that, although men still control governments, industry, and the law, one man in three (in Britain) will have committed a crime by the age of thirty? Why do men so outnumber women among the down-and-outs while, at the same time, they still earn, on average, 25 percent more than women do for an hour's work?

If men run society in their own interests, why are our jails full of men? Why are men more often victims of violence than women? Why are more men than women murdered? Why is it that more men than women take the desperate way out by killing themselves, and why do so many take out their frustration and despair on the women to whom they also turn for comfort?

If power is in the interests of men, why are so many men emotionally disconnected? Why do nearly one of every two divorced men sever the emotional connection with their own children as soon as the connection with the children's mother is dissolved? Men may have power in the world but it looks increasingly as though the flip side of power is abject failure. When it comes to the scrap heap it is the men who are piled on fastest and in the greatest numbers.

Our politicians like to look at lawlessness, rioting, the destruction of communities, as a simple matter of bad behavior and lack of moral fiber. We are told to believe that a bit more policing, a little less "nannying" by the welfare system, and these young men would be back on their feet acting as responsible citizens. The reality seems to me to be that, as youth unemployment climbs above 17 percent, an increasing number of young men no longer believe that they have a stake in society, and if they don't belong inside the society that created them, then why should they respect its rules?

Unemployment is also a problem for women, but lack of paid work, or the threat of it, does not have the same effect on women as it has on men. Girls and young women may sink under the weight of their own disappointment and depression, but they don't smash up the society that fails to recognize their value. Is it just because girls are brought up to be good? I doubt it. I believe it is because girls are less likely to feel that they need to have power in the world in order to be important to someone. A girl can also make herself important through relationships, and particularly through becoming a mother. A boy learns that relationships depend on money and power.

Boys learn early that a father is there mainly to make money. This is what a nine-year-old South London schoolboy had to say about what fathers are for:

> I think men seem to think that women are for looking after children. I think men can look after children but they don't seem to think that's what they are for. They think they are for money. I don't know if I'm going to be different. I might be the only one with a job—or I might not be able to get one.

After a discussion about what fathers and mothers do, this boy and his friends agreed that they would like to stay home with children instead of going out to work. One of them added:

> I would like to look after children because otherwise, you might feel rather lonely, on your own. 'Cause the rest of your family are all having a nice time at home while you've got to go to work and leave them.

This child was already affected by anxiety about his future role. He has grasped that one part of being different from girls is having to be apart and earn money. Of course he knows that in most families women do that too, but mothers don't derive their status only from earning—they also look after children. He is less certain that a father who doesn't earn has the right to stay home and look after the children. He has learned that mothers have an automatic right to a place in the family. Fathers are destined to be lonely. They have to buy their way in and they can fail.

A thirteen-year-old wrote: "My fears of the future are: being homeless without a job, begging for money on the streets, and I'm afraid that no one will care for me when I am older and my Mum dies."

Many young men deal with this anxiety by denigrating parenthood and family life. If marriage is a trap and motherhood represents drudgery, failure to conform is another name for freedom. But most do look forward to a time when they will have their own woman to cater to their needs, just like Mom did, and they know that that means being a wage earner.

For some the fear of failure in the world is a spur to greater effort. For others it is too big a weight to bear. For a significant minority it may seem easier to find an alternative way of being a man: opting out, hanging out on the street corner, or numbing the empty feeling in the pit of your stomach with drugs. For some,

failure starts early, as soon as society starts sorting children into
those who will rule, those who will be ruled, and those who are
destined for the scrap heap.

THE EDUCATIONAL LOTTERY

The orthodox way to success in our society is through education.
The school system is not only a way of increasing knowledge; it is
also a gateway to adult life. Academic achievement is not the only
criterion of success; those who do extremely well academically
may well be less successful than those who put more effort into
making relationships, but for a boy to get on in the world he needs
to believe in the possibility of his own success.

In the past, society protected boys to some extent from the
consequences of failure by peddling the myth that boys were
smarter than girls. They had to compete with each other but they
didn't expect to have to compete also with girls. They were destined for different roles, and different lives, and those different
expectations were built into the system. Before the introduction
of comprehensive education, all British children took a test at the
age of eleven. Girls did better but more boys got into the academically oriented grammar schools because there were more places
for them.

Selection is by its very nature a boost to confidence. Children
who are selected as the cream already have an edge on those who
are deemed "failures." With more places in selective schools, by
the age of sixteen boys were marginally ahead of girls in the overall
attainment of higher-grade exam passes at sixteen years old. In
mathematics the discrepancy was far greater. In 1967, boys were
37 percent ahead of girls, and there were almost twice as many
boys as girls going to college. By discriminating against girls, society was able to allow more boys to join the winning team.

Boys who were less academic followed different routes, most of which were also exclusively male. They could get an apprentice-ship, learn a trade, or turn their greater muscle power to use in laboring jobs. They wouldn't be rich but the future held some cer-tainty. Over the last twenty years, women have started to demand an equal role in the world, and equal education to prepare them for it, and at the same time the nonacademic routes into work have irrevocably changed.

Now boys are competing not only with other boys for academic success, and a place in the world, but with girls too. Men still have the advantage at work, they still earn more, still dominate power structures; but the route to that place is not as simple as it used to be. Being a boy is no longer an automatic passport to economic independence.

The educational changes have had some clear advantages for all children. With the introduction of comprehensive education the overall attainment level of all children has risen (contrary to com-mon myth). More working-class children finish their education with useful educational qualifications. But progress has been much faster for girls. In 1987, 17.9 percent more sixteen-year-old girls achieved higher-grade exam results than they had in 1967. They were now 6.6 percentage points ahead of the boys. Boys still did better at math, but that gap in attainment had halved. Between 1977 and 1987 the percentage of girls with higher grades had risen by 35 percent in math, 84 percent in physics, and 89 per-cent in chemistry.

By 1991 the examinations had been changed, taking account of new teaching methods brought in over the past decade. The areas of math and science in which boys had always excelled were now being taught in ways that would appeal more to girls. Now girls were ten percentage points ahead in overall attainment and were almost level in math. Boys are still far more likely to specialize in science and technology, but in the compulsory, combined science exam boys and girls are now about equal. At the advanced-level exams, taken at the age of eighteen, girls, overall, now do better than boys.

This evidence shows clearly that, at least in school, girls more than hold their own. In just twenty-five years of feminist activity, the general academic attainment levels of girls and boys have reversed. It is no longer possible to argue that boys are innately smarter, though there is one area in which boys are still ahead. It is in the expensive, elite, boys' private schools, where a select group of young men expect to get high grades and go on to the best universities, from where they will step directly onto the ladders of power several rungs higher than everyone else. These boys are not representative of a higher male intellect; they are actually bucking the general trend for higher attainment among girls.

Just as girls have reacted to the news that they have equal rights by achieving more, boys in those exclusive single-sex schools, which still peddle an idea to their pupils that they are being educated to run the world, will also achieve what is expected of them. These are the sons of men whose material success has allowed them to pay very large fees for private education. They may not see their fathers very often but they do know that Daddy is powerful—and power rubs off.

The finding that, in general, girls are doing better educationally is not unique to the United Kingdom. A recent study (Hetherington, 1992, p. 57) found that, among the stable, middle-class American families used as a baseline with which to compare divorced and remarried families, parents reported that girls at the ages of eleven and twelve were "more scholastically competent" than boys of the same age. Among black Americans the discrepancy is much greater, and in this group the greater expectations of girls cross the higher-education barrier. About twice as many black girls as black boys will graduate from college.

The greater success of girls is still not reflected in the world of work, where men still move faster into positions of power and women are still held back. (The reasons will be looked at in the last section of this book.) However, while men still hold power at the top, further down the ladder boys and men seem to be running into trouble and, where school failure for girls is a rather private affair, when a boy fails he makes himself felt.

THE FLIP SIDE OF SUCCESS

In any competitive system someone has to lose. But, as the built-in bias that boosted the success of boys starts to be dismantled, it looks as though boys are failing in larger numbers than girls.

In the United States, children who don't fit into the mainstream education system are sent to "special education," a euphemism for failure. In special ed, black children are massively overrepresented, but it would be a mistake to see their color as the major issue. Eighty-five percent are also male. In the United Kingdom the pattern is very similar. Boys labeled as behaviorally and emotionally disturbed outnumber girls by four to one. In the British inner cities, where toughness in men is prized above academic success, the all-male comprehensive schools lag behind the comprehensive schools for girls in grades and, across the country, there are nearly 25 percent more boys than girls who fail to obtain any grades at all.

Male failure starts early. Standard assessment tests, at seven years old, reveal that in communication skills girls are way ahead, and in math and science there are a roughly equal number of high achievers. However, in every single category, boys outnumber girls among the children who are below average. These tests are supposed to show which children need help to come up to standard, but what they also show, to the children themselves, is who has succeeded and who has "failed." Young children do not like to fail and they certainly don't like to have their failure pointed out to them.

If, at the age of seven, a child is already being told he is a failure, he may well go on to fulfill that promise. If, at eleven, others seem to be coping well with things he cannot do, he may put his feet on the desk, say he is bored, and pretend he doesn't care. If he is not then powerfully motivated to opt in, he may well decide to opt out. Better to fail magnificently than to fail ignominiously. Girls also fail (particularly if they live in a community in which they are expected to put their energy into catching a man to earn for them, rather than earning for themselves), but boys fail in larger numbers. I hear far more stories of boys with potential who look at the way the cards are stacked and decide that, if they can't win, they would rather not play.

The children most likely to fail are those who have the least to gain from conforming. They are the children who feel that the education system holds nothing useful for them. Some may opt out by destroying themselves, while others, seeing that nothing is to be gained by cooperation, build alternative systems in which they can have the power that has been denied to them.

The National Children's Bureau report *Highlight on Violence, Disruption and Vandalism in Schools* (1977) found that "pupils unable to achieve academic distinction turn to bullying and disruption as a way of gaining attention and status." In a study of bullying carried out in 1978 (Lowenstein, 1978) boys were found to be four times as likely as girls to be responsible for physical attacks and also far more likely to be victims of attacks. The effect of intimidation is to drag other children down to the same level of powerlessness, through fear. A child who lives in fear is unable to learn. The bully has then reduced his victim to his own dysfunctional level. Some children make deliberate attempts to harden themselves against physical attack and become bullies themselves.

Tom spent most of his school life paralyzed with fear. He tried to harden himself by joining his tormentors; he tried to harden his body with hours of weight training. Now in his early twenties, he has no qualifications and no prospects. He says of his experience in school:

I had been a bit of a nerd at primary school so when I started secondary I dressed up like a little skinhead. At first the older kids thought it was quite funny. They would talk to me and that made me feel quite good. But then I got into difficult situations where I was expected to fight. I hated it. I hated school. It was so violent. One day I just said, "I'm not going to school." I just stayed home in bed. I suppose I was depressed.

Tom talked for hours to his parents. Neither of them seemed able to find a way of supporting him, but at least he is still alive to tell the tale. Suicide is now third only to road deaths and cancer as a cause of death for people under twenty-five. In 1990, 591 people under the age of twenty-five killed themselves; 80 percent of them were male, a total that rose by 78 percent during the 1980s. Girls are just as likely to be unhappy but they are less successful at killing themselves and, crucially, far more likely to seek out someone to talk to about the way they feel. Boys abide by the vow "Thou shall not snitch" literally unto the death.

For others, self-destruction is slower. Registered male drug addicts outnumber female drug addicts by more than three to one. Boys and girls may be as likely to dabble with drugs, but boys, it seems, are more likely to make drug abuse a chosen life style. (When women do get addicted, it is often to drugs that have been prescribed rather than street drugs.)

Taking drugs is a useful adaptation if the important thing is to avoid being confronted with your failure. It is a way of simply avoiding dealing with the world, of which success is such an important part. Others don't take avoiding action but simply collapse under the strain of conflicting demands. Boys under the age of fifteen are twice as likely as girls to be admitted to psychiatric units.

DOOMED TO FAIL

Educational failure may well be merely a side effect of a life without enough parental care and support. Some of these children will have been abused, abandoned, and humiliated as children, but even among the most unhappy, who end up in the care of the local authorities, the girls are far more likely than the boys to find a way out for themselves.

A social worker, reviewing his caseload of adolescents who had spent their teenage years in care, realized, on reflection, that the young people who were living relatively stable lives by their early twenties were all girls. Two had even made it to college. The boys were in and out of prison, sleeping on the streets, or otherwise subsisting in the margins of society.

The discrepancy is partly due to the fact that girls keep their failure to themselves. As adults, women are more often admitted into psychiatric units than men, and are twice as likely to be admitted for depression. However, those men who do suffer as adults from mental health problems are more likely to fall through the social net.

MIND, the British mental health organization, has found that single men are far more likely to suffer from mental health problems than married ones, whereas the level of distress varies little between single and married women. This has been interpreted as evidence that marriage protects men from mental breakdown but has no similar protective effect for women. It could equally well indicate that a man with a mental health problem is less likely to marry and that loneliness simply compounds his feeling of alienation.

If a man fails to make money he is excluded from a male peer group that depends on beer (or other drugs) to lubricate friendship. Without the money for a pint he has no right of entry. If he uses his money to buy his place at the bar, he may well threaten his place in the home. Many mothers on welfare prefer to manage alone rather than share their homes with a man who adds nothing to the family income, but still seeks to control it. Hilary Graham, writing on "women's poverty and caring" (Glendinning and Millar, 1987), found that "not only may women feel economically better off as lone mothers, but they may also (and relatedly) find it easier to cope with their poverty."

For men, far more than for women, failure as a breadwinner may lead directly to homelessness. Housing is obtained through the knowledge of how to operate the housing system, having the money to enter it through the private sector, or, in the U.K., having children in your care, and it is overwhelmingly women who care for children. A single adult who has no income, no job, and no means of raising the deposit necessary to secure private accommodation has no legal right to be housed, and the difference in the relationships of men and women to children is reflected in the fact that men greatly outnumber women among those in homeless shelters or sleeping on the streets.

Suicide figures show how far the bitter taste of failure can take a man. During the recession of the 1980s the suicide rates for men in Scotland (with particularly high levels of unemployment) rose by 75 percent. In 1988, the male suicide rate outnumbered that for women by 125 to 45 per million.

BEING BAD

For every boy who accepts failure and opts out, through fear or through self-destruction, there are many more who refuse to accept this verdict and turn their anger against the rest of the world by being "bad" and kicking against authority. Those most likely to choose this route are the young men who recognize early on that society does not provide for them a place in which they can legitimately exhibit their power. These young men are not maladaptive. They are in a sense adapting too well. They have learned that men should have power and, knowing that they cannot get that power within the system, they build a parallel system of their own in which to rule.

Indeed, the word *bad* has itself been subverted to mean all that is strong, brave, and hard. To be *bad* is to be masculine. Bad boys need to show that they are also hard. They need to let others know that they can't be messed with but, unlike bullies, they may choose not to use violence—until it is necessary to prove a point.

When a girl "gets into trouble," the trouble will almost always be of a sexual nature, and she is the one who is most likely to pay the price: she may get pregnant or get diseased (and, with the exception of AIDS, sexually transmitted diseases are more serious for women than they are for men). Boys get into crime. They are nearly six times as likely as girls to be cautioned or found guilty of indictable offenses (criminal statistics of England and Wales). In the peak age group for crime (between seventeen and twenty) the disproportion is even greater. Fifteen- and sixteen-year-old boys are sixty times more likely to be imprisoned than girls of the same age.

Graham is black and twenty years old. Of the ten or so boys he hung around with at school, eight have spent time in prison. He was the one who really believed what the teachers at school had told him: "I thought if I worked hard at school I could get a good job in computers. I thought that color and class had nothing to do with it." At college he discovered that people like him were destined to fill the dreary, repetitive jobs. The exciting work, and the high salaries, would be going to people with qualifications that he had never even heard of: white people.

His friends with their dead-end jobs and hustling had money. As a penniless student he felt an outsider. He had nothing to spend, no way of joining the glittering world where what you wear is who you are, and he no longer believed that the legitimate route, of hard work and exams, would get him there, either sooner or later. So he dropped out of college and joined his buddies, hustling for what he could get.

A year of unemployment followed. He felt marginalized and depressed but, instead of joining his friends in prison, he started to read:

I learned all these things I wasn't taught at school. I realized that I had been totally brainwashed. School does nothing to teach about racism and why, as a black person, you feel so alien, because we all do, every black person does. You feel so restricted. You have so much potential as a human being but there is no way to express it. People don't understand, they say: "He's got a chip on his shoulder." But a black person is always asking himself who he is and where does he belong.

Graham believes that he found his way because he learned to look inside himself for values rather than judging himself, and his peers, by their external trappings. He doubts whether he would have been able to find this route if he had not been firmly rooted in a family in which he felt loved. He recognized something that many of the world's hard men fail to understand: he cared about being cared for. It has become a cliché, but the fact remains: power may get money but it won't buy love. He decided that connecting with people was more important to him than dominating them. But he had at least had the kind of family life that taught him what love feels like.

Boys who fall foul of their families during adolescence may just keep on falling. Michael (he prefers to use an English name) came to England from East Africa when he was thirteen. Within a year he had been placed in a children's home because of his uncontrollable behavior. He said:

I remember at five years old I got knocked over on my way back from school with my sister. I had blood coming out of my mouth and I was crying. Not because I was hurt but because I was afraid that my father would hit me. From the age of about seven my only memory of my father is of him getting his belt out to beat me. I think he hated me. I could see it in his eyes.

By the age of twelve he was big enough to hit back and the fight grew fiercer. The only saving grace had been his mother.

> I always believed that my mother would be on my side but, when the crunch came, she betrayed me. She and my father went to the social services. My mother didn't intervene. I felt that she had rejected me. I was taken into care for four weeks and at the end I told them I wanted to stay. I didn't want any contact with my parents. I didn't like my father, and my mother had betrayed me.

Those first four weeks were, as he now sees it, a "honeymoon." Then there was a change of staff and Michael found himself living with a regime of arbitrary violence. Nobody took any interest in him. No one had any expectations. His violent behavior was met with a greater level of violence, so that he learned to channel his rage into breaking windows rather than hitting people. He had arrived in England with high expectations of a good education. In the children's home he soon learned that there were other ways of making money.

Since leaving he has been fired from three jobs, one for fraud, one for fighting, and one because, on having been searched on suspicion of theft, he turned out to be carrying drugs. He also gambles—in fact, he will try almost anything that might make money, and he feels that fraud is really just another way of doing business. In his mind, "money is everything." It isn't surprising, really, because money is about the only thing in his life that seems capable of retaining its value.

Looking back, Michael feels that the social workers were wrong to have taken him away from home. Certainly the children's home provided him with no greater safety and succeeded only in undermining the only relationship that actually mattered to him. It might have helped if a foster home had been found for him. Unfortunately, foster parents are not keen on taking in boys, let alone Asian boys. A teenage girl stands a much higher chance; a boy is too likely to get into trouble. So these vulnerable, unhappy children are forced to resort to their peers, many of whom have been similarly damaged.

Michael's hatred of his father is, paradoxically, the thing that keeps him from arbitrary violence. He will hit if he is angry, but he is not so damaged by the violence of his childhood that he has adopted it as a way of life. He doesn't want to be in any way like the father he despises. He would like to get married and have children but, he says: "If I have kids I'm worried that they wouldn't love me and that I might turn out like my father."

There is still something inside Michael that is soft and reachable. He knows that, too often, his impulsive generosity is an attempt to buy love. He knows that love cannot really be bought, but at least he still thinks love worth having. Perhaps it was the continuing support of an older sister, or the occasional more enlightened social worker, that kept him in touch with the possibility of feeling. It may even have been that, as one of the only Asian boys in the homes he lived in, he was actually protected, by the level of racism he experienced, from identifying too closely with the others in his group and adopting their hard veneer.

For too many others, being taken care of becomes rather less important than being respected. What they want is the respect that is reserved for those who have power. For these young men, the pull toward the power and apparent wealth of the criminal world may be irresistible. In this parallel society, power is not vested in the hands of the state but in the hands of the person who is not afraid to take it. Writer Michael Brown sees this alternative image of masculine power as:

How much pain and violence you can inflict on another person;

How many girls you can impregnate and not get married;

How much reefer you can smoke, pills you can drop, and
wine you can drink;

How many times you can go to jail and come out "un-
rehabilitated";

What kind of clothes you wear;

How much money you have;

What kind of car you drive. [Brown, 1976, p. 6.]

Brown was talking about black Americans, but his painful definition could apply equally well to any young man living in a society in which men learn to define their difference from women by
demonstrating their power and wealth, and where paid work is
denied to them. I talked to a mother in the depressed northeast of
England, where a generation of young men has grown up without
ever seeing their fathers working. It is the mothers who try to keep
the community together, but their sons are turning on them. They
see the women who are fighting to keep the community going as
representatives of an authority that they totally reject. She told me:

It started with verbal abuse from the kids. Now most people
are afraid to go out at night, and more and more people are
leaving the area. Two years ago there were 75 empty houses.
Now there are 475. There is a hard core of fourteen- to nine-
teen-year-olds and usually an older man, about twenty-five
or thirty, who encourages them.

It's dead hard keeping your kids away from street culture.
These boys belong with each other. They bond to each other.
They brag about how they get away with what they do. They
do it for status and the girls stand and watch, then they get
pregnant and provide a place for the lads to hang out.

At one time you would get a job after school. Now there
are no jobs. These kids are ground down with poverty. They
spend their lives on the streets or watching TV and seeing
the advertisements for running shoes and electronic goods.

They hear, so the story goes, that they can make up to £300 a week with petty thieving and far more through organized crime. These kids see that as a legitimate goal.

Status in the community comes not only from greater economic power. These young "hard men" also derive power from the admiration of their peers, and it is the boys who steal the cars who get the girls. Young women who have no status of their own can only bask in the reflected glory of the men in whose company they are seen—until they have a child of their own and become mothers themselves, with a different tale to tell of the hard men.

I met one young woman aged sixteen who already had a child and another was on the way. The father of her children is her brother-in-law. He cannot decide which sister he prefers, so he makes use of both of them and he doesn't do so discreetly. This young woman is so starved for affection that she will accept any crumb of comfort, however much it humiliates her. The young man turns his self-loathing on her and all the other women he abuses. She thinks he loves her, because she has never experienced love and doesn't know what it feels like. From this unpromising home her children will, in their turn, play out on the streets, watch the television peddling dreams, and then look for a means to make their dreams come true.

The disenfranchised use violence to get the money with which they can fulfill the promise held out on television. Another group of young men, those who did jump through the hoops set out for them, often find themselves in jobs that provide them with money, yet they still find that they have no status. They have been good boys, they have done what Mother asked—now they are waiting for the prize. They want to be recognized as people with power in society. While they are waiting, they are inclined to demonstrate their power in other ways.

In an article (3 August 1989) entitled "Holiday Island Where British Means Brutish," Nick Cohen of the *Independent* interviewed a British tourist in Spain who said: "You can do what you want. Get pissed, fight and if you're lucky get a woman. But keep away from Spaniards. I hate them. They've got shit teams." He was flying the flag for his country and his sex and proving that the Brits are "hard men."

RESPECT AND THE MAN

The boys who are bad have recognized that hard men are not pushed around. They don't want to be pushed around and so they harden up. The power structures they create are a mirror image of the structures in the legitimate world, where it is just as important to have power if you don't want to be pushed around. Those men who crave the sense that they can be "on top" may, like the tourists in Spain, use their two-week vacation pretending to be powerful by throwing their weight around in a place where they are unlikely to be called to account. Others have real power in the world, the power that is vested in the state or the financial institutions of the industrialized world.

These men may be generals or presidents or heads of corporations, but their values may differ from those of Michael Brown's list only by the fact that their power has been come by legitimately. They too have been through a process of socialization that has hardened them and cut them off from meaningful relationships. They also see cars and clothes as badges of rank, and women as commodities to be used and abused.

The similarity in the behavior of men who are successful inside and outside society occasionally becomes crystal-clear. The entertainment industry and its close ally, the press, like nothing better than the opportunity to glamorize hard men. It is here that we see the way in which the legitimate hard men prop up the status of the illegitimate: two sides of the same coin.

Sometimes the two sides come together to do business. After the 1992 riots in Los Angeles, in which rival gangs all but destroyed the neighborhoods they live in, Martin Walker wrote a feature for the *Guardian* (30 May 1992) titled "LA Gangs Give Peace a Chance." This is the opening paragraph:

> The scars on his hand and his arm and the long furrow across Clyde Barrow's scalp are the visible marks of bullets he has taken during his 17 years in a Los Angeles gang. There are five more bullet scars on his body, but his hands are gentle as he picks up the toddler from the basement floor, wipes the bottle on his immaculate white T-shirt and sniffs warily at the child's rump.

No, he doesn't proceed to change the child's diaper, but hands him over to his mother, "a pretty girl with long fingernails and thick gold chains at her neck." Clearly in awe of the power of the man with scars, the long list of convictions, and the pretty girl, Walker then goes on to write about the gang leader's vision for making peace in Los Angeles, providing "security patrols" for rebuilt shops, and quotes their demands, that

> our communities are patrolled and policed by individuals who live in the community and the commanding officers be 10-year residents of the communities in which they serve. Former gang members shall be given a chance to be patrol buddies in assisting the protection of the neighborhoods.

At no point does Walker appear to spot the irony in giving the job of law enforcement to the people who are mainly responsible for terrorizing the community. He clearly believes that there are two equal forces at work—the power of the hoods against the power of the state—and that it is reasonable for the two groups of hard men to make treaties with each other over the corpse of their bleeding community. More than that, this attitude buys into the racist assumption that all black people understand is violence, and that the power these men have taken by force gives them a legitimate status as community leaders.

It was a similar reverence for hard men that gave the Mafia its grip in Italy. Mafia men there do indeed have power, and they have used it, but it would be hard to suggest that they have used it for the good of their communities. Charles Richards wrote in the *Independent on Sunday* (31 May 1992) about a funeral service after the death of an anti-Mafia campaigner:

> Quietly at first, fighting back the sobs, Rosario Costa began to speak. It was meant to be a short prayer, but it became a poignant statement of the despair of many Sicilians and their feelings of being abandoned by the state.
>
> "Jesus said on the cross, forgive them for they know not what they do. To the men in the Mafia who are certainly here within these walls even if they are not Christians, I want to say that I can forgive them." Her voice rising, she went on: "But you must get on your knees, if you have the courage to change." And then the searing, despairing lament: "But they never change."

In Italy the hard men live on the other side of a legal system that fails to reach them. In Eastern Europe, Northern Ireland, Angola, and the Middle East, the hard-man mentality has been grafted onto the twin cancers of nationalism and religious fundamentalism. These men kill and rape not for self-glorification but for a cause. They fight because they want their team to win. They have followed the call, which tells them that a real man strikes the first blow: for his home, his team, his country.

It's a message that has been swallowed even by as mild-mannered a person as self-improvement guru Robin Skynner, who wrote (*Guardian,* 19 December 1992) of man's innate aggression: "First as a hunter, killing animals to feed the family; and second, as a warrior defending mother and children, and the social group against aggressors. Violence is, or was, what he was for." Maybe they believe that they really are protecting women and children, but without these hard men there would be no need for protection. Every child who dies in a war is dying because a man somewhere has decided that the children on his team are more important than the children on some other man's team.

The world would be a better place without hard men, but it will take a revolution in thinking to change the way in which men are made. Hard men do not make themselves. Lessons in violence, indifference, and separation are provided every day for every male child. Learning them is a part of learning to survive as a boy, and unlearning them is a great deal to expect of anyone who has to make his way in a competitive and class-ridden world. As Herb Goldberg puts it (Goldberg, 1976, pp. 43–44): "The man who 'feels' becomes inefficient because he gets emotionally involved and this inevitably slows him down and distracts him. His more dehumanized competition will then surely pass him by."

Our sons are growing up in a world in which it helps to be less human. Few of them will turn into murderers, but most of them will have learned by the age of ten that the world expects them to "toughen up." The gun-toting drug barons and their couriers who terrorize housing projects are products of a system that believes it is better for a boy to hit the person who upsets him than it is for him to cry. So are the men who need to drink before they can allow themselves to feel, and those who kill themselves rather than confess that they have lost their jobs. The process is so effective that few of our boys escape it entirely, nor will they, unless we understand more clearly just what it is they are facing.

II

WHATEVER HAPPENED TO MY SWEET BABY?

2

In the Beginning
There Are Babies

The making of a man starts from the moment of birth, or even before then, when the eye of the ultrasound scanner picks up the shadow that marks out a boy baby and Granny starts knitting in blue instead of pink. In many cultures the birth of a boy is overtly celebrated as a matter of more significance than that of a girl. A Pakistani friend told me that her husband had been considered very odd when he chose to celebrate the birth of a girl with the same show as he had the birth of his son.

Fathers in less traditional societies may not be able to make an overt display of their pleasure when they father a son, but surveys of fathers' behavior (Lewis, in Hargraves and Colley, 1986) show that they still tend to take more interest in their male babies than in their female babies. They stay longer in the delivery room, handle them more, ask more questions about them, and stimulate them more. Girl babies are cuddled; boy babies are stimulated.

The research doesn't show nearly as much difference in the way mothers handle their different sex children as in the way fathers do after the first few weeks. To begin with, mothers tend to touch their daughters more than their sons—though they take care not to do so in the presence of their husbands—and they are also more likely to stimulate their daughters and to cuddle their sons, but after this early period the major difference lies in the fact that boys tend to be breast-fed for longer.

The similarity in the mothers' handling of boys and girls may lie in the fact that the physical demands of a small baby take up most of a mother's time. She doesn't differentiate her behavior because it is the baby who sets the pace of her care. A crying baby needs to be soothed no matter what its sex. Someone who only plays with a baby when it is clean, fed, and happy is more likely to initiate communication rather than simply responding to needs.

Nevertheless, while mothers may handle their small babies the same way, many express a very early sense of their sons as "different" and their daughters as extensions of themselves. One mother said to me: "I never expected to be the mother of sons. I don't know anything about boys." Another said: "My first sight of him was as very separate. My first thought was that he was very self-confident." I was reminded of my own first thoughts about my son that it wasn't me who knew how to feed him. He knew and showed me himself.

A newborn baby has no way of knowing that it is a separate being. As far as it is concerned, the body of its mother is an extension of its own body. When the baby cries this body is there. It is the difference between the person who mainly cares for the baby and other adults who come and go that helps the baby to understand both that people are separate creatures with their own boundaries and that people can leave—and come back.

The process of learning their separateness takes place between the ages of six months and eighteen months. At the same time the baby is also absorbing information about its gender. Indeed, some studies suggest that children as young as twelve months old can tell whether a strange child is male or female and will favor the child of the same sex (Kujawski, 1984, quoted in Hargraves and Colley, 1986, p. 110). Most parents will testify that, once words come, they will very soon be used to divide and codify the world: big, little; boy, girl; man, woman.

For a girl, the road at first seems simple and straight. She realizes very early on that she is to become a woman. A woman is what her mother is. She is going to become a mother just like her own. She will be powerful, loving, and wise. Later she may come to understand that her father has a greater power, out in the world; but in these first few years identification with the mother means that she is firmly rooted. She has already identified her future— she simply has to grow into it.

For a boy, the way ahead is not so simple. He learns that the person who leaves (if he has a resident father at all) is the person he is going to be like. He is not going to grow up to be like Mommy. For the girl, the moment of recognition is also a moment of power. For the boy, it is a moment of uncertainty. Even in families in which both parents go out to work, the mother is, almost always, the biggest and most important person in his universe, but he will never be like her. His destiny is to be different. He is going to grow up to be a man, and from the moment he discovers this difference the search is on to discover the elements of masculinity.

If his father is accessible he will provide him with a sense of what it is to be male. He will play rougher games, talk to him differently, offer him "appropriate" toys. However, in most families the father is rarely available, and in an increasing number of families he is not available at all. So the things that the father does are distant, remote, difficult. While a girl finds, in these early years, an easily available model of what it is to be female, her brother is floundering. In the first two years he is much the same as the girls he sees, but in order to be a boy he must define his difference from them. He starts looking for clues.

Research indicates that, even in the very first year of life, boys tend to be more exploratory, whereas girls are more "person-oriented" (Hargraves and Colley, 1986, p. 110). Yet these little explorers are also more anxious and more easily upset when the object of their exploration proves frustrating. Perhaps this little boy is searching for himself, for the person he is going to be, whereas the little girl stays close to Mother (or a female caregiver), the living model of her future. Indeed, it is the inherent difficulty of this search for masculinity that, according to psychoanalyst Robert Stoller, is the reason why there are so many more men than women who grow up biologically normal and yet feel themselves to belong to the opposite sex (transsexuals).

The first clues are the easy ones. He finds that he has a little thing at the front that makes him different from girls. Depending on the culture he comes from, quite a lot of fuss may be made of this little thing. It will be given a name, it may be played with while his diaper is being changed. It may be the object of interested comment. It is outside his body, easy to see, and, what is more, feels interesting.

Soon he will start picking up other clues. If there is a man around his house he will gravitate toward him. Fathers tend to play more with their sons than with their daughters and, when they do play, tend to play more physical rough-and-tumble games. For most boys the intervention of the father is an event. Most of the time he is not there. In his absence, his mother and the other women who care for him have to provide verbal evidence of what a man is. Marianne Grabrucker, in her diary of her daughter's first three years (Grabrucker, 1988), noticed that mothers of boys were constantly referring to their "manliness":

> Whenever Martin has managed a little crap in the loo, it's praised as being just like a man's; if Martin has hurt himself and bleeds a little, it's described as being real man's blood; at mealtimes he's told to eat his food, just like a man, just like Daddy. . . . No one has ever told Aneli that she should eat up her food like a real woman.

Grabrucker sees this as part of the way in which a boy learns that men are more powerful. However, it could also be seen as one of the only ways in which mothers can present an image of the male to a boy who rarely sees his father. It isn't necessary to tell Aneli that she will grow up to be a real woman. Mommy is there and she can see her. A boy has to do much of his learning about men through what his mother says about them. His mother's view of men will become part of his own view—for good or ill.

When a female child is cared for wholly by a father rather than a mother, she too is likely to feel unsure of her gender role and need to be reminded that she will grow up to be a woman, "like Mommy." The few girls I know who have been brought up mainly by their fathers displayed very little interest in the homemaking games that occupy so much time for most other girls. Without the model of a mother to follow, housework games had little appeal. That is not what, in their eyes, Mommies do.

In families where both parents are equally involved in child care, gender difference in the behavior of children may still be quite marked, not because of what the parent is deliberately feeding in but because of what the child is looking for and adding to the sum of his or her own identity.

This father of two has a firm commitment to bringing up his children as equals. He works from home and has a high level of involvement with their day-to-day care. I asked him what games he plays with his children. He told me: "Football, Frisbee, kite flying, swimming, board and card games. Different only due to their ages." He then added: "But my daughter likes to play with the Playmobile [a construction set with people in it], while my son likes to construct complicated things with rope, wood and engines [real or imagined]. He liked cars best; she played with dolls from an early age."

Already these children seem to be selecting the characteristics that apply particularly to their same-gendered parents and practicing those with more diligence than the others. Of course, they are helped with their selecting by clues from elsewhere. Both these children have been cared for while their parents work. The alternative caregivers are female. Most of the other adults encountered during the first two years will have been female. The other male adults will have been, on the whole, fairly remote.

As soon as they start mixing regularly with other children, they will start picking up new clues. This same father says: "I remember my son playing with the toy stove and other homemaking things and being chased out by a girl who said boys weren't allowed in there. He was clearly shocked." A mother of three sons, who have mainly been cared for by their father, reported a similar experience:

> Claudio had two friends home from nursery and they played in my old doll's house. Claudio put the father doll in the kitchen and said, "Daddy's making dinner." His two male friends giggled and said, "Daddies don't make dinner." Claudio said, "Mine does," but he never played with the doll's house again.

In fact, boys have very little idea of what fathers actually do. Boys in a London primary school were asked: "What do fathers do which is different from mothers?" They answered: "Sit down a lot; laze about; smoke a pipe." Asked what fathers in the olden days might have done, one said: "They might have been challenging each other with duels and swords and stuff." Another suggested, "Pirates." When asked what fathers were for, two said: "To look after us." Another suggested: "To be sensible and don't rob banks and that." A third: "Helping you to live because they buy your clothes."

They were then asked what it would be like if the men had babies. One child said: "Maybe they might decide to give the women more difficult complicateder jobs, where you get more money and more sort of dangerous jobs like being a diver, which I don't think women are allowed to do." Another added, "Also being a police officer or a fire officer."

When my daughter and her friends play with boys, they always insist that the boys play "Daddies," which in this context always means getting bossed around or being sent out to "work"—whatever that means. Given their understanding of what their own fathers do, it isn't surprising that the boys quickly tire of such a role and ask to play the baby instead, where at least they can clown around.

So while most girls are industriously home-building with whatever they can lay their hands on, boys have no simple role to inhabit. Even those boys with no men in their lives will have picked up pretty early on the fact that men drive cars, trains, buses—and they will drive them too. Those with the coordination to do so may start making things (though boys often lag behind in the fine motor skills that would allow them to paint, draw, and color). Given encouragement, they will also dress up—though they soon work out that most dressing up includes dresses, which are intended for girls; men in our culture don't dress up, and boys have to make do with firemen's helmets while girls are swathing themselves in lace.

So just how can a three-year-old boy play out the fantasy of being a man? Is it any wonder that many of them are running around being loud and silly, trying to find a role to inhabit? In any given situation, small girls are more likely to be quietly getting on with something, learning to do something that their mother can do, while their male peers are still running around like mad things, as if trying to divine from the air a sense of what it is they would like to be getting on with. Perhaps this is one of the reasons why boys from as young as a year old appear to be naughtier than girls and are more often reprimanded (Snow, Jacklin, and Maccoby, 1983, p. 101).

However vague and imprecise the information about masculinity, there is no more dedicated detective than a small child in search of knowledge. Superheroes provide the most obvious and overt messages, just as folk and fairy tales have done in the past. If your son is behaving like Hulk Hogan, Superman, or Captain

Planet, it is hardly surprising. These figures are very clearly identified as male. They are mostly involved in fighting and protecting
other, more fragile (often female) people and they are also, clearly
and unambiguously, *good*.

WHO'S A BAD BOY?

While the messages pumped daily from the television are powerful, there are many more clues provided unconsciously by the way
in which adults react to children's behavior. Pat's son, at two,
seemed "unable to sit down and play. His idea of a good time was
to run around pushing the other children over and disturbing
their activities."

When he was two and a half, Pat says:

> He went to a playgroup and loved it. He was still being loud
> and silly but was very interested. Shortly after he joined, he
> pushed a child downstairs just as her father arrived to pick
> her up. The father raised the roof and so it was decided to
> cut down my son's days, "to give the other children a rest."
> To the father of the child who had been hurt, this boy was an
> aggressive monster who should be punished, though his
> mother was told by the playworkers that he wasn't really
> naughty, "just impossible to discipline."

Of course, it is quite natural for a parent to be alarmed when his
child is pushed down the stairs. It is equally necessary to give the
pusher a clear sense of the fact that his behavior is wrong. However, a two-year-old who pushes is simply a two-year-old who has
not yet learned that pushing is wrong. He is not an axe murderer
in waiting. The way in which this kind of behavior is managed will
give the child some very important information about himself.

Pat's reaction to her son's exclusion was to take it on herself:

"Great, I had spawned a monster!" She was pregnant at the time and living in a partly renovated house. His exclusion simply increased the tension in which they were all living. Pat said: "I felt that I was being penalized for my son's behavior." Her son, at two and a half, was learning for the first time about his own power, learning to use it and to test the reactions of others. In learning, he had discovered that he had the power to disrupt the lives of all the people around him, including those whom he looked to for guidance, strength, and support. Terrified by his own power, he then started soiling himself as well. Perhaps what he wanted was simply to return to being a baby, when everything was simple and nobody expected anything of him.

Now mother and son both felt that they were failing: she was failing to control her son; he was failing to control any part of his life. Finally, alarmed by the prospect of bringing twin babies into this disaster area, she persuaded her partner (he had to be persuaded) to attend a couple of sessions of child guidance. She was told by these outsiders that she was a fine parent, that she clearly loved her son, and that she need not worry. They explained that some children react to stress by becoming "loud and silly," as if somehow that could cover up the worry inside.

Once she believed that she was not responsible for everything her son did, she could relax and he gradually became calmer. Now she was able to establish a more consistent and less anxious authority. When her son reached six years of age, she could look back on this as a period he had passed through.

What would have happened had she not sought help and reassurance? Her child would have been very aware of her anxiety and fear and started to absorb a sense of himself as a bad child. He might have reacted by becoming passive but, just as likely, he would have become defiant. A world that is arbitrarily punitive to his newfound need for autonomy is a bad world. Its authority is to be denied and defied.

This child was not behaving aggressively but, at this early age, even aggressive outbursts cannot be seen as evidence of future behavior—unless they are handled in such a way that the child starts to see him- or herself as a bad person. In a report by Mavis Hetherington on children after divorce, it was aggression in girls at the age of four that was most closely correlated to later socially inept behavior. For boys, early aggression did not predict later behavior at all. It seems likely that in these traditional American families, aggressiveness in boys was considered normal and the child was given some time and space in which to organize his feelings, while aggression in girls was considered "unfeminine" and met heavy disapproval.

In a family in which girls are encouraged to stand up for themselves and any sign of aggression in boys is seen as socially unacceptable, the reverse may be true. The girl will grow out of her aggressive behavior and the boy will internalize a sense of worthlessness, which will make his behavior much harder to change.

I came across a rather startling example of this difference when I talked to the parents of an eight-year-old girl. I met them initially when their child was three. She had been creating havoc in her playgroup because of her tendency to take out her feelings with teeth and nails. I knew little of her older brother other than that he seemed rather quiet and was perhaps a little overshadowed by his tempestuous younger sister.

Five years later I bumped into their father. He told me about the difficulties they were having with their son.

I used to believe in nurture, but now I think it's all nature. My son has always been a problem. At eighteen months he was always the child who had to be followed around in case he thumped someone. That made me feel pretty guilty. It was a real problem for us and we always came down on him quickly but with very little impact. His sister is completely different. She isn't aggressive and has many friends.

I was amazed. In fact, their daughter's aggressive behavior had been a feature of her life well into elementary school but, as she was an aggressive girl, it was seen as an individual problem and she was given a lot of space and understanding to try to learn how to control her own behavior. Aggression in a boy was seen, by this family, as a symptom of being male that had to be curbed and controlled, not something that rated special attention.

The son's partly suppressed hostility, punctuated by bursts of rage, is now the focus of the whole household. It is perhaps not surprising in the circumstances that much of his rage is directed at the little sister who somehow always comes up smelling of roses.

Families in which parents are attempting to control what they see as "aggressive" male behavior, while at the same time encouraging what they perceive as "assertive" female behavior, may find that they are actually preventing their male children from learning to control their own feelings in a more socially acceptable way. They are relaying messages telling their sons that rough aggressive behavior is what *bad boys* do.

For a child searching for clues, the most important information will be that this is what *boys* do and that they are *bad*. His anxiety and confusion start to rise. If this anxiety manifests itself in uncontrolled behavior, in lashing out at those around him, more often than not his mother will be drawn in to "deal" with him. She too will add to his confusion by her own feeling of guilt and the fear that, as Pat put it, she had "spawned a monster." If a woman has experienced violence with adult men, this will even more surely color her view, making her fear a similar tendency in her own son.

The anxiety of these particular parents had been increased by the fact that, in their milieu, where families are trying to adjust to bringing up "gentle" boys, rough and aggressive behavior is particularly frowned upon. So, in order to satisfy the disapproval of other parents, they find themselves labeling their own children as "problems." This is not to suggest that aggressive behavior shouldn't be controlled, but that it is the behavior, not the child, that is bad. A three-year-old who scratches another child needs to learn that scratching is bad, not that he or she is a bad person.

A male child who is already irritable, easily roused, and physically uncoordinated is particularly likely to get trapped into a cycle in which caregivers actually encourage the very behavior they are most concerned with curbing. Parents who have basic confidence in their son's goodness may be better able to rise above these early difficulties.

Carl, at twelve years old, is one of the most thoughtful and pleasant adolescent boys you could wish to meet. Those mothers who knew him as a preschooler might be surprised to see how he turned out. Says his mother: "He was a tricky, demanding child from one to four. I can remember some women friends being very disapproving of his roughness and almost hyperactive boisterousness. At around four he became much calmer and easygoing." She always defended her son to the hilt and says: "I want the same for both my children—that they be gentle and fearless. Self-esteem is probably the best route to those qualities."

A three-year-old who is told regularly that he is a bad child is unlikely to build up the good feeling that is necessary for self-esteem.

MORE MIXED MESSAGES

In families where the role of the man is seen as that of brave warrior and adventurer, a child may be encouraged to hit back, or even to hit first, to establish his place in the pecking order, on the grounds that a boy must learn to defend himself. However, if a boy who has been brought up to see himself as a warrior then enters a system in which warrior behavior is frowned upon, his messages will start to get scrambled. One mother I talked to told me that, though she wanted to bring up her son and daughter as equals, her efforts were constantly undermined by her father, who offered a continuous stream of propaganda about the superior attributes of the male.

She told me: "My dad has told Abdul, 'You've got to look after your sister when she's at school. If anyone troubles her you must fight them.' He sees school as a place with a lot of fighting and rough stuff, so he encourages Abdul to be like that." Abdul, two years younger than his sister, is being encouraged to act "like a man" and protect his "weaker" sister. He is being given a sense of pride in his masculinity and at the same time being told that, as a man, he must face danger. He is getting a clear message that a degree of aggression is positively good.

This message might have been appropriate in some circumstances and it might even be seen as a rational response to the perceived racism of the school system, but as his mother well knows and Abdul will pretty soon find out, three-year-olds are not only not required to behave this way at school but are positively discouraged.

This child will have come up against the first and most puzzling contradiction of his life. Granddad is an important person, the most important male figure in his family, and yet his schoolteacher (almost certainly female) says that Granddad is wrong. So what does that mean for his carefully collected clues about what it is to be male?

Erik Erikson, a Freudian psychoanalyst, writing in 1950, described the case of a little Jewish boy whom he had occasion to treat for stress-induced fits. Sam had been born in a Jewish neighborhood. His problems started when his parents moved into a middle-class suburb and he was required to behave in a different way:

In dangerous situations, Sam used what we call the "counterphobic defensive mechanism"; when he was scared he attacked and when faced with knowledge which others might choose to avoid as upsetting he asked questions with anxious persistence. These defenses, in turn, were well suited to the sanctions of his early milieu, which thought him cutest when he was toughest and smartest.

In the new situation, his parents were anxious to curb his behavior because, as Erikson observed, "a little Jew had to be specially good in order not to be specially bad." As a result the defenses that had worked so well for him at first started to lead him into trouble. In the confusion he found himself utterly defenseless. He could not figure out how to behave. Where once there had been a simple set of rules, now he found that defense left him even more open to attack.

In a sense, the severity of his physical reaction to stress did protect him. It ensured professional intervention. Most children suffering from similar confusions about the way they should behave will stop short of such obviously pathological behavior and either behave wildly or withdraw from the battle.

A similar sense that their sons have to be "specially good in order not to be specially bad" provides many black parents with a deep sense of both anxiety and grievance. One mother I spoke to had two boys, aged five and seven. The younger child had early on learned that being utterly charming is the best way of getting on in the world. His older brother, an extremely intelligent and energetic child, had more difficulty finding a way of interacting. She told me:

> I worry that he might get into trouble. I worry that he might get involved with the police. I often wish that I had sent him back to Gambia, where my family is. He would have had a sense of belonging there, a sense of direction. I feel such fear for him.

There is no doubt that her fear for the future of these children will affect their view of the world and of themselves. Should they be tough in order to survive with their peers, or will this toughness bring them into conflict with authority? Just how can this mother bring up boys who are both safe and strong enough to stand up for their rights?

LEARNING NOT TO BE GENTLE

What of the many boys who are not anxious, aggressive, and excitable? While most surveys confirm that boys are more likely than girls to be naughty and aggressive, they also show that the gender difference is not universal. In any group there are likely to be more aggressive boys than aggressive girls, but there will also be almost as many unaggressive boys as there are unaggressive girls. Gentleness is almost as often a male attribute as it is a female one, but it is not *labeled* as masculine behavior and it is not counted in surveys.

Between the ages of eighteen months and three years it is very common for both boys and girls to go through a phase in which they push, grab, and defend what they see as their own territory from others. Some children may take longer than others to learn how to control what is theirs and work out how to allow another child to "borrow" something without fearing that they will lose it forever. This behavior may be described as aggressive. Other children are so fearful that they never really manage to work out how they can hang on to what is theirs, nor do they learn how to lend. They feel perpetually at the mercy of more powerful forces.

Girls and boys may belong to either category. This is how one father described his son and daughter: "My son has been more dependent, more easily frightened and hurt, less communicative emotionally, and more likely to brood." A mother talked about her son's experience of starting nursery school: "He was desperately unhappy and I was desperately worried about him. He couldn't cope with the number of people and the range of options. He spent much of the time hiding under the table." A third parent said: "I stopped going to my NCT [National Childbirth Trust mothers' group] after my second child because his brother, at three, was being victimized by the other boys."

These parents worry about their children's lack of assertiveness, and they may not be aware that many of the boys who spend their time running around and shouting, or losing their tempers and screaming, may also be demonstrating their anxiety. When John started nursery school at two and a half, he went into a small group of five children with one staff member. The day was well organized and he clearly felt safe and happy. After a few weeks, the staff decided that, since he was physically bigger than the other children and seemed more advanced in his play, he should join the older group of three- to five-year-olds. His behavior immediately deteriorated. He reacted to the bigger space, larger numbers, and less structured activity not by withdrawing but by running wildly around the room.

A child who is running wild and apparently out of control is far more likely to hurt someone else than a child who is sitting quietly building with Lego. This doesn't necessarily mean that he is aggressive, but it may well be seen that way. John, "promoted" because of his maturity, was now in danger of being labeled as a problem. In the preschool years boys are persistently scored as more aggressive than girls by researchers. The difference is more marked than at any other life stage.

The fact is that there is no socially sanctioned way in which boys can show their anxiety and ask for help. If they are rough and anxious they are seen as aggressive, but they are given precious little encouragement to show weakness. While girls are encouraged to seek help from adults, boys are expected to learn to cope. This encouragement may, again, not be explicit, but it is worth noting that girls and boys get different responses both to aggressive behavior and to defensive behavior.

Little girls quickly learn that by crying they will enlist adult help on their side. Crying is therefore a more effective defense than hitting back. It might be in the interests of boys to learn the same strategy, but too often crying in boys will elicit a very different and far less positive response.

In a study on the effects of divorce (Hetherington, Cox, and Cox, 1982, p. 270), researchers discovered that in all the family groups they studied: "Crying and distress in boys received less frequent and shorter periods of comforting and more ambivalent comforting than did distress signals from girls." By *ambivalent* the researchers meant responses such as "a hug, combined with: 'There, there! Boys don't cry.' Girls were far more likely to be given unqualified reassurance."

Because there are no models of gentle boys, these children may find that they also receive confusing messages about the way they should behave. Says Clarissa:

At four, Justin seems to get on better with girls. He loves singing and dancing and playing musical instruments and he also likes imaginary play, which is as much to do with things like going on holiday, going to a restaurant, or being Peter Pan and sprinkling people with pixie dust as it is with playing monsters.

I really do love him just as he is, but sometimes I feel slightly anxious. Are we making him too gentle, in a way which might open him to bullying later on? Are we overly soppy and affectionate with him, and might that make him different from the other boys? Should we toughen him up a bit? And that's really the dilemma. I am an avowed feminist. I want him to grow up to be gentle and kind. I want him to respect women as equals. But I also want him to hold his own in a world of men, and I don't want anyone, male or female, to regard him as a wimp. I keep thinking it's something of a battleground out there. But then I think, Would I even be asking these questions if Justin were a girl? I think not.

3

Mother, It's Hell Out There: Turning Boys into Men

Jacob is seven, a gentle child who loves colors, flowery patterns, dressing up, playing with a puppet theater. Until he started nursery school, his parents went along with his preferences. Then, his mother told me:

> I dissuaded him from wearing dresses to nursery. I just said I thought the others would make fun of him. I said I thought it was a shame. I would point out that, in Africa or the Far East, he wouldn't have this problem. I made efforts to find him clothes which are colorful and flowery. He's very interested in clothes and spends ages choosing them. He would have liked to wear red strap shoes this summer but we persuaded him to have sandals instead.

These are particularly liberal parents who are unusual in their tolerance. Their fear is that he will be teased. Had they been parents of a less tolerant kind, their son's behavior might have led them to seek professional advice. Lim and Bottomley (1983) describe the "symptoms" of a five-year-old boy whom they treated for the condition of being too feminine: "a wide range of articles used inventively, a preference for girls as playmates, choice of feminine toys, avoidance of boys and rough-and-tumble play."

This child "neither believed nor wished that he was a girl" and yet he was treated using behavioral therapy, which involved rewarding him for behavior considered masculine (toughness, fighting, playing with cars) and reprimanding behavior considered feminine.

There are practically no cases of little girls whose behavior is considered insufficiently feminine being treated in this way, and it is impossible to conceive of parents of girls having these worries. A girl can dress up as a fairy princess or wear sneakers and jeans or she can switch between the two, and no one will worry about her "femininity." A boy is forced to sublimate all his love of beautiful colors and textures if he is to become one of the boys. One mother told me rather sadly:

> He loves pretty things but he knows they are not for him. He sublimates his own desire to dress up and takes a great interest in what I wear. The other day I watched him brushing his sister's hair. He clearly enjoyed the feeling as well as the look of it but, for a boy, pretty is what you look at, not what you are.

There was a time when girls who were "tomboys" and enjoyed climbing, running, wearing shorts, and cutting their hair short were also considered deviant. Efforts were made to feminize them, to make them more passive. In the 1950s, in Enid Blyton's "Famous Five" children's books, George was a girl who wanted to be a boy because she didn't want to do the sissy things that girls did. She wanted to be out in the world having adventures, and a generation of girls grew up also hankering after the freedom their brothers had.

These days little girls have no real reason to envy boys. My seven-year-old daughter is amused by the notion in Louisa May Alcott's *Little Women* that Jo wants to be a boy. She can see no particular benefit in being a boy, because there is nothing a boy can do that is not also open to her. Clearly this has been a big change ·(and it still varies according to where a girl lives today). Part of the change has to do with a general reduction in the freedom that children enjoy.

Twenty years ago, almost half the seven-year-olds surveyed in a study on mobility were allowed to go to "leisure places" unaccompanied (Hillman, Adams, and Whitelegg, 1992). Today the figure is only 20 percent. In 1971 three-quarters of this age group went to school unaccompanied. Today less than 10 percent do. More boys than girls have this freedom but, on the whole, the freedom to wander in the woods all day is no longer available to anyone, regardless of sex.

Today's little girls see a version of *Beauty and the Beast* in which Beauty is more intelligent and braver than all the men, and teenagers can enjoy the film *Fried Green Tomatoes,* which traces the attempts made to force a tomboy to conform. Looked at from today's perspective, this fight for autonomy and against the passivity that women were forced to accept appears heroic rather than deviant, but we have yet to provide similar role models for boys who want to opt out of the masculine mold.

For a girl, being more boyish means being more powerful in the world. For a boy, to be more female is to be less powerful. The pursuit of equal rights with men has inadvertently confirmed the preeminence of traditional masculinity by seeking to emulate it. In so doing, it has actually narrowed the options available to boys. To be better than a girl, a boy has to be more of a man. The only way out of becoming a masculine man seems to be becoming a failed masculine man or separating yourself from notions of "normality."

Those men who stop competing with other men and opt for more openness in their behavior, flexibility in their dress, and emotional expressiveness are often assumed to be homosexual. Indeed, for some young men homosexuality is not just a sexual option but a positive choice to live a less rigidly bound life. (However, for most boys the fear of being thought to be homosexual is enough to ensure that, at least in public, they keep any "feminine" tendencies very firmly in check.)

Messages about gender roles come thick and fast as soon as a boy starts school, even if his parents have tried to be more flexible in their own approach. (The question of what happens at school is an important one, which will be dealt with in more detail in part V.) As far as parents are concerned, the boy they see at home is changing fast. A father who had been an equal participant in his children's care said:

> Coming into contact with other children, my son has become more "masculine" and my daughter more "feminine." They have responded to the expectation placed on them to behave in the ways needed to fit in with other children.

It is in school that boys really start learning the rules of what it means to be a boy, not in easy stages from a consistent adult figure but from their peers, and it is the most dominant figures on the playground who will convey most forcibly what it means to be male. These are lessons that he cannot easily avoid. Since the first realization of gender, a boy is caught up in a battle in which the need to identify with men requires him to separate from his mother. The silence that mothers so often encounter as their sons enter the outside world is bound up with their need to be separate, to find a life for themselves, to discover what it means to be male. For a girl, the battle will come later.

While girls continue to identify directly with their mothers, boys, in that vast majority of families in the industrialized world in which fathers play only a minor part, "identify with a cultural stereotype of the masculine role" (Chodorow, 1978, p. 176). A girl will be good to be like Mommy, while a boy, according to Nancy

Chodorow, starts "to deny identification with and relationship to the mother and reject what he takes to be the feminine world; masculinity is defined as much negatively as positively. Masculine identification processes stress differentiation from others." Robert, a graphic designer in his thirties, told me that his earliest memory of starting school was being teased for having a so-called girl's middle name—Francis.

Few boys have the self-confidence to insulate themselves from this process, and it is not only the boys who enforce it. Girls, feeling their superiority, their greater social confidence and competence, their greater sense of themselves, and their stronger relationships with other children, tend to treat boys as contemptible inferiors.

Some boys do refuse to join in. Jacob, mentioned earlier, refused to accept the need to enter the world of men. Says his mother: "He doesn't aspire to being one of the boys. He likes girls and likes to play with girls. His pain at the beginning was that the girls would only play with him at their own discretion. He had to work hard to be accepted." Jacob is fortunate that he goes to a school in which his preferences are respected and where, so far, he has been allowed to maintain his distance from the male culture without being teased.

James, now in his late twenties, says he always felt different from the others. He never played football, never got into fights, and always associated with boys who felt as he did. He just didn't want to be "one of the boys" and so he was beyond the range of their scorn. By the age of eleven he realized that he was not just less interested in rough-and-tumble games; he was also gay. In a sense this was a protection. As a teenager, he no longer had to compete within the established masculine hierarchy. He had a passport into a different world in which his behavior was not considered unusual.

A child who is helped to feel confidence in his own choices will, in the end, be able to resist the pressure to conform without suffering too much. It is the boys who want to join in, and don't know how to do it, who are most vulnerable to coercion by other children. By the age of seven a child's own need to join in, often aided by his parents' (particularly his father's) fear of homosexuality, ensures that very few American or British boys will be seen playing with girls or holding their mothers' hands—let alone kissing them goodbye—in public. The ones who still do are regarded slightly anxiously as "immature," "babyish," or, worse still, in danger of becoming homosexual.

If he is not yet ready to define his masculinity by separating from the female world, the world will itself leave him with little doubt about his separateness. David Panter, a psychologist who studied the transition between nursery and elementary school, noted the relief of one father who commented that his son was "getting better at fighting now" and that he was glad the child was no longer interested in dolls because "if a boy plays with a doll you think he is going to grow up into a poof."

Nowhere is this fear of homosexuality or effeminacy made clearer than in traditional upper-crust British society, where boys are whisked away from their mothers' skirts to the male-dominated world of the boarding school. The fear, as royal biographer Ann Morrow pointed out in the *Mail on Sunday,* is that too much mothering might be bad for a boy. (Not that this is in practice a very useful way of enforcing heterosexuality. Homosexual affairs as well as sexual harassment seem to be a feature of almost any all-male environment, from young offenders' institutions to the top boarding schools.)

Writing about the future of Prince Harry and Prince William, who were just eight and ten at the time, she quotes "a doctor with 30 years' experience of psychological problems in a Kensington practice" who says reassuringly:

There is a danger that the princes may be mummy's boys, but the separation that comes with boarding school soon puts that right ... loving the boys as she does, she must know that it cannot be good for their long-term development to be under her beautiful wing for much longer.

More recent comment, after the breakdown of Charles and Diana's marriage, has focused on the psychological health of Prince Charles and his fitness as a father, pointing out that he was bullied at his boarding school and very unhappy, which may have contributed to the problems he has had with relationships as an adult.

It seems incredible to me that an eight-year-old child could possibly be considered old enough to emerge from his mother's wing at all—let alone be thrust out against his will. Yet there is no doubt that even those among us who would be horrified at the idea of sending an eight-year-old boy to boarding school do start expecting more independent behavior from our sons at that age, even if we welcome the fact that they still want to be cuddled at home. For a girl, public anxiety and shyness are quite acceptable. They may even be considered ultrafeminine. The other girls may react by "mothering" her, but once in school it is even harder for a boy to find a respectable way of demonstrating anxiety.

Roy's mother wrote: "His younger sister had no problems starting school. Roy was weepy, clingy, and devised ways of staying at home. While his sister became more confident, I feel school has made him a sadder person." Roy is big for his age and clumsy, and his tearfulness is not cute; it is irritating. Whereas his sister quickly realized that, by putting her thumb in her mouth and looking sad, she would get sympathy, Roy's experience was totally different. He would either be ignored or "jollied" out of it. If quiet misery did not elicit a positive response, loud and angry misery did at least create enough noise to cover the pain inside—and to keep Mother close by a little longer.

At home he had always had both physical affection and a degree of cheerful rough-and-tumble. At school he discovered that the only way to get close to another boy was through "play fighting." According to his mother: "Roy's problems started when another boy, who was also his best friend, started hitting him. The school never seemed to take it seriously." Indeed, it would have been hard for the school to single out these incidents. These two boys were friends and at any given time, in a school playground, there will be bundles of boys all over the place screaming with laughter and apparently kicking the hell out of each other. To a female observer, the only difference between play fighting and real fighting is whether or not the participants are smiling.

For Roy the contradictions and confusions were overwhelming. His friend kept hitting him, and when he complained to his parents they would go to his school and make a fuss. In the past he had always believed that his parents were strong enough to fix anything, so why couldn't they fix this? Why couldn't they make his friend learn to be gentle?

Of course, what Roy didn't understand was that his friend was just as confused but a little further down the road to understanding that at least one of the things that distinguish boys is that they are *not* expected to be gentle and they are supposed to learn not to cry. An only child of a single mother, this friend felt an urgent need to separate, and he understood masculinity to be a process of learning to give, and to take, a carefully measured dose of violence. Without much experience of rough-and-tumble in his own home, he had simply misinterpreted the rules.

It is important to know the rules. If a boy goes too far, and hurts someone, he will be considered violent and unpleasant by both adults and children. If he opts out, he will miss out on the central activity by which boys make friends. If he is lucky he will find another boy who doesn't want to get involved, and they will pair up away from the playground violence, quite often forming intense, close relationships. But the way to be in the center is to understand the rules of this game. If a child is not anxious when he starts school, he may pretty soon become anxious—if he doesn't know how to play by the rules.

When Saul started school he was a happy, ebullient child, a bit loud and noisy, but not bad with it. His father was at home but rarely played with him. His mother was not interested in physical play. He had little opportunity to channel his considerable energy. On day one he entered his new classroom eager to be involved. He had met the children before and was looking forward to joining them. A group of boys were play fighting in a corner. Saul went forward eagerly to join in, clearly seeing that people were having fun. He had never experienced anything quite like this but decided to try it. He kicked the nearest child. There was a silence. The children got up and moved away. He had transgressed. He had not learned the rules. He was cast out. His mother said:

> For the next three years, most of Saul's energy was used up just trying to work out how to "get in" with these boys. Sometimes he would be allowed to play, or even to visit their homes, but he never felt sure that he was one of them. He always felt uneasy in their presence. He seemed to have no internal sense of how to behave. Every day and every new encounter was an experiment. While learning these rules he was also supposed to learn to read and write and add and take away, but he didn't have much time. The effort of learning how to be a boy took up all the available space.

Eric is the son of gentle, perhaps rather anxious, parents. His mother's childhood was overshadowed by her father's violence, a fact that may have made her particularly anxious about any signs of aggression in her own children. He went to a nonsexist, antiracist nursery school where aggression was frowned upon and playworkers reasoned with children rather than ordering them about. Nevertheless, he was wild and difficult. When he started kindergarten he almost immediately got into trouble.

In spite of the fact that his mother, Jane, was worried about his behavior, she was also proud of what she saw as his "confidence and energy." She told me that, very soon after he started school, she had watched him on the playground and he was busily trying to get other, much bigger boys to play his game, just as he had always got the little kids in the nursery school to join in with what he wanted to do. She clearly set some store by the fact that he showed "leadership potential," but she was equally concerned that he should be kind and gentle.

What she saw as confidence and energy could also be interpreted as anxiety and desperation to be noticed, to be accepted, to be in the middle of things. He often alienated and irritated the other children because he seemed driven and out of control. He would be red in the face, eyes sparkling with effort, and simply not understand why the girls, in particular, were put off. Perhaps he had taken on the idea of himself as the leader, seen that this position was appreciated at home, and now, a small fish in the big sea of school, he needed to prove that he was still "a big boy," still "in control."

He initially got into trouble for hitting a couple of girls (had they been boys, the adult retribution might not have been so swift). One mother was extremely upset and, said Jane:

> I felt so guilty. Any lapse in a child's behavior and you feel that you have done everything wrong. I wanted to understand why he had done it but, of course, he didn't know. He must have been very aware of my anxiety and distress. It was not just that he got into trouble for hitting a girl; all my anxiety was being laid at his door as well.

What upset Jane was the fact that her son was behaving in a way she believes he has always been taught is wrong. He was clearly caught between the expectations of nonviolence from adults, the demands of the playground, and his own feeling that he ought to be top dog as he was before. The more often he got it wrong, the more often he would get into trouble and the more anxious and uncontrolled he would become.

Gradually, as Eric found his feet in school, the anxiety lifted and his behavior grew more controlled. He was perhaps fortunate to be in a class with a particularly ebullient and self-confident girl who acted as a link between the girls and the boys. Competing for her approval set a slightly different standard of behavior. Playing with her was important, and to do so he had to modify his behavior. As he did, his popularity with the other children increased.

This child was lucky; in most schools, gender divisions are still rigorously enforced, from both sides of the gender divide. To be accepted, a boy has to learn to be like the other boys, even if that means doing things that his mother doesn't like. Few seven-year-olds can articulate the conflicts they are facing at school. A ten-year-old whose mother remonstrated with him for name-calling and unpleasant behavior said: "You just don't know what I have to do to survive at school."

Perhaps this is why mothers hear so little about what is going on. How do you tell your mother that today you learned how hard you could kick someone without hurting him? Perhaps this explains why boys who ran home with their first drawings to show them to Mommy later refuse to discuss what they are doing at all and seem to move into a sort of minimalist crypto-speak, where the dialogue goes something like this:

Mother: How was school today, darling?
Son: OK.
Mother: Well, what did you do?
Son: Nothing.
Mother: You must have done something. You didn't just sit still all day, did you?
Son: Can I have something to eat?

Being not gentle is only one way in which boys seek to differentiate themselves from girls. They also have to find a way of being together that allows them to be separate, guarded, not caught being in breach of the rule to be "not girly." Boys playing together seem to need a joint interest or game to act as both barrier and cement to the relationship. Intimacy is avoided by gathering in groups rather than intense twosomes. One mother, describing the way in which her son and daughter make friends, seemed to sum up the gender difference: "Carl has a far wider circle of friends with a general feeling of bonhomie to most people. His sister has very intense relationships with a best friend."

Boys may want to engage directly but may well find that the other boys won't let them. Jack had been brought up in an all-female household and was cared for with a group of girls, which is perhaps why, when he started school, he expected to be able to have close relationships with other children, just as the girls did. His mother says: "He tends to be more passionate about relationships than other boys. He is not good at being cool and laid back, but for a couple of years now he has been more careful. He is less prepared to make himself vulnerable. He keeps his distance more."

One ten-year-old boy, who is extremely gentle and spends much of his time painting and model-making, handles the demands of the male world by reserving the quiet, gentle part of himself for the times when he is with a close female friend. The girl in question comes from a two-parent family in which her father is the main caregiver. She identifies very strongly with him and doesn't enjoy the stereotypical homemaking activities of her female peers.

The two of them, thrown together on a regular basis, have carved out a space in which they can simply be themselves, unfettered by social expectation. Yet, as his mother points out, when he spends time with boys his behavior is as loud and boisterous as theirs. He has learned how to function as a boy without losing touch with the other person inside. He has not lost his ability to respond with warmth and spontaneity, nor has he become suspicious of closeness, but he has learned how to behave like a boy when need be.

Sports provides one common key to togetherness without dangerous intimacy. Boys with parents who take them to the park, play ball, teach them to swim, and encourage tree climbing and bicycle riding will have gathered together a useful repertoire of behavior that is acceptable to other boys, providing a means of coming together and yet remaining separate.

One extremely gentle son of a loving, warm, and very much present father had a terrible time at school until his father sent him to soccer training. Once he had acquired a skill with which to operate successfully with the boys on the playground, his anxiety levels dropped and he found it easier to make friends and to avoid being victimized by bigger boys.

It's pretty tough on those boys who lack the coordination for these activities. Physical coordination is not something that happens at birth; it is slowly acquired. Some boys start school lacking the physical coordination to stand on one leg. The chances of using the other to kick a ball are remote. The child is condemned to the sidelines. Jack's mother said of her son's sudden interest in soccer: "He tried hard and it was excruciating that he wasn't very good at it. He even joined a junior soccer club for a bit. But then he discovered fishing. A very male activity without the physical side."

Some boys discover another boy with a mutual interest in something that is not physical, such as computers or modelmaking. Then the relationship may seem quite close and intense and the boys may seem desperate when it breaks up and they find themselves exposed to the unfriendly world of masculinity without an ally. However, even when there is a mutual interest, as the children leave childhood behind the intensity and exclusiveness will lessen; other boys with similar interests will be allowed in to dilute the relationship. The interest is the thing, the safe middle ground.

A conversation between boys—of virtually any age—will start off not by a review of who that other person is, and how he feels, but by what they know in common. The tone is carefully modulated to ensure that the only emotion that comes through is (where necessary) scorn. It's like a verbal swapping of baseball cards:

Boy 1: What team do you support?
Boy 2: Big Feet United.
Boy 3: What, them? You don't support them, do you?
Boy 2: Yes, I do, but I like the Flat Foots too.
Boy 1: Yeah, Johnny Mack is good.
Boy 2: He's pretty good. I think Big Feet are going to buy him next season. (Neutral safe ground now established.)

It is perfectly possible for this sort of conversation to go on for some time without the participants discovering anything about each other at all. Participating in this verbal game, in which the rules are clearly set, gives them all a feeling of safety. They have made contact with other human beings without running the risk of breaching the rules. If you say nothing out of the ordinary, you can say nothing wrong. If you say nothing wrong, you cannot be laughed at and no emotional damage will occur.

In this atmosphere, in which the slightest step out of line can bring scorn upon your head, the other line of defense is to be silly. If you don't try to do something well, then you cannot be laughed at for having failed. A child may act the clown at school and at home, and never reveal to anyone that he is unhappy. It is extremely common to hear mothers of sons say that they didn't know he was being bullied for a year, or a term, or until another mother told her.

One of the more chilling side effects of this process is that boys often fail to learn the language with which they could describe their feelings, and without language it is hard for anyone to make sense of what he feels. Alison Leibling, researching young-offender institutions, found a high level of depression among the young women. The young men seemed to be experiencing exactly the same things: total lack of motivation, sleeplessness, lack of contact with others, and, for 17 percent of them, thoughts of suicide, but they described the way they felt as "boredom." Leibling suspects it is the lack of a language that prevents these young men from alerting prison staff to their real state of mind. One mother told me that her son was able to talk about what had happened to him only when she gave him a passage from Margaret Atwood's book *Cat's Eye,* with its graphic account of bullying within a group of girls: "It was as though he finally had a name for what was happening to him—and he knew that it had happened to others too. He was not a uniquely terrible person."

Karen's son was eight years old when she told me:

> I finally discovered from another mother that the children in his class had collectively decided to ostracize him. He had been having a difficult time since his father had just left and was feeling very vulnerable, so he must have been in absolute emotional agony—but he never said a word to me. It is as if he believed that this was the way the world was and nothing could be done. I don't think there was anything particular that he had done. It was just that he was a little bit awkward socially; he couldn't cope very well with teasing and would take it too much to heart.

She believes that he had decided not to tell her, but it is just as likely that he didn't know how to. He just didn't have the words.

This mother decided to have a quiet talk with the parents of some of her son's former friends. The message she received was that none of them were prepared to "break ranks" and befriend him because they would then become vulnerable themselves. Thanks to a determined effort to find friends for him outside the school and a move to a different class the following term, the problem blew over, but it had left its mark. Her son is now more wary than ever of forming close relationships. Friendships last only until the first disagreement. At the slightest hint of trouble he withdraws.

As boys get older they become more practiced at distancing themselves. I have heard many mothers complain that, while their ten- and eleven-year-old girls organize their own social lives and simply ask their parents' permission and assistance, boys of the same age seem loath to make any arrangements at all. The more casual an arrangement, the less the emotional investment. Perhaps it's not lack of imagination, or lack of maturity, but an anxiety never to be the one who makes the first move—never to be the person who moves closer.

This distancing does have some advantages. Once boys have learned the trick of distance, they find it easier to avoid the pain that characterizes the falling in and out of love, which seems to be such a big part of intense female friendships. Saying nothing, revealing nothing, building a wall of silence between you and those who may be able to get at you: this seems to me to be one of the ways in which the process of socialization turns boys into men.

4

The Gateway to Adulthood: Freedom and Risk

Puberty is the point at which, in many societies, boys are put through religious rites that will lead them forever out of the world of women and children and into the world of men. We have replaced the ritual of the past with a more down-to-earth rite: the move from primary to secondary school. For many children the entry into secondary school is marked by a clear change in their relationship to adults. Children who have been accompanied to school every day are now allowed to make the journey alone. Their world grows wider than the few streets between home and primary school, and they have moved on from friendships established in early childhood into a bigger social group where they have the chance of making new alliances with people their parents may never see.

But, of course, independence has its risks too. A twelve-year-old boy may not yet have built the protective shell with which he will learn to face the world. As he flaunts his newfound freedom from adult control, he is vulnerable. He finds that he is the smallest fish in the sea, and his freedom from the ties of family may appear to be sending him straight into the jaws of a more worrying authority: that of older, rougher, tougher boys who, he fears, will exploit his open innocence and steal his money, snatch his backpack, run off with his brand-new sneakers.

It is much harder for parents, particularly single mothers, to allow the freedom their sons need in order to grow if they fear that freedom is fraught with danger. African-American writer Eugene Perkins, in *Home Is a Dirty Street* (quoted in Kunjufu, 1985), writes about the role models and mentors of black youth in an American ghetto where, he argues, society has failed to provide for boys a safe place in which to learn about being men. He could as well have been writing about the white boys on some of the rundown estates of Britain's old industrial cities:

> It is on the streets where the black child receives his basic orientation to life. The streets become his primary reference because other institutions have failed to provide him with essential skills he needs to survive in the "ghetcolony." And for the child to survive the ghetcolony he must undergo a rigorous apprenticeship that will enable him to compensate for the lack of guidance from other institutions and adults. He becomes the student of the "asphalt jungle" because that is where he can learn the skills he needs.
>
> The instructors consist of hustlers, pimps, street men, militants, gang leaders, and working men. And though these men do not have master's and Ph.D. degrees, their credentials have been earned from actual experiences and not from the sterile laboratories of formal academic institutions.

Boys living in these circumstances have to have someone very strong in their lives to act as a counterweight to the peer pressure of the streets. However, no adolescent boy is completely insulated from danger. Sharon, a middle-class city-dwelling single mother, was appalled when her son came home in tears from a trip around the corner to buy a paper. A couple of older boys had stepped out of a shop and demanded money. Transfixed with fear, he had given them all he had. She was quite unable to decide what to do. Was this the beginning of a life of terror? Should she immediately plan a move to a more genteel neighborhood? Should she stop him from leaving the house without her?

Deciding that her own sheltered upbringing did not equip her to make a judgment about what to do, she consulted a male friend. He was relaxed about it and reassured her that "it could happen anywhere. It happened to me at the same age and I lived in a quiet suburb. It's just part of growing up—learning how to look after yourself."

The social assumption has always been that it is girls who are in need of protection. While we want to encourage them to be independent, most parents would be extremely cautious about allowing girls the same freedoms that they encourage in boys. Indeed, most girls are themselves acutely aware of the need to defend themselves—not against robbery or violence so much as sexual attack. It is much easier for girls to ask for protection from each other and from adults.

This may be partly the reason why boys are in reality so much more vulnerable than girls. According to British Home Office statistics, ten- to fifteen-year-old boys are more than twice as likely as girls to be victims of violence, and the vast majority of all male victims of violence will have been involved in an incident in a public place. Forty-six percent of violence against women occurs in their home or the home of the assailant. However, the fact that girls are better protected is not the only reason why boys are more often hurt. Boys have to face an additional danger: girls rarely attack each other physically, and practically never attack boys. Boys are a great deal more likely to attack another boy than to attack a girl.

Yet boys are not brought up to be aware of their vulnerability. On the contrary, they grow up in a world in which they are seen as either the protectors or the aggressors and they cannot easily ask for protection without appearing "wimpish." As they topple from the nest and get caught in the crosswinds of life, they have to find their own equilibrium, their own way of coping. Parents find themselves sitting on the sidelines, hoping that their sons will have the sense to ask for help when they need it, and not to take on anything they cannot handle.

Not that the streets are the only places in which boys come into contact with aggression. *Bullying: An International Perspective,* edited by Elaine Munthe and Erling Roland (1989), cites one study (Lowenstein, 1978) in which the number of physical attacks on boys in school was four times as high as those against girls.

In the same book, boys were asked to report on incidents over a one-week period. Fifty percent of fourteen-year-olds said that someone had tried to kick them at least once, and 36 percent said that someone had tried to break something belonging to them. Among twelve-year-olds, 19 percent said that someone had demanded money from them. Astonishingly, only a minority of the children were made unhappy by this behavior. Indeed, the authors suggest that there is "a continuum of acceptable violence which a large minority of children experience at one time or another."

RITES OF PASSAGE

Episodes of theft, extortion, and bullying appear to be so prevalent among boys at secondary school (irrespective of social class) that they can almost be classified as initiation rites set by older children as the start of the hardening process that leads to adult masculinity.

The timing would be right. In many cultures and religions this process of change is institutionalized and directed by adult men. It may be marked by a ceremony. For Jewish boys, for example, a bar mitzvah is a symbolic moment at which boys need to start moving out of the care of their mothers and thinking about their responsibilities as adult men.

Societies that carve out a role for these pubescent boys, even if it is purely symbolic, may be attempting to contain their behavior as they test out their newfound freedom from mothers' apron strings. However, they also seem to be exhibiting a fear that their sons will look at the world of men and beat a hasty retreat back to Mommy's skirts.

The division of girls and boys into separate institutions at the age of eleven is still common in Britain, the assumption being that in an all-male group boys can more easily be turned into men. However, there is no evidence that boys behave any better, or are more socially responsible, if they are kept in male-only groups, and the biggest concern lurking in the minds of those who advocate boys' schools is not that boys will be too tough but that the influence of mothers is so awesome that boys might not learn to be tough enough. In the more sexually egalitarian society of Scandinavia, all secondary schools are coeducational. The Scandinavians do not seem worried that their sons will fail to become men if they are kept too long in the company of women.

The desire to prove that you are male is not something society needs to force on boys; they are usually pretty eager to prove it themselves and will almost certainly find the means to do so if they are given the space.

Geoff was the quiet younger child in an extremely exuberant family. His childhood had been dominated by a very assertive older sister who was the apple of her father's eye, and Geoff had been very badly teased, mainly by a group of girls at school. Geoff looked to his mother for protection but, at the same time, struggled fiercely against her to gain a sense of autonomy. At the age of nine he took to boasting about the things he could do: he could water-ski, ride horses over hurdles, carry heavier weights than anyone else. Once he had said he could do something, it became a matter of principle to him that he should indeed achieve this end.

His parents had little interest in sports but they were amused by his need to compete physically, and even more amused when his sister insisted on proving that she could do anything that he did—better. Finally, at the age of twelve, he discovered the game of rugby. Here no one would follow him. His sister, by this time, had moved on to other interests and found his involvement in this "macho" sport faintly contemptible.

He opted for the toughest position on the field. He had made himself strong enough mentally to withstand a battering. It was as though he was determined to set himself goals in an arena in which no other family member could possibly compete. Here at last was a place where no woman would follow—except to cheer. His parents were baffled by his decision but did not discourage him. His self-confidence grew by leaps and bounds. He didn't last long on the team. It turned out only to be a means of separating and, once the step had been taken, he went back to the quieter pursuits he actually preferred. Geoff chose a socially sanctioned way both to mark his difference from the women around him and to show that he could be one of the in-group.

Early adolescence is also a time when a boy may start to take an interest in things that his father likes to do. Adrian, a thirteen-year-old whose anti-authoritarian attitudes were inducing despair in his parents, suddenly took to playing the guitar. He had never shown any interest in music (his father's passion) until this point. Now they had a territory in common, which allowed them to be close without any of the embarrassing intimacy that they both found hard to cope with.

By the age of twelve or thirteen most boys, whether they are divided from girls or not, know that their future lies in the external world, outside the family. Yet they are bound to feel some ambivalence too: it's scary out there. One mother told me a story that illustrates just how differently the world treats a boy child and a young man:

My thirteen-year-old son got run over at an intersection near his school. I was contacted and arrived at the hospital to find him in the teacher's arms. A nurse took him, and wheeled him through. He was prioritized because he was still small for his age and considered vulnerable.

His brother, two years older than him, was knocked down at the same intersection. I got a call from his friend and arrived at the hospital to find him pouring with blood. No teacher had accompanied him, no nurse had spoken to him. He had not even been given anything to mop up the blood. When I arrived he just said, "Don't embarrass me, Mom." He had been totally ignored until I arrived. His friends had done really well but their help was not even acknowledged.

Teenage boys, particularly if they are in a group, are registered by adults as threatening and treated accordingly. Of course their loud, physical, swaggering behavior contributes to this perception. These young men, barely out of childhood, are trapped in a stereotype that they are helpless to undo, and which is almost universally reinforced by the people around them. A large twelve-year-old who is laughing and fooling around on a bus may have no idea that, to others, his behavior is threatening. He still feels like a child fooling around. It is the reaction to his behavior that will begin to teach him he has the power to frighten people—a power that he may not actually want at all or, on the other hand, may enjoy.

It isn't surprising that these boys, with their skittering voices, pimples, and sudden lurch upward in height, feel ambivalent about their newfound freedom. This mother commented that her thirteen-year-old "swings from one extreme to the other. At times he is very close and affectionate with lots of hugging and cuddling. Then he swings to real dislike, frustration, and arguments, most of which have to do with his defining and challenging limits."

One way of dealing with ambivalent feelings is to ensure that your parents continue to organize your life. Adolescent boys will adopt strategies in which they can vent their anger and frustration about the limitations parents make on their freedom, while at the same time doing everything in their power to prove that they are not yet ready to be kicked out of the nest.

One mother of a thirteen-year-old boy who had taken to aggressively demanding his right to be treated as an adult said:

> My daughter is so organized. She is always making demands because she knows exactly what she wants. I have to treat my thirteen-year-old son like an eight-year-old and give him careful instructions, otherwise he would never get anything done, he would miss appointments and forget to go where he is meant to be. Words just wash off him. Sometimes I feel like pinning instructions to his coat.

If something happens at this crucial stage to shake the foundations of his security, a child may find it very hard to steer himself through these choppy waters. This mother said of her son:

> As a young child he lacked courage but he was the easiest child in the world. He saw life as a challenge to be avoided. He had very few friends and was not at all interested in sports. He just wanted to be at home. He survived by keeping his head down. He plodded along, a bit uncoordinated, a bit of a loner.

He and his younger brother lived with their mother. However, they saw their father frequently and their parents made an effort to maintain a good relationship. When he was fourteen his father committed suicide. It was an experience that thoroughly shook him up. As his mother said:

> The boys loved their dad—he was an exciting and inspiring person. The older one was completely wiped out by his

death. I think it was partly the realization that his dad wasn't a hero. When he killed himself he was letting them down.

For their mother his death was also a blow. In spite of their differences, and his history of depression, he had always been there for his children. When, two years earlier, the younger boy had been seriously ill, his parents were both there at his bedside, taking turns to provide support. When the father died there was no one else for her to turn to in order to share the difficulties of being a parent. She tried to get professional help but was unable to find the support that she needed to help her cope.

Within a year of his father's death, this easygoing boy started to go off the rails:

> He became very hostile and angry. There would be door banging. He would leave home and then come back. He did very well in his GCSE exams [those taken at sixteen] but then, after one term at school doing A-levels [exams taken at eighteen], he decided that he couldn't stand school any longer, so he dropped out. It was a terrible time. It was really wearing me down, and I wouldn't discuss it with any of my friends because I didn't want my son to be labeled as a troublemaker. I had to cope with it all alone.

Looking back, she feels that her son was badly let down by his school (a popular school with a pretty good academic reputation):

> My kids have been through dreadful personal experiences: divorce, disease, and death. They have learned that the worst can happen, that you do nothing wrong and all this pain is dumped on you anyway. They needed attention and sympathy but they didn't get it. I think it's about boys being expected to take it like a man. They are just expected to cope.

At eighteen, this boy seems to be recovering his equilibrium. He has returned to college to study agriculture. He is still angry but his anger is no longer focused on his mother. He has extended it to the whole of Western society. His intention is to get away from it all and go and live in a Third World country. In the meantime he just learned to cut himself off from the mainstream, macho culture of the school by, says his mother, "giving up the competition for peer-group approval." As a result he was thrown back on his own resources, had few friends, and spent much of his time at home. She feels that he has come through his crisis and is deeply relieved that he is able to make his own decisions, however unorthodox.

For this child, the death of a loved father triggered a surge of rage. Many teenage boys go through similar periods of fury that may be much harder to understand, let alone sympathize with. Girls, it must be said, go through a similar spasm as they enter adolescence. Indeed, for many mothers, used to a companionable relationship with their daughters, the pain of a daughter's separation is far more devastating. Many boys have started the process of moving into the world much earlier and for them the teenage years may, by comparison with their sisters, seem positively peaceful. However, as we shall see a little later, when a boy does go off the rails, parents are often in for a far rougher ride.

For some boys, rebellion takes the shape of opting out. They seem unable to move away from the television or computer, they rot away in their rooms getting pasty-faced and puny, and their parents worry that they will never rejoin the world. It may be worth thinking about the stress they may be facing on a daily basis. No wonder they want to flop, to hide away in a fantasy world, to opt out of the real world, which forces them daily to hide their emotions, wear a shell over their vulnerable true selves, and bide their time until they are strong enough to do to others what has been done to them.

BECOMING A MEMBER OF THE TRIBE

Riding the storm of puberty, when your body is changing and the demands on you are increasing, both boys and girls find the need to form alliances with others who will be traveling this road with them. These alliances are a way of helping to define a personal identity. In order to develop a sense of himself or herself, a boy or girl becomes more particular than ever about friends and clothes. As Erikson says (1950):

> Young people can also be remarkably clannish and cruel in their exclusion of all those who are "different" in skin color, or cultural background, in tastes and gifts, and often in such petty aspects of dress and gesture as have been temporarily selected as *the* signs of an in-grouper or out-grouper.

This clannishness may manifest itself as cruelty to outsiders, but its main impulse is to establish common ground and greater closeness among those within the charmed circle. The young person is gathering around him- or herself a handpicked group to transfer trust and affection as a stepping stone out of his or her own family. The first signs of this outward identification may seem incredibly trivial. The boy may refuse to wash, not notice if yesterday's breakfast is still clinging to his jeans, never look tidy, and yet worry if a hair is sticking up on the back of his head.

Girls at this stage are even more body-conscious, but much of that concern is about body shape (a subject that has been exhaustively discussed elsewhere). They will also start to wear clothes that define them as fashionable, but the category allows for some degree of individual adaptation and self-expression. For boys, dress codes are narrow. Like the language that younger boys develop (see the previous chapter), they serve as a means of identification to like-minded people and a warning to those who might attack their budding, but fragile, identity.

Sports clothing may be the first step: it is distinct and allows a boy to make an instant assessment of those on his side—and the rest. A boy who feels uncertain about his standing in the group can be fairly sure of acceptance if he joins an already existing and sanctioned clique, such as those who follow a particular team. Says Jack's mother: "For a year he became an ardent football fan. I found that total identification with a team quite upsetting."

There are many other ways in which adolescents show the clan to which they belong. Young black youths in inner cities have developed a number of distinct subgroups, defined by clothing and hairstyle. A Ragga youth, for example, has zigzag patterns shaved into the back of the head and wears baggy clothes. For Matthew, a young white boy who joined a skinhead gang, the first outward sign was the way he wore his tie. In a school where uniform is the rule, such small signs are a way of indicating your relationship to a particular group.

One of the more peruasive badges of identification in American and British cities in the 1990s is footwear, specifically, the designer sneaker. Teenage boys have been known to kill for possession of these trophies of inclusion in the group, a fact that manufacturers cynically exploit by pricing their products at the very top of the scale at which they think parents will still be prepared to buy them.

Once the boy has found himself a niche, and feels a little more confident of the group with whom he identifies, some of these dress codes will evolve. He no longer needs the safety of a particular team uniform; he can venture out—a little—into the world of teen style. To most parents this will probably seem just as hideous as the shiny goalie's sweater with breakfast down it, but that is part of its charm as a way of marking the child's separation from the world in which Mommy bought his clothes for him. Erikson goes on:

Adolescents not only help each other temporarily through much discomfort by forming cliques and by stereotyping themselves, their ideals and their enemies; they also perversely test each other's capacity to pledge fidelity.

Those with more confidence may set out to establish their own clique. Adrian is one of a small group composed of half a dozen boys and girls who demonstrate their separateness by showing contempt for everyone else. They dress in the same way (although they believe themselves to be totally individual), they listen to the same music, and all have the same interests. The boys in the group have decided that work is contemptible because it's imposed by adults. The girls are rather more selective in their contempt, and they don't allow their identification as outsiders to interfere with their grades.

Adrian sees himself as different, but it is striking just how much his own feelings of his uniqueness coincide with those of his father at the same age, who remembers:

There was a central block of boys who conformed and grew up to be bank clerks. There were nonconformists who were cool. To be cool you had to have disrespect for authority and humor—the badge of identification in the group. It's always been very important to me that I haven't capitulated, I haven't conformed to things most people of my age and background conform to.

For Adrian, then, nonconformity is in itself a way of following in his father's footsteps. He is secure in his own sense of identity, and Adrian's mother feels that she can rely on his inner sense of self-preservation: "He is essentially a cautious child—he doesn't take risks, he just shows enough self-confidence to let the others think that he is a risk taker."

For those whose foundations are less firmly established before the age of twelve, the need to make alliances can lead to trouble.

Children who are attempting to define their own unique place will victimize those on the outside in order to prove themselves tough, impress their peers, and secure their place in the in-group. Bullying, which may have been quite random in the lower grades, gradually starts to focus on a much smaller group: those who by their vulnerability show themselves to be out-groupers, loners, those without a group at all.

Those who find themselves on the outside are easy meat for recruitment into gangs, where rules of loyalty are clear and attachment to someone big and tough brings with it a sense of security in a shifting and terrifying world. Erikson, writing in the shadow of the Second World War, made an analysis that holds a frightening message for the young people of Europe and America in the instability of the postcommunist society:

> The readiness for such testing [of fidelity] also explains the appeal which simple and cruel totalitarian doctrines have on the minds of the youth of such countries and classes which are losing their group identities and face worldwide industrialization, emancipation and wider communication.

Matthew's group and personal identity was not clearly drawn. His parents had grown up in the country and came to London to find work. They split up when he was eight and after a sheltered childhood with his gentle and creative mother, Matthew's entry to a large boys' secondary school was traumatic. It coincided with the time when his father remarried and his mother returned to college. He was desperate for support but quite unable to ask for it from his mother, Sara. She remembers:

> He did tell me that some boys had stolen his dinner money and we talked about that, but he never told me how frightened he was. Now he says I never listened, but in fact we

used to talk for hours and hours. I think perhaps he was trying to protect me. He must have thought that I was living on
a different planet. I had no idea of the reality of what he was
living with at school.

Matthew had always relied on his mother's understanding, but he
simply couldn't square her explanations of the oppression of black
people with his own experience of being bullied by a group of
black boys. He was just entering the phase of his life at which it
was necessary to define himself as separate from the person he
loved most in the world. His father was preoccupied with his own
life and unable to provide any alternative support.

Matthew soon discovered that, by dressing in skinhead gear, he
could attract the attention of bigger, stronger boys—and the protection too. Soon he was a part of the gang and before very long his
brother Peter had joined too. He had found himself an alternative
family. His loyalty to the group was unshakable. By the time his
mother realized what was happening, Matthew was unreachable. He
had pledged his fidelity to a cause that she found totally repugnant.

Sara was in an impossible position. The more she argued with
him, the firmer he became. She blames herself for what he
became, but this boy was not failed by his mother. She was the
only one in there battling for his soul. She, and he, were failed by
all the other people in their lives, who didn't see what was happening and failed to offer support. She says: "I was desperate and crying out for advice from anyone: doctors, teachers, psychiatrists,
therapists, friends, or family. I went everywhere, obsessively asking
for help to stop the nightmare getting worse."

At that time there were few schools prepared to take on board
the reality of cultural change. Bullying was not challenged, the
younger boys were left at the mercy of antisocial older children,
the growth of racist organizations within the school was ignored.
The attitude of the principal seemed to be that parents were
responsible for their children's behavior, and while they were at

school, the least said, the soonest mended. Matthew found that the only people who seemed willing to show him the way, teach him to be strong and manly and how to survive in the alien world in which he found himself, were a group of young fascists. He clung to them as models and mentors.

To his mother, Matthew, at twelve, seemed a responsible and serious child whom she looked to for support. At school these things were not valued and he did not have enough self-confidence to withstand the pressure to conform. His gentleness and soft voice made him a target for other boys, who could boost their own image by victimizing him. Of course, the fact that the children happened to be black was not the issue—there are bullies in every community and every stratum of society—but because the school did not acknowledge bullying for what it was, Matthew was left to draw his own conclusions from his extremely limited view of the world.

Unlike Matthew, Danny was the sort of little boy who was always in trouble. His mother remembers him as "always doing something that you didn't want him to do. He was a bit of a wild boy—a leader, he always wanted to be the star." When he started secondary school his confidence was shaken because he had a medical condition that made it hard for him to participate in sports. In elementary school he had been able to judge for himself when he should play and when he had to stop. His new phys. ed. teacher assumed he was malingering, humiliated him in front of his peers, and then, when it became evident that this child really wasn't physically strong, covered his confusion by barring him from participating at all.

It was a bad start for a boy who had always wanted to be the center of attraction. He was also spending a lot of time in the hospital, which further marginalized him. From being a bright, attractive, small boy, his world had shrunk and turned gray. But he kept the pain to himself until, at about fifteen, he found common cause with a group of similarly bright, but disenchanted, dropouts. Says his mother: "In a moment he seemed to go bananas. He started avoiding school, getting into drink and drugs, partying, and hanging around with shady people." By now his behavior appeared to be uncontrollable. His mother tried family therapy but everything kept getting worse:

> He had started dealing drugs and got knifed several times. I took advice from a drugs project and they suggested that I force him back to school, but that didn't last long. I would be at work and come home to find his friends in my house stealing things.
>
> As a liberal parent you rely on reason and love. I had no sanctions I could use. If I withheld money he would steal. For three years I have been hauling him out of police stations. I've told him I won't do that anymore, that he is on his own. His brother thinks I should throw him out. He says he is ruining all our lives. Maybe it would be better if I did send him away.

Sara did send her sons away. She said:

> Finally I snapped. I told them to pack a few things and go to their father's. I told them that I loved them more than anything in the world but I was finished. I had no more resources left. What they were involved with was no part of my life. What they were doing was wrong and if they were continuing with it they couldn't have it both ways. They could come back anytime but only when they finished with their fascist activities.

The time with their father did nothing to shake the boys' political convictions. Estranged from the mother he loved, Matthew, then sixteen, dropped out of school and found himself with the

time on his hands to get even more deeply involved with the antisocial group he had joined. His father, unused to the day-to-day
responsibility of taking care of children, did nothing to intervene.

Ten years later, Sara says:

What happened with me and the children is a wound inside
that never heals. How could I, who had considered myself
such a caring, loving mother, who shared such a close bond
with my children, how could I have failed so desperately? I am
haunted by the whole disaster. How easy it is to destroy a life.

In a sense this book is dedicated to people like Sara and, in
spite of the fact that he has grown into a person who represents
everything I despise, it is for Matthew too. Until we can understand what happens to turn a gentle, creative child into a thug, we
can do very little to stop it from happening to others.

Matthew and Danny are not special. They were not predestined
for their fate. Their parents are not bad people and they have
never stopped loving their sons. Why did it happen to them?
What happened to turn the little boys who were so loved into
young men who, in Danny's case, seem set on a course for self-
destruction, and in Matthew's case, set on dragging down as many
other people with him as he can? Now in his early twenties,
Matthew is a racist thug known to the police and implicated in
many racist attacks.

The rest of this book is an attempt to understand more clearly
the influences that turn boys into men and how very hard it is to
resist them, because wherever and whenever a boy meets the real
world of men he will be called upon to show that he too can be
tough. He may be able to take on the protective coloration of a
group or escape by tucking his softness well down behind a mono-
syllabic address, unremarkable clothing, and a basilisk stare, and
hope to emerge unscathed when the worst of the "proving time" is

over. He may come through the process relatively unscathed, still remembering how to laugh and how to love. He may get so used to operating within a group, rather than as an individual, that he spends his life seeking the safety of group structures to remind him that he has any existence at all. He may lose sight of his humanity altogether.

III

ALL MEN OF WOMAN BORN

5

Where Do Mothers Come From?

Many of the books on gender and sex equality written over the past twenty years have opened with a discussion of maternal instinct. Does it exist and, if so, is it important? Is it the reason for the inequality of women or just an excuse for it? The desire to protect babies seems to be something that all adults (and animals) have in common, but it is the feelings of mothers that have been separated off and called an instinct. Somewhat perversely, this has meant that mothers who do mistreat their babies are protected, while fathers in a similar position are not. A mother who kills her baby in the first year is rarely punished. She is assumed to be ill and in need of treatment. A man in the same situation has no similar defense. He is despised.

If instinct guides women as distinct from men, how does it operate? Surely it should guide us in providing the most basic care without which a baby could not survive, such as the knowledge of how to provide the milk without which our children would die? Nevertheless, in less than 100 years of bottle feeding, in some countries the ability to breast-feed has been all but forgotten. Mothers who do want to breast-feed often find that they are struggling because they have never seen another woman feed and have never been in a position to learn the skill. Midwives are now going back to turn-of-the-century descriptions of breast-feeding to try to relearn the technique so that they can pass it on to the mothers in their care. The baby's sucking reflex may be instinctive, but clearly the mother's role is not.

It isn't just in providing food that modern mothers often feel at sea. Many women come to motherhood with no understanding even of how to hold a baby. Their only preparation for parenthood has been the period in early childhood in which they spent hours and hours playing at being Mommy: cradling dolls, dressing dolls, feeding dolls. However, the obsession with dolls fades in time for most girls to become obsessed with boys, and, since the majority of women these days leave their own childbearing till their late twenties or thirties, the lessons are rather hazy—little wonder then that so many new mothers spend the first weeks of parenthood in a state of panic or depression.

However, before long, something does reach through the mist to guide us, but is that something an instinct or a memory? Those people who have worked with abused children have little doubt about this. They believe it is a mother's history, not her instinct, that she brings to the role of mother: the distant memory of the way in which her own mother handled her, like a mirrored reflection, passed on from generation to generation. If those memories are secure ones, she may enter into parenthood with confidence. If they fill her with dread, she may find herself veering wildly between her intellectual beliefs about how parents should behave and her deeply repressed memories of what happened in her own life.

Our children have no way of knowing whether our actions are driven by intellect or by the remote control of memory. They will pick it all up as a package. Our unresolved fears become a part of their understanding of the world. So, if we are to understand our children better, we must first try to understand ourselves and the influence of our parents on our lives.

Women's memories of their mothers may be particularly power-ful. Michele Collins, a young mother who sought the help of New-pin (an organization that helps mothers who are having difficulties with their children to come to terms with their own childhood), wrote this poem:

> *She stared down dark eyes.*
> > *Looking into my face,*
> *The fear would whelm within.*
> > *God I didn't sin.*
> *Her face would be so white.*
> > *Her hand would rise.*
> *Words would tumble out.*
> > *Of that empty space,*
> *between her lips,*
> > *The hand would fall slap.*
> *It sounded like a clap.*
> > *The blood warmed my cheek*
> *so red.*
> *I KNEW THEN THAT SHE REALLY WANTED ME DEAD.*

Michele's experience of being mothered had little positive for her to hang on to when it came to her turn. Others grope into their minds and find more fruitful memories: of being cradled and warm, of being rocked and sung to, of being loved. But there is another image in the mirror too, one that, for the mother of a son, may be even more important, though it may well be hazy. It is the reflection of our fathers, often wholly absent and rarely wholly there. Estranged fathers are less likely to keep in touch with daughters than with sons, and even a father in permanent resi-dence may spend very little time with his daughters and teach them very little about his world.

Nevertheless, the daughter will look for him. She senses that he holds something special for her, even though she doesn't

know what it is. This is what one thirteen-year-old girl said of
the father she had not seen for seven years:

> I ask Mom to drive past his house just so that I can see what
> it looks like, but she won't. And whenever we go to my aunt's
> I always look out because I know he lives near there. Last
> year I did see him. He was walking towards us and we waved
> and I called to him. He looked a bit puzzled, but then the
> lights changed and we had to move. He just went away.
> When I was younger I used to write to him, saying I wanted
> to see him—but I always changed my mind and didn't give
> the letter to my mom to send. I would like to tell him when I
> do well at school. Sometimes I dream about him and then,
> when I wake up, I really want to see him. I hope he thinks
> about me too. Sometimes I think he probably doesn't
> remember what I look like. I would like to see him, to go out
> to places with him, and get to know him because, whether he
> agrees with me or not, I still think of him as my dad and I
> miss him.

He is the Prince Charming of the legend, and the more absent he
is in reality, the more present he will become in her mind. The
daughter with a father who is real will play with him. She will
learn to kick a football, play cards, build Lego, work computer
games. The girl who has only a fleeting image of her father will
spend hours acting out fantasy games in which she is rescued from
her tower and carried off.

These fantasies will weave in and out of her other main life
work, which is to understand and emulate the role of her mother.
The female role she can build with ease: the bricks are all lying
around in front of her; she has only to pick them up and slot them
into place. The man is an enigma—he comes in from the outside;
he lifts her up out of her mundane world. He flatters and teases
her but she never has enough of him. He is never wholly hers; she

must share him with her mother and her brothers and sisters. He is like the Saturday afternoon treat that she thinks about on and off during the week: it's not entirely essential to life, but it sure cheers things up.

Of course he may not be Prince Charming at all. He may be the monster in the story. Nevertheless, whether he is angry, abusive, or merely absent or abstracted, he is still not a whole person and he still cannot fill her emotional and physical need for love in the way in which her mother does. She continues to imagine the man who can and, in the meantime, relies on first her mother, and then girl-friends, to fulfill her emotional needs.

Some women give up on Prince Charming and seek both emotional and physical fulfillment with women, but most find that the need to take possession of a man becomes an urgent one as adolescence awakens erotic needs. According to long-term surveys in the United States and Britain, girls in single-parent families are more likely to find themselves involved in sexual relationships and motherhood before they are ready. It seems then that girls without the secure love and esteem of two parents are most likely to start looking for love elsewhere—and most likely to be disappointed when they don't find it.

While young women are looking for Prince Charming, their male counterparts are involved in a two-way struggle. Having finally broken free of the world of women into the world of men, they find that their sexuality is leading them straight back in. Is it a trap they are entering or is it a return to the perfect love of their infancy, which Michael Balint described as the final aim of all erotic striving: "I shall be loved always everywhere and in every way, my whole body, my whole being—without any criticism, without the slightest effort on my part"? (Balint, 1935)

The young woman may also want this unconditional love. She may well be looking for and believe that she has at last found the relationship she craves with the man who will satisfy both her erotic and her emotional needs, the man-mother that she never had. She may soon discover that she is expected to provide emotional support rather than receive it, but she continues to wait, as she has been trained to do, for the moment when he will come up trumps. He will provide the emotional resting place she craves. So she oscillates between displays of physical weakness—in an attempt to force him into the father role—and mothering him—to prove that she is worth loving.

Into this relationship she will bring a child. Is it instinct that leads her? Or is it the need for a love in which she can totally lose herself at last? After all, a child must return her love and a child cannot go away. A woman often begins pregnancy knowing that her partner's enthusiasm does not match her own. She hopes that he will learn to love the baby and that, in the meantime, his love for her will ensure that he provides the emotional support that she will need for the task ahead. For, after all, aren't men supposed to be the strong ones? Don't they tell us that they are the ones who can run the show?

Maybe he will or maybe he won't. Studies show that the man she had hoped would stand beside her too often disappears at the crucial moment. Between 30 and 50 percent of men withdraw emotionally into depression, or physically into longer hours of work, after a baby is born. Daddy, feeling the trap of mother love close around him, deprived of the total attention he feels is his due, has disappeared into the world of men.

This is how one thoughtful man talked about his own introduction to fatherhood and the loss of the warm spot near his partner's emotional fireside:

> When she was pregnant she became very detached, and I felt very lonely and frightened of not doing the right thing. I was very committed to the idea of having a baby and being involved, and supporting her, but I didn't really know what it meant and I think I was scared of being found out, so I didn't talk about any of it.

Like most men I had got so used to emotional support from women that I didn't even realize I was getting it. I couldn't see it. When that support got refocused on the baby, I didn't know what to do. I knew the baby needed attention but I just didn't know what to do about the sudden, yawning emotional gap. I'm not sure that I even realized what it was. I just felt violated.

He reacted, just as a child might do to the birth of a sibling and the realization that Mother must be shared, by veering between attempts to "be good" and acting out his frustration and jealousy with tantrums. However much he tried to be supportive, he couldn't control his behavior because, at the time, he couldn't understand it:

I'd seen how so many women cope with their husbands' emotional demands by just treating them like another child. I so much didn't want to behave like that. I tried to be the perfect dad. To be boundlessly joyous. I couldn't think about what I was feeling at all, and nobody else was interested. I was just expected to be totally supportive. So I treated all my fears as weaknesses and just tried to ignore them. I veered between being a brick of unswerving support and just exploding.

This father was utterly committed to fatherhood. He too longed for the total love of another human being and held on until he found his equilibrium. Many partnerships don't survive the shock of fatherhood. With the level of divorce climbing steadily toward one in two marriages, according to Zelda Westmeads of Relate, the Marriage Guidance Council, "it is very common to discover that problems emerge after the birth. The first baby is not just a change but a crisis in many marriages."

For many new mothers, then, the bubble of Prince Charming

bursts on contact with reality. She reverts to her old ways, turns for help and emotional support to other women, and, angry at this betrayal of her dream, shuts the father out. Once again she has learned that Daddies are only there on Saturday afternoons. If you happen to fall over and cut your knee on a Tuesday, you will have to make do with Mom. She now knows that it wasn't her mother who kept her father away from her—it was the outside world that claimed her dad and then claimed her partner too.

The father quoted above refused to be shut out. While he was unable to provide the emotional support that his partner wanted, he was not prepared to give up on the emotional fulfillment that he wanted for himself—with his child. Gradually his partner learned to trust him enough to open the door and let him back in. Many fathers take one look at the closed door and head for a bar.

These mothers have two choices: they can learn to accommodate to a partner who isn't part of the partnership or they can get angry. If they get angry and force confrontation, perhaps they will both learn to find a new way. They might, on the other hand, decide to part. Most marriages that fail do so while children are under five years old. Many partnerships soldier on with a mother who runs the whole parenting side of the venture. These are the women who have decided that accommodation is less painful than war. They may, like Roseanne Arnold, grumble about their partners' inadequacies and small incompetencies while embracing them in the love that they also provide for their children. They might live on in smoldering resentment with a man they have learned to view with contempt, or they may simply lower their standards, like the middle-class mothers Ros Coward describes in her book *Our Treacherous Hearts:*

> While researching for this book, I received the strange impression that a large number of women were actually married to the same man! One after another women repeated,

often verbatim, the same feelings about husbands and partners. These men were described as more stable, more balanced, kinder, nicer and more fun than the women themselves. They were "successful," "ambitious," "secure,"
"kind" or "the perfect father." The women described themselves as "lucky." Far from listing men's inadequacies, women
seemed pathetically grateful for any small amount of domestic input.

The explanation of why so many men, try as they might, are
unable to come up with the goods and become equal parents is a
large part of what this book is, in the end, about. Right now we are
talking about the mother and her relationship with her newborn
son, and it is the image of her relationship with her father and her
partner that will shadow their encounters.

Many mothers find that the love they feel for an infant son is
different from the love they feel for their daughters. There is a
sense of continuity with a daughter and a sense of difference with
a son. A woman who feels positive about herself, and her female-
ness, will embrace her daughter within that comfortable self and
establish a companionable intimacy. A woman who feels bad
about herself may well treat her daughters badly, as though pun-
ishing them for being female, being like she is.

A son may arouse quite unexpected feelings. Some mothers talk
with a surprised delight about how much they love their sons,
almost as though they hadn't really expected to find so much to
love about someone so alien. The differences are intriguing and
the similarities possibly even more so. When mothers talk about
their sons, it is often as though they had found hidden treasure—
underneath the often gruff exterior is a special something reserved
only for them.

Chodorow (1978) summarizes the cases of two psychoanalysts,
Burlingham and Sperling, who describe

girls who act as extensions of their mothers, who act out the aggression which their mothers feel but do not allow themselves to recognize or act on. They describe boys, by contrast, who equally intuitively react to their mother's feelings and wishes as though they were the objects of their mother's fantasies rather than the subjects. Girls, then, seem to become and experience themselves as the self of the mother's fantasy, whereas boys become the other.

At a parents' group I visited in Newcastle, one mother's self-loathing was directed in a very physical way against her two daughters, whom she abused both verbally and physically. Her own history was of constant betrayal by her father and then by the man who had fathered her three children while living with another woman. Instead of hating the men who had disappointed her, this woman had taken that anger on herself, believing that all women are "stupid" and "useless." She hated herself for her powerlessness and had longed to have a son of her own—a man who would stay with her, share her life, and make her stronger. When she finally had a son she was overjoyed; at last she was reconciled to being a mother—although she was still abusive toward her daughters.

Already, in infancy, she is feeding her son a myth of masculine superiority, although he will actually grow up in a world that is peopled entirely by women (his mother and two sisters). How will he live out his mother's fantasies of his masculine power in a world in which his only real power will lie in his ability to cause trouble? In this area of Newcastle adult male unemployment has become normal. His only real chance of economic independence will be through hustling, the only way to show his power through fighting. This child has been told that he, the youngest in his family, is also the most important. He has been preprogrammed for a life in which he will be impossible to discipline and will never discipline himself.

The shadow of absent fathers reflecting their images in her

mind has created a longing that she cannot fulfill, just as she is now creating a boy who will be unable to fulfill the needs of the women in his future. This woman's pathological self-hatred marks her out as extreme, but the other women in the group, when asked, could think of nothing positive to say about having daughters other than that it was fun to dress them up.

For every woman who projects her own self-disgust onto her daughters, there must be as many who take into the experience of mothering a sense of betrayal by their fathers and then find themselves unconsciously playing it out in their relationships with partners and sons.

Disappointment breeds resentment, and those men who castigate feminists for breeding man-hatred would be appalled by the level of antipathy toward men expressed by very ordinary women who have never been remotely touched by ideas about separatism and would certainly not classify themselves as feminists, women for whom contemptuous grumbling about male incompetence is matched only by their fear of the "strangers" who stalk the street, grab innocent children, and wreak vengeance on women through violent sex.

These mothers may well see their own sons as exempt from this condemnation of the male world, but it will be harder for their sons to exempt themselves. One sixteen-year-old boy told me: "There was a lot of passionate man-hating going on. She used to say it didn't apply to me because I was only a boy. But I was going to grow up into a man." A boy who grows up being told that men are bad can choose either to be bad as well, to side with his mother and despise himself, or to reject his mother and everything she stands for.

Steven wrote to the *Guardian* newspaper in January 1990:

She used to talk for hours with her woman friends on the telephone. "Dissolve the marriage," she would say when they moaned about their husbands. But I have had 23 years of that and I am sick of it. What am I supposed to say? "Yes, men are morally inferior." Either I say that or I turn round and say, "No!" Which is what I did . . . I turned round, held her by the shoulders and said, "Mum, you are full of shit!"

Parents who are engaged in a dance with the reflections in their own mirrors cannot see what is happening in their partner's mirror. Perhaps if they could, they would turn and start dancing with each other, creating new reflections for their own children.

6

The Making of Mother Power

The mirror dance of the last chapter plays fast, or slow, as the backdrop to the daily care of our infant sons. In the foreground is the mother. After nine months inside their mothers, our sons spend the next nine months gradually learning that they exist as separate beings from this warm, soft, sweet-smelling body. Studies show few consistent, observable differences in the ways in which women care for sons or daughters in the first year, though they do show that mothers, on average, breast-feed their sons for longer than their daughters, and they tend to respond more quickly when their sons cry.

Some writers have seen this as evidence of the mother's preference for boys, or perhaps as a way of enforcing the "boys don't cry" rule at an early age. It seems more likely to me that it is a fairly simple response to the fact that, as the last section pointed out, women are more likely to feel a sense of continuity with their daughters and a sense of difference with their sons. Their relationship with their daughters can be more matter-of-fact because they feel at ease with them, while with their sons there is an edge of anxiety generated by difference. Physical affection is a good substitute for understanding, and mothers will use it with their sons just as they do with their lovers.

So our sons, from the very start, are being handled most of the time by someone who loves them wholeheartedly but does not expect—quite—to understand them. For our daughters, love is tempered by the mother's knowledge of who they are. From birth, mothers are teaching their daughters, by their example and the stimulation they provide, to become women like themselves. Of course, this involves dangers as well as advantages, because mothers will project the things they don't like about themselves as well as the things they do, but that is the subject of another book.

To start with, the mother is the whole world to her child. Then other arms will hold him. He will learn that there is a world outside and other people to care for him and that Mother is not always there. He may even transfer his deepest bond to someone else if that person spends more time with him, but in the vast majority of families it is still Mother who is the apple of his eye. When he learns to crawl, he will follow her. Now he can find her, but he cannot hold on to her. She can leave and he cannot make her stay. He does not control this important part of his life. She controls him.

The realization of separateness is a difficult time both for boys and girls, but it is boys who react with more fear (Hargraves and Colley, 1986, p. 106). Researchers have no convincing explanation for this difference, but it seems possible that the greater confidence that mothers feel with their daughters is reciprocated. A crawling girl baby will move toward her mother at the first sign of stress. A boy is more likely to "freeze" and then to cry.

Perhaps more interesting is the finding of researchers Martin, Maccoby, and Jacklin (in Hargraves and Colley, 1986, p. 109) that mothers who were more responsive to their baby sons produced sons who were more exploratory at two years old and more sociable at three, while girls whose mothers were similarly responsive were more clingy and less exploratory. It was the mothers who were less responsive whose daughters proved more sociable at three years old. Once again there are no clear-cut theories as to why this should be, but perhaps the secret lies with the sense of difference that many mothers feel with their sons.

Girls whose mothers are less involved tend, like boys, to be more prepared to explore. It seems that both boys and girls need a fine balance of loving involvement and a sense of separateness if they are to be both confident and exploratory. For boys with less responsive mothers, the sense of separateness is too great and the child becomes fearful. For girls with overly responsive mothers, the sense of separateness doesn't start to develop at all and the child is afraid to explore her own world for herself.

SOME HAVE AND SOME HAVEN'T GOT . . . BALLS

For a child living with parents who are not concerned to emphasize gender, the first introduction to the idea of "difference" may arise with the birth of a sibling. The first child in this family, in which both parents were very involved in care, was a boy. He was, according to his father, a gentle child who played with cuddly toys and enjoyed homemaking games. His first realization of difference was that classical moment that Freud described. He was three and was bathing with his six-month-old sister. After the bath they were both naked on the bed when he asked: "Was her willie chopped off?"

Freud suggested that the realization that girls, and Mommies, don't have a penis triggers in the boy a fear that his may also be chopped off. He believed that, in infancy, a boy identifies solely with his mother and, in fantasy, fights his father for possession of her. The boy then learns to fear that his father, in retaliation, might cut his penis off, and it is this fear that provides the motivating force behind the boy's move from the all-embracing love of the mother to identification with the father—and the start of opposition to the mother. It is an "if you can't beat them, join them" situation, which seems to assume that it is fear that lies at the heart of the acquisition of masculinity.

In families in which the father does take a sufficiently warm and involved interest, his sons can make the transition without feeling that they are burning their bridges behind them. They can be like Dad without betraying their love of their mother. However, in most households, even loving fathers are not necessarily available fathers. Peter Moss and Julia Brannen, in their study of dual-career families, discovered that full-time working mothers spent nearly five times as long as their partners in sole charge of their infants. Where mothers do not work full-time, the discrepancy is far greater. A survey of American men has discovered that, on average, fathers spend eleven minutes a day in the company of their children (Brannen and Moss, 1991).

In today's macho work environment, many men seem to feel that they have to outdo each other in overtime and weekend work to keep their place in the rat race. In Britain, 42 percent of men work more than forty-six hours a week (and that doesn't include commuting time). In those homes where fathers do provide care for their small children, it is often at night, while the children are asleep. Even if Dad doesn't work at all, he is unlikely to become the major caregiver. Women, on the whole, abandon paid work when their partners are unemployed, rather than leaving them to care for the children. So even when the father is there, he rarely provides the emotional underpinning of their lives.

If he has no contact at all with his father, or another man with a similar role in the family, the boy will not learn yet that men have a higher authority in the world. He will not have to face separation from his mother or identification with his father. He will derive all that he needs from his mother, growing close and learning to identify, as a girl would, with the mother. Most research makes clear that it is fathers, not mothers, who are most concerned with marking the gender difference, to claim their sons as "like them" and their daughters as "different."

Studies of single-parent children under the age of two (Cheryl Keir, University of East London) show no evidence that, at this age, the lack of a second parent presents any difficulties at all. With no knowledge of his difference, the boy child feels no need to establish difference from his mother. He may well be more gentle and cooperative than the "average" boy.

Some psychologists see this as a problem that may lead to distortions in a child's gender identification and, eventually, to transsexualism (the desire to be a woman). Dr. Richard Warshak, a clinical psychologist from Texas, says:

> People call these boys "Mama's boys." Some become so frightened to leave the safe "womb" of their mother's home that they refuse to attend school. They usually have difficulty getting along with other boys and prefer to play with girls and younger children.

It's an interesting theory and one that makes clear the fragility of our notions of masculinity and femininity. Clearly, if a boy cannot become properly masculine without lessons in how to be male, then masculinity—as we understand it—cannot be something a boy is born with. It is added, like icing, to a ready-made cake. In the example quoted in the last chapter of a child who was "treated" for supposed gender confusion at the age of four, the problem was not in the child at all. He knew he was a boy and was quite happy being a boy. What he had not realized was that his version of being a boy was not compatible with the world's view of how boys should be. The confusion was imposed from the outside.

If this boy had lived with a father in the house, the psychologists would have been less concerned, even if he was still interested in playing with dolls. They would not have been able to construct his preference as something "imposed" on him by women. Children who stay longer in the company of women, or among men who are themselves concerned about being gentle and nurturing, may well construct an idea of themselves as gentle, nurturing people. The difficulty they face is not with their view of themselves but with the way the world views them.

If a boy has no father to fight for the love of his mother, clearly the scenario Freud described cannot take place, at least in the way he suggested. Nevertheless, the recognition of gender will, in itself, usher in a new era for a small boy. He will learn sooner or later that he is different from the mother, grandmother, aunts, or other female caregivers who form the inner ring of his daily protection: the women who provide the secure base from which he will learn to go out into the world. So, in order to discover what it means to be male, he is faced with the awful task of tearing himself away from the sheltering protection of the people he loves most. Is it any wonder that we hear that boys are more "difficult" than girls?

CONFRONTING MOTHER POWER

As the baby discovers that he can have some control over his own environment, he will soon start to realize that adult power can be used to thwart him. The clash of wills often peaks at the time we call the "terrible twos"—when children are testing the limits of their newfound capabilities. As the child learns to run, so he must learn not to run into a road. As he learns to turn switches, he must learn also that some switches hold dangers. As he learns to climb, he must learn also that he can fall.

Since it is his mother who cares for him, a boy's first experience of opposition will be with a woman. He will learn that women exert control and that men stand far away. His first understanding of power relationships will tell him that he is not destined for power, because the fact that men are in reality more powerful is not one he can yet grasp.

Pat, whose difficulties with her two-year-old son were described in the last section, was left with the entire onus of responsibility for her child. Child care was her job; her partner gave her no backup at all until she managed to persuade him to visit a child guidance clinic with her. Probably the most significant moment was, she told me, "my husband telling me how patient he thought I was. He had never said that before."

It is perhaps an interesting reflection on the importance of a mother's own self-confidence that Pat needed the approval of two men—the psychologist and her own husband—to give her the confidence to control her son more firmly. It is this backup role that many fathers prefer to the hands-on approach of the mother. Sometimes the backup will be far less helpful. Mothers often complain that fathers break all the rules they are trying to establish with their children and undermine their efforts to provide boundaries. As one mother complained:

> I worry a lot about the children eating sweets. Their father will go to the store with Jerome, who will come through the door saying, "I'm going to tell Mommy I've got candy." His father says, "I couldn't help it. He doesn't respect my authority like he does yours."

Both these boys are learning that Mother has power but, at some higher level, there is a man who has power over her and can be used against her. They cannot yet construct this power hierarchy entirely to their own benefit. They love their mothers too much to be glad that Father represents a higher power, but already it is sowing the seeds for rebellion against mother rule. They see that Father lives in a different realm and that that realm is also going to be theirs.

One of the first sites of the battle for separation from Mother may come when the boy finds that she is intent on controlling a part of him that, until then, had belonged entirely to him. Psychoanalysis has much to say about the importance to child development of the moment at which the mother temporarily takes control of a child's bodily processes in order to hand back a more orderly control to the child. Modern child-care experts, taking the lead from psychoanalysis, suggest that toilet training should not take place until the child has enough understanding to see the purpose of the exercise and to take control himself or herself.

Nevertheless, the transfer from the baby state, in which the child has been allowed to excrete at will, to potty training, where the child is trained to predict when these bodily processes will take place and then act on that understanding, is a big step. It is also a step that boys are more likely than girls to find difficult. Part of the difficulty may be that boys simply mature more slowly and take longer to be able to predict their bodily functions, but boys are also more inclined to perceive toilet training as a battle of wills and to utilize it in the attempt to wrest control of their world from their mothers.

So right at the beginning, at the tender age of two, while the girl sees the introduction of a potty as a way to be grown up—to be more like Mommy—the boy is likely to perceive it as an attempt to control him, to take something away from him. Of course, both girls and boys can have problems and may regress under stress to a baby phase in which the world seemed a more benign place and they felt less responsible for their actions. But boys are four or five times more likely to visit clinics for help in controlling this basic bodily function (Blackwell, 1989). Perhaps they need the involvement of another adult to take control from the hands of their mothers and put it where it rightly belongs.

At the height of Pat's problems in coping with her son's behavior, he took to soiling himself. He would quietly go off into another room and then return with a trouserful, even though he was well aware that this would upset his mother and cause him more distress than simply asking for a potty. This problem was resolved when she and her husband sought help. When Pat became more confident and calmer, her son gradually felt able to take control for himself.

Another mother told me that she felt closer to her son than her daughter, that he was more "like" her, and yet this loving son,

from the age of two, entered into a battle with her over the contents of his body. By the age of eight, the problem of soiling was
compounded by the ostracism of his peers. His mother wrote:

> Poor child, he seems a shadow of the happy little boy he was
> three or four years ago. Or a shadow has fallen on him. The
> day before yesterday was his birthday. He came into our bed
> and started opening presents. As each one opened he
> seemed to compose his face into what he felt was the right
> expression of gratitude. How is it that he is so unresponsive?
> He casts himself into a state of noninvolvement, a kind of
> waking oblivion where he is hard to reach.

This child was the quietest member of an ebullient family. Highly
imaginative and creative, he seemed to feel totally overwhelmed:
by a mother who took, perhaps, too much pride in his creativity,
robbing him of his solitary pleasure by the intensity of her interest;
by an extrovert older brother and a father who set a standard of
achievement that he felt he could never hope to emulate.

His father wrote down the following snatch of conversation
when the boy was nine years old:

> Sometimes in dreams I am flying over this line of houses.
> Seeing the woman inside writing on the same page of a
> book. She sits by the bottom window, just by the door. The
> woman in the dream is like my thoughts, my conscience.
> She knows about right and wrong. She believes that she has
> to finish the book. Sometimes I think I might not be what I
> am. I have to be allowed to think my own thoughts because
> they are mine.

It was at this stage that his parents decided to seek the help of a
child guidance clinic. Gradually the problem was resolved. Her
son, reflecting on the experience a while later, said:

I couldn't get all the things I felt out of my system. I didn't tell people what I felt most of the time but this man [a psychologist] asked questions so that you had to say how you were feeling. It was a relief to find an adult who was listening.

Clearly his parents were listening. What they were unable to do was to create the space into which he could speak, or the words in which he could articulate his anxiety. He felt desperate to preserve some sense of his integrity, so he held on to the contents of his body just as he hid the contents of his mind. But he discovered that things cannot just be kept in. They leak out; they demonstrate to the world that something is wrong.

This mother's love was never in doubt, nor was his love for her. According to the theory of psychoanalyst Christiane Olivier, in *Jocasta's Children,* it could be that at the bottom of the problem lay his fear of growing up—entering a world in which he would leave his mother and learn to compete with his brother and be like his powerful father. Says Olivier:

For various reasons it may happen that the little boy can't make it on to the classic road to "maleness" [transferring the opposition of toilet training to a more generalized opposition in the games he plays]. He will go off in a different direction, giving up the struggle because the "enemy" is too strong. The direction he takes is one of regression. Seeing the effort that is called for, he just gives up, he dies: becomes apathetic, goes on wetting and soiling himself, shows no interest in anything. In a word, he would rather not grow up.

BECOMING A REAL BOY

For some children, opposition is triggered not from within the home but through contact with the outside world with the first move to the nursery school. Here they will come up against other children, and adults, who may have a more developed sense of gender and need to enforce those divisions to prop up their own identity.

The boy who has been happy to help Mommy clean up after a meal suddenly refuses to do anything she asks him to do. He may regress into tantrums, which are put down to his being "over-tired"; he may simply refuse to tell her anything about the things that happen at school, or greet her with an outburst of anger when she picks him up from school. If he feels totally overwhelmed by the expectations put upon him, he may simply refuse to go to school, inventing headaches, tummy aches, and any other reasonable or unreasonable excuse to avoid the world in which, he now realizes, he is expected to start the business of turning into a man.

The little boy is not only feeling the pull of the male world; he is also experiencing the tug of the female world of home, love, comfort, and mother. He may choose to stay in it a while longer and emerge more slowly, or he may feel the need to make a sharp and aggressive show of defiance in order to prove that he is indeed different.

One child of five, in the midst of an argument about what he could and couldn't be allowed to do, picked up a toy and threw it at his mother. She was deeply shocked, but it turned out to be a pivotal point in their opposition. It was as though, at that moment, they had established an understanding. His aggression dropped off as his masculine identification intensified. He insisted on absolute control over the clothes he wore, and his behavior became almost a pastiche of the tough, macho stance of the oldest boys in the school. Once he found acceptance as the smart cookie he wanted to be, his aggression toward his mother lessened. He felt safer to show affection without getting overwhelmed by her love and turning back into a baby.

This child has a close relationship with his father, whom he sees regularly, but they do not live together. At the point of the worst conflict with his mother, he was getting along well with his father, who simply saw the problem as evidence of his ex-partner's inability to handle her son. This child was clearly using his father as a role model for the man he wanted to become but he was, at the same time, reflecting back to his mother the hostility that he knew his father felt toward her. The conflicting loyalties were difficult to deal with, and the showdown provided him with an opportunity to back off, as well as providing his mother with the evidence of his difference.

John also found a way of marking his difference. In his case the opposition was far less intense. His father is a warm, engaged, and central figure in his life and, in moving closer to his father, he did not feel the need to reject his mother aggressively. He decided that, at the age of almost seven, he wanted to have his hair cut as his father did, at a real barber's. His mother said:

> He watched a man having his hair cut first. He was having zigzags cut in the back and looked very stylish. Then Sam realized that he was having his hair cut by the same person. He was overjoyed. He felt so proud and grown up. When we left he said to me, "I want to have my hair cut every day."

For other boys the separation may be the refusal to talk about school life, which was discussed in the last section, or an insistence on wearing a particular kind of clothing, but it will not be complete. Just as a boy displays aggression one day, he will want the total love he has come to expect the next day. He may stand tough and tall on the playground and then dissolve into tears if someone knocks him down. He wants his mother but he wants to be male too, and it may at times feel very hard to have both.

THE MOTHER'S DILEMMA

Most mothers feel a sense of loss as their sons start to identify as male. It is the mother, not the father, who feels upset the day her son has his curls cut off, who enjoys his plump babyness and feels sad as she watches it disappear. She loves her daughter too, but the closeness of their bond is not threatened in the same way. Her daughter may not feel the urgent need to break away for many years yet. Indeed, in these first school years, her desire to be nurturing, pretty, and loved by Mommy intensifies. For the girl and her mother, the problem may be not one of separation but of overidentification. For the daughter, growing up is becoming more like Mother. For her brother, growing up means being less like Mother.

However, the desire to keep their sons close a little longer is not Mother's only motivation. They look at what the world does to boys and they feel afraid. They know that their own child is not hard, tough, cynical. They do not want him to be like that. Virtually every mother I have ever talked to believes that her son is uniquely sensitive. He is not unique; it is just that she is the only person who is allowed to glimpse that softness. Women everywhere, whether their agenda is political or practical, express the same dilemma: how to bring up the boys they would like for their daughters—and themselves—without exposing them to danger. For women recognize that the male world is dangerous and that they cannot just keep their boys at home.

The child who stays close to his mother and totally identifies with her in the preschool years will not necessarily stay that way. He may become even more difficult and unruly than his peers. He may have learned late what the difference is, but, having learned, he is anxious to be accepted as "one of the boys." As he takes a crash course in masculinity he may well alienate the very people he is trying to attract—and drive his poor mother mad as she wonders whatever happened to her gentle little boy.

Finding a way to respond to opposition can be both difficult and extremely distressing. No mother coping with a difficult child can escape feelings of fear and shame about his future and her abilities as a parent. A child who is unruly is seen by the world as a reproach, a judgment on our abilities as mothers.

I have lost count of the number of times mothers (usually mothers of girls) have told me that such-and-such a mother does nothing to curb her son's aggression and seems unaware of the havoc he is causing. I find this hard to believe. Mothers who beat their children into sullen good behavior perhaps don't care about them. Mothers who don't seem to respond do care about their children; they just don't know how to react to their opposition, and they feel helpless. One mother said:

> My first child needed constant vigilance. I couldn't leave him for a second. He seemed to have no idea of right and wrong. I felt that I was constantly shouting at him. My second child, a girl, hardly needed to be corrected. She just seemed to know how best to behave in order to get what she wanted. With the second child I felt completely relaxed in company. With the first I felt constantly anxious about how he might behave and also about how I might respond.

The way in which parents respond to their child's opposition will provide him with his sense of himself and the world and will shape the kind of child he will grow into. Research indicates that parents who react to difficult behavior in preschool children with verbal or physical attacks, power assertion, or withdrawal, rather than compromise, are more likely to end up with aggressive, insecure adolescents.

A difficult child is often an anxious child desperately covering his own anxiety. What he needs is to feel safe, and it is warm, authoritative, and consistent parenting that will provide that safety. Acting with calm authority is very different indeed from being authoritarian. An authoritative parent provides firm limits, until the child is old enough to take over the reins of his own life, without attacking a child's sense of his own worth. An authoritarian parent imposes her will without concern for her child's feelings.

It is not easy to be an authoritative parent who can generate a calm security while one's children are ricocheting off the walls. Where there is conflict between parents, it is particularly hard for either parent to maintain a calm and authoritative structure for the children, and sons, far more than daughters, seem to react by becoming disorganized, excitable, and difficult.

Psychology professor Mavis Hetherington compared the behavior of children in high-conflict and low-conflict families, both divorced and intact. At a year after divorce, the sons in both divorced groups were more oppositional and aggressive, lacking in self-control, distractable, and demanding than those in intact families. By the second year after divorce, the boys in low-conflict divorced families were doing better than those in high-conflict intact families, and those coping with both divorce and conflict were doing worst of all.

It seems likely that these boys (all between four and six years old) were suffering from a conflict of loyalty that the girls were less sensitive to. The boys would have just entered the life stage in which they were beginning to move from the mother's world into identification with the father. His sudden disappearance, particularly if it was accompanied by hostility toward (and from) the mother, would have disrupted that transition and caused an internal conflict that the girls are less likely to face. If this man with whom a boy is just learning to identify is now an enemy of the person he needs and loves most in the world, how can this identification be right?

During the elementary school years, then, a boy is creating his identity from the clues he finds around him. If his father is close and warm, he will find the job little more difficult than his sisters, who have their mother's role to follow. If his parents are fighting over his head, he will be anxious and confused. He needs his mother's love badly but he also needs to show that he is different. He doesn't know whether to stay with the women or leave with the men.

SINGLE MOTHER, DIFFICULT SONS

Though conflict between parents will affect boys in all families, boys in divided families have an additional problem. It is hard to indicate your difference from someone who is all you have in the world. In research by Mavis Hetherington (1982), boys of four and five whose parents had recently divorced were rated by teachers as "more aggressive, impulsive, resistant and lacking in task orientation" than girls or than boys in nondivorced families. Hetherington also reports

> high rates of negative exchanges between divorced mothers and their sons. Analysis showed that divorced mothers of boys were not only more likely than other parents to trigger noxious behavior, but were also less able to control and terminate this behavior once it occurred.

On closer examination the researchers found that these mothers were not any worse than other mothers in coping with their children. The problems they faced were bigger. Their sons were swinging violently from clingy, anxious behavior to aggressive outbursts as they rode the roller coaster of their own feelings of abandonment and came to terms with the loss of the masculine image upon which they were starting to model themselves.

For all mothers and sons, the first year after divorce is likely to be hard, but as the grief associated with divorce recedes mothers start to find their feet and sons start to behave in a more manageable fashion. The father at this stage may also move into the background of the child's life. According to Hetherington:

> Two years after the divorce we found that the father was becoming relatively impotent at shaping his children's behavior just as the mother was becoming more powerful. At that time the mother's authoritative control, consistency, use of rea-

soning and explanation, family organization, maternal warmth and marital conflict were related to self-control in boys.

Fathers could no longer intervene to provide the necessary balance if mothers were unable to provide a clear and loving framework for their sons. Indeed, where there was a high level of anger between parents, the continued involvement of the father often exacerbated problems of adjustment between sons and mothers. However, where estranged parents had the maturity to negotiate a low-conflict relationship, the father, just by being available and continuing to exert a degree of control, could back up a mother's efforts and help their son grow to maturity.

Since all the boys in Hetherington's study had lost a father through divorce, they may be more upset by the loss of a parent than the lack of a male figure per se. However, there were other differences too. Boys whose parents were divorced "spent an increasing amount of time playing with younger children and with girls rather than showing the more characteristic developmental pattern of a marked and increasing preponderance of time in play with same-sex peers."

Without a clear role model these boys are apparently slower to pick up typical "boyish" behavior. That could be a good thing for mothers who want to bring up gentle boys, but Chodorow (1978, p. 106) sounds a note of caution. She refers to work by John Whiting, who studies children living in societies in which they are cared for exclusively by their mothers for the first two years, and men live separately.

He describes boys who are overwhelmed by the intensity of the bond with their mothers and find the effort of separation and achieving masculine independence very difficult. These cultures, far from breeding boys with a flexible gender identity, breed a pattern of continued sex segregation and sex antagonism. It seems that boys with a fragile sense of their masculinity may have more need to define themselves, stereotypically, as male, in order to stop themselves from being "sucked back" into the warm, safe world of women.

Boys without fathers tend to gravitate toward men they meet in other ways. If there are male teachers in their school, they will try to get close to them both physically and emotionally. These men will have a powerful influence because, alongside the images of superheroes, they provide a big chunk of what the boy will learn as male behavior. If, as in Whiting's study, the men they encounter have a fragile sense of their own masculine identity, and are antagonistic toward women, they will shake the child's identification with his mother and increase his anxiety and antagonism toward her. If, on the other hand, they can reflect for the boy an image of a man who can be both strong and gentle, they will help him to recognize that the identity he has started to build in the image of his mother is not incompatible with masculinity.

Tandi, a South African exile, was acutely aware of the difficulties that her son was facing at school in trying to join in with activities he had never learned at home. Her son had never known his father, who was killed in action when his son was three. Tandi talked about him often and he was a hero figure to his son, but his idealization was not grounded in everyday reality:

> At home he is really a very gentle boy but at school he models himself on superheroes and charges in fighting. He has no models of how men should behave. Women friends take an interest in children, but the men who come here ignore him. A girl would have me and my friends as role models. I could rely on myself more to help her. I would be more conscious of the pitfalls. I won't be able to do that for him. There are things he won't be able to get from me—or believe from me.

Tandi's response was to find a man to befriend her son through a city agency. He would take him out one afternoon a week to the park or to a film. The strategy worked. The tension between them started to decrease, and her son's self-confidence increased as he gradually learned to trust his new friend.

Many divorced mothers remarry and, if remarriage occurs before the son's puberty, it can be an extremely useful prop to the mother's relationship with him. Hetherington found: "With younger children, maternal control and monitoring increased and conflict decreased over time, as the family adjusted to the remarriage." This beneficial effect did not occur when remarriage took place during adolescence.

While boys need to learn about the male world, they can manage without a resident male, provided that their mother can establish a safe enough base from which they can explore. It is a great help if the mother has some emotional backup, but that doesn't have to come from a man. Ben was a highly excitable child who became almost manic in any unstructured group. His mother lived first in a house with a number of adults, both male and female, then moved into her own house and, shortly afterward, entered a relationship with another woman who later had a son of her own:

> For a long time he was very uncontrolled. He could cope at school; it was in groups of people without any structure that he fell apart. Now that I am not living alone, things have improved. I know I was very bad at limiting him to begin with. Now we are both much clearer about limits. It's been much better for him, having two parents. He's gained enormously from it. She has a very close relationship with him and that's been good, and he has also had to learn to deal with an adult relationship and the jealousy that goes with that. It is having two of us that makes the difference.

It is quite likely also that, living in a harmonious, all-female household, this child was spared the problems that some boys face of having to deal with a mother's anger about the way in which she has been treated by the men in her life. The way the boy perceives the "man in his mother's head" will make a big difference to the way he is able to see himself. If a child learns that his father is a worthless creep or a dangerous monster, how can he be happy about growing up "like Daddy"? If he isn't to grow up like Daddy, then who is he? If, on the other hand, he has already decided that Daddy is a hero, he won't go along with his mother's assessment. He will stay, in his heart, with Daddy, and take out his aggression on his mother for sending his father away.

Either way, his search for an identity will have been dealt a mortal blow, and it may take some time for him to recover his equilibrium and start reconstructing his idea of what it is to be male. The man in his mother's head may, in the end, invade even those homes where Father has never been present at all. A woman who has lived with her son since his father disappeared during the pregnancy talked about her son's growing need for her to show approval of men:

> I've just ended a very brief relationship and my son is very angry with me. It brought a whole host of issues to a head. He said, "What's the matter with you? The trouble is you don't want an ordinary man, you want a perfect man. What was wrong with him?" It was almost as though he was standing up for his whole sex. He has a sense that no man is good enough for me—and I think that he fears that includes him.

In spite of her concern for him, her son, now into adolescence, is an attractive, popular, and apparently self-confident young man with a sense of ease around girls that many boys his age envy. Life for single mothers with sons is undoubtedly harder, but that does not mean that they are doomed to dreadful relationships with aggressive offspring. However, they do need to recognize that boys have particular needs. Above all, they need mothers who understand their vulnerability as well as recognizing their need to be free. Where most girls thrive on responsibility and derive confidence from a mother who is successful in the world, boys (though they will never admit it, and seem constantly to kick against it) seem to need more reassurance that they are listened to and cared for. ·

7

The Breaking of Mother Power

In early adolescence both sons and daughters move away from the intense emotional involvement they have had with their mothers and start to establish a separate identity in readiness for forming adult attachments of their own. If, in the first half of childhood, the mother's power seems far-reaching, in the second half her power may be found to be an illusion. Father rules the roost even if he is hardly ever in it, and this is something that gradually dawns on his children as they get old enough to see the world beyond the home and the school.

For children, the first inkling of male domination of the outside world may come when they start learning the names of people and jobs. They see the world is divided into specific areas. Women rule the home and men rule outside. At first the girls seem quite happy to cede all the outside jobs to boys and men. Even the daughter of a female doctor may say, with determination, that only men can be doctors. For, after all, who knows what these empty titles actually mean? What does a fireman actually do once he has put the fire out? The real business of the world that children know takes place in the home and that is where women rule.

The boys hang on jealously to these empty titles: a girl can't be a builder, driver, pilot, doctor—only boys, who are going to be "like Daddy," can go out into the world as he does. At last they have found a territory they can own—but at first it may seem a very bleak and empty one, away from the warmth of home and Mother. Inevitably they feel ambivalent. They envy girls their secure place by the fireside, and must stiffen their own resolve and face the inevitability of their fate. At the age of eight that fate may seem frightening. By the age of eleven, the lure of the outside has become strong. The boy is finally coming into his own, and it is at this point that the power of fathers will be felt most strongly.

I asked eleven-year-old children at an inner-city elementary school what they thought was good about being a boy. They all declared that their toughness was a bonus but added to the list "a better choice of jobs." One of the girls observed: "Boys have a better choice of things to do," and "You don't get many male servants." One child picked out the pleasure of "doing things with your dad, like fixing cars." However, even those boys who rarely "do things with Dad" are extremely aware of his presence.

In two-parent families all over the industrialized world, the preparation for the real world starts with the idealization of the world outside the home, and the subtle (or not too subtle) denigration of home, Mother, and all she stands for. Even when a boy has ample evidence that the world outside has little to offer him, he needs to believe in it and to believe that he has a place in it.

I have watched the process and heard mothers describing the way their authority is undermined not only by their sons but also by their partners. Sometimes these men are dismissive and aggressive, but even fathers whom society would regard as "good fathers" may wittingly or unwittingly collude in the process. These mothers describe a scenario in which the father is seen by the children as part of the outside world—to be looked up to—and the mother is seen as part of the furniture—to be sat upon.

Typically, Dad arrives home in the evening to a scene in which Mother and children are already locked in conflict. If she works, she will have arrived home earlier, taking on the brunt of the parental controlling role: "Have you done your homework? Take your socks off the sofa. When did you last wash? Don't be so rude. Please clear the table and turn off the television." It is she who deals with the brunt of opposition from children who want to be treated like adults without recognizing that adults also have responsibilities.

When Dad breezes in she may initially be glad to see him because she associates him, just as her children do, with the outside world, with something less constrained than the life she is leading. She may feel glad that she will no longer be the focus of their unending needs and can find a small corner of brain space for herself. Then the scene plays itself out rather like this.

The daughter, who has been sulking and door-slamming, suddenly brightens up and starts telling Dad all the things she has avoided telling her mother. These gems are for *him,* not for her, not for the woman who nags and harries and demands from her. The daughter alone can capture his attention, make him her own, and relieve her unending boredom—locked in here with the dreary little brother and that nagging old woman.

The boy bides his time. He doesn't need to compete for attention. He knows that his father belongs above all to him. For are they not both men, and don't men belong together? "OK?" asks his father. "OK, Dad," he replies, enjoying the familiar pattern of wordless reassurance. If Dad asks him, man to man, to pick his softball cleats up from the living room floor, he will do it. No matter that, ten minutes earlier, his mother made the same request and he completely ignored it.

The daughter asks, with the little simper in her voice that she keeps only for Dad, if she can go out to a party. "Of course," he replies, glad to be asked, flattered by the direct appeal to his masculine authority. He doesn't know, and she doesn't tell him, that she has already asked her mother and that her mother said she couldn't. Now she has split them apart. She has him on her side against *her.* She has won.

The son hears her and feels angry. Why does she always get her own way? Typical woman, he decides, using all that baby stuff to wheedle her way in. Wouldn't catch him doing that, *oh, no*. When he wants something, he takes the direct route. If he wants something, he will fight for it. None of that underhand yucky stuff for him. Men don't need it.

Later Mother will rage silently when she discovers that, once again, her dwindling authority has been undermined. She argues with herself, not with her partner. Her emotional being tells her that she has been betrayed; it rages at him for once again failing to consult her. Her reason takes command and reminds her that he doesn't know he is undermining her, that she should be grateful, really. Some fathers don't bother with their children at all.

She looks forward to a few moments with another adult, someone who will relieve her of the awful feeling that she gets from her children, that she is a nobody, a person only to be opposed. But he disappears behind his newspaper or slips out again to the local bar. Her heart sinks. She feels the raging inside of the small girl who so badly wanted her dad to notice her. Then her rationalizing voice comes to her aid and tells her, in a soothing sugar tongue, "You should feel fortunate. He works so hard, he makes more money than you do, he does it all for you—and the kids."

The next day Father has already gone before the children wake. Mother faces the daily battle to get them out of bed, dressed, and off to school. When she returns from work it will be her duty to ensure that they do their homework, put their dirty clothes in the hamper, pick up the empty glasses and cereal bowls from the rug. Once again they will settle into the daily grind in which she nags, they growl, and life is hell—until a breeze blows in with Dad.

This is how so many "good fathers" rule by their absence. This is how a son learns that, out there, in the world of work, lies his destiny, the place where he will learn to be a real man, free himself of all this feminine nagging, and rule his own roost. This is how a daughter learns that Mother represents not a higher form of humanity, but drudgery, an earthbound dreariness that she must at all costs leave behind. The mother whose life has been set alight by the love she feels for her babies finds herself, as they hit puberty, cast aside in their rush for the door.

Conventional psychologists see this as a healthy pattern and see the father's role as a vital one in helping teenage children achieve separation. It is, however, a profoundly unequal role in which the mother suffers a terrible blow to her self-esteem, while the father's self-esteem is enhanced. A paper given by Elizabeth Monk at Trust for the Study of Adolescence in February 1993 shows how bad this is for daughters. Mothers who are depressed, or have unsupportive relationships with their partners, tend also to have depressed daughters.

It also perpetuates a system in which the son learns to despise the woman whom he loves and to admire the man whom he hopes to emulate. If his father is not there, or is not worthy of his admiration, he may look to other men, to his peer group, to other representations of adult masculinity, to fulfill this role. In the very process of separation are sown the seeds of a system in which men admire older men but feel contempt, perhaps mixed with fear, for older women. Where (as in some of the postindustrial areas) mothers provide not only the sole authority in the home but also the sole controlling force outside (through their involvement in community schemes to combat crime and joy-riding, for example), the scene is set for a rejection of all authority.

It seems to me that this cycle in which women are used up and then discarded in this way is not a good one for women or men, and that it sets up many of the stresses and strains that plague relationships between the sexes in adulthood. Looking to psychology literature for clues as to how women can avoid this trap and rear boys who treat women, and each other, with warmth and respect, it seems clear that a key issue for parents is not so much the relationship of mother and son (though that is obviously important, particularly in single-parent families) but the way in which fathers treat their partners and, by extension, men treat women.

Research by Mavis Hetherington (1982) discovered that a father who admires his wife, encourages a warm relationship between mother and son, and is himself emotionally expressive is the single most important factor in producing boys with a capacity for emotional expressiveness themselves. A father who does not encourage warmth and respect for women will deepen the division and increase the aggression of his son's effort at separation. As this mother complained:

> My husband says that I deal with it all wrong. He maintains that I just waste my time keeping on and on to no effect. My opinion is that if I ask the kids to do something and they ignore me, if he's around he should reinforce my request, not put me down in front of them.

Every child must learn to move away from the close control of childhood and find his feet in the adult world. If, during this process, the father is hostile to the mother, the son's desire for autonomy may take on the hostility of his father. He may learn that part of being a man is learning to denigrate women. If the son is close to his mother, the hostility may prevent him from moving away from her because to do so would be to side with his oppressor. Or the anger at home may make the son turn against both his parents, make him doubt the possibility of loving relationships and of his own worth as a human being.

ESCAPING FROM THE NEST

The withdrawal in early adolescence is a mirror image of the first period in early childhood when a boy starts to identify as male. It can be a very painful period for any mother. She may know very little about his world and yet she knows that this is the time when, above all, he needs a strong safety net. It is the time when boys are most likely to get drawn into antisocial activity and yet, at the same time, most need to be free to find their own feet.

Throughout the teenage years a boy will oscillate: fearing the world on one day and fearing entrapment by home and mother the next. As he pulls away and finds that there is still firm ground under his feet, he starts to feel confident. Perhaps he will survive out there after all. He relaxes a little and his mother finds that her loving son has returned. He dares to be affectionate again because he now feels sure that he will be all right out there. Then comes another test. He wobbles, he feels fear, he brings his fear home and lays it at his mother's door. Once again there is conflict as he fights against his fear of being trapped again in her love.

Sarah's son has been dividing his time between his mother's house and his father's house for ten years. They have had the wisdom to put their son first and allow him to use these two bases according to his own developmental needs. When Dave first started school he found it hard to cope with living in two places, so they decided that he should live with his mother and that his father would visit. At around the age of seven his need for his father started to grow as he began to identify more with him but, having established himself as male, he retreated once more into a close relationship with his mother. Then he began secondary school and, once again, started asserting himself against his mother and identifying very strongly with his father. They arranged for him to stay with his father two nights a week.

I first spoke to Sarah when her son was twelve. She said:

When he and his dad are together I feel invisible. I am helpless to know how to be interested and involved. I spend a lot of time trying to make contact but he just says, "Stop asking all those questions." He's talking to me and I'm not listening, and I'm talking to him and he is not interested.

We have our moments of closeness—sometimes late at night—but he'll never talk to me during the day. He just won't communicate with me, and that is getting worse. All we seem to talk about is his room, putting his clothes in the laundry box. I think he is coming to see me as a nag.

For the first time I feel lonely. It's right that he should move away but I wish he could communicate better. We used to discuss everything in great depth. Now, if he experiences something bad at school he won't tell me anything for a couple of weeks. I know that he knows his own mind, that he is perceptive about himself and others, but his thoughts are no longer available to me. I have to trust that, in the end, the things I have put in will show. I just have to wait until he comes through this.

For mothers who have no viable relationship with their sons' fathers, this period can be traumatic. As the son pulls away it feels as if he is tearing the foundations of her life with him. What is the son to do? She is the only important person in his life and he may feel overwhelming guilt about opposing her and, at the same time, an overwhelming need to create a separate existence. He may become hostile, aggressive, and apparently unreachable, or he may withdraw from the problems of his peer group and the outside world and take to his bed.

Occasionally a boy will turn all his anger on his mother. Steven, twenty-three, writing in the *Guardian* (January 1990), had this to say about the mother who brought him up alone:

Feminism allowed my Mum to bring me up without a father. She says she left because he was an alcoholic, but I don't believe that. And if that was the case she should have chosen her husband more wisely. She dug her own grave, so she can bloody well suffer. How can she blame it on him when she was the one who left?

I think she should have done better. She could have made a bit more effort and stayed with my Dad. She should have put me before herself. If I married a woman and she had my children, I'd expect her to stay with me and fulfil her part of the contract, at least until the children came of age. As it is I have never had a decent relationship.

Of course, most young people find that adolescence is a difficult time. They are unsure about how to deal with relationships with the opposite sex, and they feel afraid of failure and rejection. This boy has a ready-made excuse for everything: it's Mother's fault. The more he blames her, the less he will be able to take over the reins of his own life and the more vulnerable he will be to peer-group pressure.

Having only one adult in your life on whom to dump all your love and all your anger is a burden, both for the dumper and the dumped on. Some mothers, sensing future difficulties, make efforts to involve other adults in their children's lives in a consistent way. Joanne's son had never known his father. He disappeared during the pregnancy, turning up briefly when her son was three and then disappearing again.

Joanne decided: "It was better for him not to see his father at all than to be rejected. I told him not to come back, but I let my son know that he was free to contact his father if he wanted to." When the child was nine she embarked on a relationship with another man, which lasted until her son was fifteen. Then this relationship ended, and this man also failed to maintain any involvement with her son.

Joanne at this point entered a relationship with a woman. It was a difficult time, not because her son minded about his mother's girlfriend but because he was desperate to establish his own identity and felt that her life style was irrelevant to him. Says Joanne:

I had another friend who I had been briefly involved with when my son was eight. He, unlike the others, had kept in touch. Now he stepped in and acted as my son's friend, mentor, sparring partner. When my son was in difficulties, he was there for him. I think biological fatherhood is irrelevant. This man had earned fatherhood. Commitment is what fatherhood is about.

IN FREEFALL WITHOUT A NET

Some mothers find that, without this help, they don't have the resilience to cope. Matthew's story first appeared in chapter 4. His start at secondary school had coincided with his father's remarriage and his mother's return to education. In an effort to find a safe masculine identity, he had gravitated toward a group of racialist thugs.

This young man now says that his mother didn't listen to him. He doesn't seem able to understand that he had pushed her beyond endurance. Sadly, for both of them, there was no one else to take his hand and guide his flight in a more productive direction. He fell out of the nest and learned, fast, how to fight. Now he believes that the only way to survive is to hit the other person first. Boys like these turn for solace to their peer group—a move that, according to Hetherington, may be constructive if the peer group is well adjusted. "An antisocial or delinquent peer group, on the other hand, will usually have disastrous consequences."

Once this boy had pushed his mother away, he turned his anger on the world. He discovered that the love of a mother cannot be so easily dispensed with or replaced, and he withdrew, learning to stutter as he spoke and becoming more and more isolated in his hatred of himself and the world. Having cut himself off from his mother he missed her power, and her love, but found no one to replace it.

Matthew's mother never stopped loving her child but, without anyone to support her and tell her that she was OK and valuable, she could not provide the strength that he needed. For single mothers this can be the most difficult aspect of coping with adolescence. It is not surprising that, facing this crisis alone, some women with no one to bolster their own self-esteem may cave in and return anger with anger, forcing the boy onto his own meager resources and those of his friends.

One mother wrote to the *Guardian* about her attempts to get the social services to rid her of her troublesome son:

> Our problems began in 1984 when my son refused to attend school. He became increasingly abusive and eventually Social Services got involved. They instigated a system of rewards but it did not work. By then he was stealing from me and could gain more from me that way than by being good.
>
> He is now 15 and I have been struggling with his behavioural problems, alone, for six years. I am now tired and cynical, sick of being abused by him and of seeing our few possessions sold to feed his insatiable appetite for chocolate and crisps.

We know little about the background to this story, but one thing is clear: a mother who feels unable to cope with her son's behavior at nine years old is going to find it hard indeed to instill in him the sense of his own worth that he needs to carry him through adolescence. Boys often lack the language to describe how they feel; they act out their rage instead of swallowing it and turning it into depression, as their sisters tend to. Their misery is uncomfortable to live with and hard to cope with (particularly for a woman who is herself feeling vulnerable, as most women do in the immediate aftermath of divorce), but it is hardly surprising that, when they feel that no one cares or understands, their sons turn against them. A child who feels unvalued cannot easily value himself and will value others even less.

Mavis Hetherington talked about children like these in an address to the Society for Research into Child Development (1989). In her talk about the effects of divorce and remarriage on children, she described the kind of children who wind up non-compliant, impulsive, aggressive, prone to sullen, brooding periods of withdrawal, and unpopular with their peers. In other words, lonely, unhappy, angry, anxious, insecure children. Who were these children and why had their lives gone so badly wrong?

There were three times as many boys in this group as girls, and their mothers were more likely to have recently remarried or divorced. Many of these boys had been difficult as young children and their problems had been exacerbated by family conflict. They tended to have no relationships with adult men, or to have fathers or stepfathers who actively rejected them.

There seems little doubt that, for many single mothers and sons, adolescence is a rough time, but it doesn't have to be. Another study by Eleanor Maccoby (1992, pp. 261–91) looking at the difference in adjustment for children living in different family arrangements after divorce found that a low level of hostility between separated parents, stability, and closeness to the resident parent were the things that mattered most. A study by Richard Kinsey in Scotland also underlines the importance of closeness. There was 25 percent less criminal behavior in homes where children were supervised after school—a finding that cuts right across class and neighborhood.

For boys, even more than girls, time is important. Girls thrive when their mothers go out to full-time work; boys tend to feel neglected. Just as they felt more anxiety about their exploration as toddlers, these young people, feeling the void beneath their feet as they step out into adult life, need to have a rock to cling to. They may seem to want only to hang out with their friends, but underneath the independent exterior, most adolescents still need the guiding hand of involved and caring adults.

A study of children in the care of local authorities, by the Trust for the Study of Adolescence, found that overwhelmingly these young people turned to adult staff members rather than their peers for "someone you can trust and tell your feelings to" and "someone to confide doubts about your own abilities." And research into children who attempt suicide found that the single most important factor preventing children from further attempts was the knowledge that their parents had listened and tried to understand their feelings. Teenage children may not appear to want adults, but they tell us by their actions that they need us.

CREATING A SAFETY NET

Society has always assumed that mothers will provide the rock for their children to lean on and will always be there for them, but there is no reason why mothers should carry this responsibility alone. As more and more women move into full-time work, we need to find other ways of providing the safety net that our adolescents so clearly still need. In two-parent families there are more financial resources and more support, so children spend less time without adult supervision. A single parent can feel stretched beyond endurance at this time and allow her children more freedom than they may be able to use safely. Boys, on the whole, get more freedom than girls, and yet all the evidence so far indicates that it is boys, more than girls, who are most vulnerable in early adolescence.

Providing a child with a safety net does not mean tying him to apron strings and preventing him from experiencing the independence that will, in the end, help him to grow up safely. There are a number of ways of providing boundaries that will allow a child to feel safe and, at the same time, free to explore. Some single mothers make a point of getting to know the parents of their children's friends; others encourage organized after-school activities, or make an effort to ensure that theirs is the home where teenagers congregate. It helps also to be absolutely clear about where children are at all times and when they should be home.

One mother said: "He says I am a fusspot. I tell him that is exactly what I am, and that if I haven't heard from him by five P.M.

I will telephone all his friends until I find him. He would rather phone me than have me out searching for him."

Of course, they will want more freedom and independence as they get older, but it is better to negotiate calmly than to give in after a screaming match. They will inevitably buck the system on occasion and these are the times when single mothers feel most vulnerable and alone. Nevertheless, it is worth keeping in mind the fact that a son may still depend on his mother to create boundaries that will help him to negotiate tricky situations. Too much freedom too soon can be frightening.

Jenny's son, at fourteen, had asked permission to go to a couple of overnight parties. His mother felt that this was a safer option than having him use public transportation to get home. Later she found that there had been drugs at the parties and she promptly banned him from future involvement. She said: "I expected him to fight and sulk and make a fuss but he took it surprisingly calmly. In fact I think he was relieved to be kept in. I suspect he felt that he was out of his depth."

With another child this might have been the wrong decision. It might simply have undermined the child's belief in his ability to make sensible decisions for himself and made him feel angry and resentful about being mistrusted. Parents need to know their children very well to be able to make the right decisions about when to hold firm and when to allow a child's own good sense to take over and just how firmly to keep the rules in place while the process unfolds.

It takes some strength to make boundaries and stick to them when you are coping with the onslaught of a newly emerging adult who is fighting for autonomy and testing you in the process. It is far easier to cope if you yourself have the support of someone who helps you to feel good.

A supportive adult doesn't need to be a husband, or a live-in lover, though it can be. Some parents find that support groups provide them with unflagging help through the hard times, and the friendship of other parents can be absolutely invaluable. The important thing is that they back up the mother's authority and increase the child's sense of security.

Someone who distracts the mother from parenting and fails to provide her with supportive backup may have the opposite effect. Children who acquire stepparents as they enter adolescence often suffer greater feelings of alienation and rejection as they feel the bonds with the only adult in their life being stretched and strained. A new partner who attempts to be directive, rather than supportive, to the child at this point is asking for trouble. Tact and patience are vital if a new partner is to be able to provide useful support at all.

COMING UP FOR AIR

With luck this testing time will last only a year or two, but it might drag on throughout the teenage years. Joanne's son, at the low point of his adolescent struggle, dropped out of school and failed most of his exams. Now, at twenty-three, he has a college degree and a promising career. Sarah, who two years earlier had been talking sadly about her loneliness and alienation, felt very different the next time we talked about her son, now fourteen:

> Not long after we talked last time, there was a terrible row. He was seeing his father three or four times a week and seemed to be coming home only for meals and to get his clothes washed. He was also being very stroppy. I said, "Perhaps you should go and live with your father. I'm just doing the housework and getting nothing in return, while your dad gets the pleasure of your company without any of the work." He thought about it for a while and then said: "I don't want to live with Dad; he's not organized. He won't remember to wash my clothes. I think I would like to stay with you."

It might not be the most flattering reason to stay with Mom, but it seemed to be the turning point in her son's move toward maturity. He realized that he was free to make a decision to change his life, but he chose to stay with his mother and she was then able to get him to see that he must also take some responsibility for the decision. He must learn to pull his weight and not reduce her to a nagging hotel keeper. Having struggled through the worst part, they now have a very different relationship:

> Now, if we have a row, sometimes he will insist on talking through what's happened. We are beginning to pinpoint areas where we cross the line and irritate each other, and we can say we are sorry. That is the role I used to take on. I'm pleased he can do that. I realize now that he has a strong sense of fairness. He is also more critical of me and of his father. He sees us more as individuals, not just as parents.

Sarah can probably look forward to clearer sailing now. Her son has moved and changed his perspective, and he can see that he has a degree of control over his own life, that he has to take his share of responsibility if he is to be given more freedom. The fact that his father was, and still is, so positively involved with him allowed him to move away from his mother without fearing that he would lose everything—and it also allowed him to move back.

STUCK WITH MOTHER

Professor Eleanor Maccoby (1992) researched deviance (substance abuse, getting into trouble at school, and various kinds of antisocial activity) in postdivorce families and found that it was a bigger problem in father-custody homes than in dual-custody or mother-custody homes because, the research suggests, the fact that fathers in sole residence were less likely than other residential parents to have intimate and open relationships with adolescents in their care may have made it more difficult for these fathers to keep track of their adolescents.

It is this intimacy that provides the solid ground on which a boy can build the foundations of his independence. He can get that intimacy from men too but, in the world as it is currently constituted, it is mothers who are most likely to provide it. Mothers who are strong enough to provide the boundaries that an adolescent still needs, intimate enough to sense when something is going wrong, and wise enough to know when to stand back can be both mothers and fathers to their sons if need be, but it is a lot to ask and it's amazing that so many mothers manage it.

However, the balance between close emotional involvement and gentle disengagement is a matter of fine judgment. A child who breaks away too far and too fast will find himself in freefall and may be unable to steer. A child who feels that he is earth-bound for too long may become increasingly surly and hostile as he attempts to force a separation not just from his mother but from women in general. Boys are not given masculinity; they take it. If it isn't available at home they will go and look for it and, if you stop them, they may well, as we have seen, turn on you too.

Sometimes, in attempting the parental balancing act, a mother will bind her son too close. She will start to rely on him for her own emotional support, trapping him in her own need, rather than leaving him free to make his struggle for autonomy. He may seem, on the outside, to be the perfectly dutiful son, always at his mother's side, while inside he feels resentful and deeply ambivalent about his relationships with his mother and women in general. Ian, now twenty-nine, travels miles to get away from his mother, but he always comes home again—and he is usually broke:

When I am around, my mother becomes intentionally helpless. She wants me to look after her and I feel angry. I get the
feeling that she wants me to be there forever. She talks about
"us" as though we were having a sexual relationship. It's not
just her. The thought of being with anyone for the rest of my
life makes me feel claustrophobic.

Robert Bly in *Iron John,* the book that brought the concept of
Wild Men into popular culture, latched on to the anxieties of a
generation of American men who feel that they have never quite
"made it" as men. For Bly, the villain of the piece is the mother.
He writes about the boy's need to separate from her, to get "the
key" to his masculinity from "under the mother's pillow," where
she has hidden it:

> Attacking the mother, confronting her, shouting at her,
> which some Freudians are prone to urge on us, probably
> doesn't accomplish much—she may just smile and talk to
> you with her elbow on the pillow. . . . Mothers are intuitively
> aware of what would happen if he got the key: they would
> lose their boys. The possessiveness that mothers typically
> exercise on sons can never be underestimated.

Bly does not see the dilemma of the mother, but only the struggle of the son, and his answer is for the boy to steal the key and to
go far away, leaving his mother behind in order to dwell with the
Wild Men (a subject I will return to in the next section). Bly is not
the first man to dwell on the power of mothers. Indeed, it is pre-
sumably because the struggle to break free from Mother seems so
necessary—and so difficult—that it has become a recurring feature of male literature.

Perhaps one of the best examples is Ken Kesey's *One Flew over
the Cuckoo's Nest.* Kesey is writing about the inmates of a mental
hospital and the battle for autonomy against the authoritarian

presence of big Nurse Ratched. It takes a very small change of perspective to see that the bones of the story are about a boy's attempt to detach himself from the power of the mother with very little help from the remote father figure: the doctor. Here McMurphy and another inmate discuss the big nurse:

> "Miss Ratched may be a strict middle-aged lady but she's not some kind of giant monster of the poultry clan, bent on sadistically pecking out our eyes. You can't believe that of her, can you?"
>
> "No, buddy, not that. She ain't pecking out your eyes. That's not what she's pecking at."
>
> "Not our eyes?" he says, "Pray, then, where is Miss Ratched pecking, my friend?"
>
> McMurphy grinned. "Why, don't you know, buddy?"
>
> "No, of course I don't know! I mean if you insi—"
>
> "At your balls, buddy, at your everlovin' balls."

And this is how they sum up the doctor:

> Doctor Spivey . . . is exactly like the rest of us, completely conscious of his inadequacy. He's a frightened, desperate, ineffectual little rabbit, totally incapable of running the ward without our Miss Ratched's help and he knows it. And worse, she *knows* he knows it and reminds him every chance she gets.

McMurphy fails in his bid for freedom and is punished for trying with a lobotomy, which reduces him to the status of infant again.

A more lighthearted approach to the male fear of entrapment appeared in *Cosmopolitan* magazine (U.K. edition) a couple of years ago, when Dave Berry wrote "Cracking the Guy Code," about men who fail to call again after the first date:

You go out with a bloke, and you have a great time, and at the end of the evening he says, quote "Can I phone you?" and you—innocently interpreting this question to mean, "Can I phone you?"—answer, "Sure!" The instant you say this the man's body starts to dematerialize . . . eventually you start to wonder if there is something wrong with you, some kind of emotional hang-up or personality defect that your dates are detecting.

This is silly. There is absolutely nothing wrong with you. In fact you should interpret the behaviour of your dates as a kind of male compliment to you. Because when the guy asks you if he can call you what he is really asking in Guy code is, will you marry him? . . . So when you say "Sure" in that cheery voice you may think you are just indicating a willingness to go out again but as far as he is concerned you're endorsing a lifetime's commitment that he is quite frankly not ready to make after one date, so he naturally decides he can never see you again.

So my advice to single women is that if you're on a date with a man you like, and he asks you whether he can call you, you should give him a non-threatening answer like "No," or: "I guess so, but bear in mind that I'm a nun." This will make him comfortable about seeing you again.

While this makes an entertaining read, the issues underlying it are serious ones and they are important for all of us, as Christiane Olivier puts it in her book *Jocasta's Children:*

Because the woman has been kept at a distance by her husband, she will invest in her son and prepare in him the ground of "distance" for the other woman, the one who is yet to come. Misogyny is a crop sown by one woman and reaped by another. The circle has been closed, the loop looped.

Bly sees all-male groups as the answer to the boy's need for separation but, in fact, the formation of all-male groups is not a new idea, nor is it progressive; it has always been the way men have reacted to their fear of entrapment. In ancient Greek society, where wives had no status and were isolated in their homes with their children, boys grew up with just such a potent mixture of love and hostility as so many boys do today. Their hearts were tied to Mama but their heads were out in the world, where they alone could be in control.

In a study of Greek mythology, Philip Slater (1968) noted:

> The most striking fact is that of all the clear instances of madness deliberately produced on one being by another, none can be said to be caused by a truly masculine or paternal agent. Most are afflicted by Goddesses . . . nor is the relationship between the sex of an agent and the sex of the victim a random one; in the overwhelming majority of cases madness is induced by a person of the opposite sex.

So boys learn that to need what you fear is a recipe for madness. This fear haunts adult relationships between men and women and forces men into a jolly camaraderie from which women must at all costs be excluded: it is the reason behind the men's clubs, the stag nights, the all-male gatherings that are a feature of any society in which men fear that their masculinity is built on shaky foundations—a fear that so often undermines relationships between men and women.

Women cannot bring up their sons in their own image, no matter how much they might wish to, because a boy needs to discover for himself what it is that makes him different. He cannot learn that from her. He must find the information elsewhere. Yet, at the same time, it is just as important for him to hold on to the parts of himself that he learned from his mother, because men and women are not only different from each other, they also, potentially, have a great deal that is the same. I cannot believe that the way to rear boys who feel clear about their masculine identity, and secure in their relationships, is through greater separation. While men have an important role to play in the rearing of boys, I cannot believe that it is in their interests, and I am sure it is not in the interests of women, that their role should be to split the sexes even further apart.

IV

FATHERS AND
SONS

8

Where Do Fathers Come From?

Back in the 1950s, child psychiatrist John Bowlby expounded his theory of maternal deprivation. For many years women have asked why paternal absence from child rearing has not also been a focus of concern. Now, in the 1990s, fatherless families are being blamed for everything from poverty to the level of youth crime, and yet there has still been no public discussion of the nature of fathering and no attempt to think about the possible effects of inadequate fathers. A mother can be good or bad, but so far we seem to be expected to believe that a father just is.

I once wrote, in an article on men and custody, that judges tend not to look kindly on giving custody to parents who had learned their interpersonal skills playing with toy trucks. A female editor asked me to remove the sentence on the grounds that it revealed my bias against men! Are women so desperate to believe that men can deliver their half of the package that would lead to equality that we can ignore overwhelming evidence that, so far at least, they are finding it an uphill struggle?

The fact is that in virtually every society throughout history (*pace* the Trobriand Islanders), women have taken on the whole responsibility for the intimate care of young children. Grannies, nannies, and female relatives may have differing degrees of involvement, but fathers hardly figure. Indeed, as recently as 1979, British child-care guru Penelope Leach, in her book *Who Cares?* delivered these immortal words about a mother's absolute responsibility for the care of children:

> Suppose that you were an architect [she clearly didn't imag-ine that some mothers might actually *be* architects!]. Every-one grumbles from time to time about their working condi-tions: the architect-you will yearn for a bigger office or a different firm of builders just as the mother does for an eas-ier house or a washing-machine. But as an architect you will not moan that it is intolerable of society to expect you to shoulder the responsibility. You wanted it because it was an honour. You will not seek a state employee to do some of it for you because it would reduce your status and share of the credit. And you will not seek weapons with which to force your sexual partner to share the job with you. It is yours and he has his. Doing it well is worth every effort you make. The game is worth the candle.

Few people would dare to say such a thing these days, but most homes still operate on a similar model. So most baby boys are still cared for by women and come to parenthood with memories of early nurturing that are much the same as their sisters'. The differ-ence is that, in men, the memories are overlaid by other memo-ries—of Father. Since they are men trying to be fathers, it is pic-tures of their fathers, not their mothers, that emerge out of the cloudy depths of consciousness to give a helping hand.

For some men these memories are rich and fruitful even if their fathers spent little time with them. One father I talked to said: "A green truck would take him to work every day at six A.M. In the evening it would bring him back and he was always overjoyed to see his son. All the gentleness, the singing, and bedtime stories I remember are about Dad, not Mom." These memories had been submerged during a stormy adolescence and didn't really reemerge until his father died and he found himself taking over the mantle of paterfamilias in a second marriage with his first son.

This father was able to tap into the warmth of his own relationship with his father to provide a similar emotional engagement with his own sons. Many men find that their memories of Dad fail to provide a useful guide for a relationship with their own infants. Reading accounts of relationships with fathers, I was struck by how different these memories are to the blurry, running-together, fuzzy sort of memories that people tend to have of their mothers. They are the hard-edged memories that people reserve for important but rare events. Sherwood Anderson (1942) wrote of his contempt for his father as a young child who was entirely excluded from his world until, one fateful day, his father came home to find him alone:

"You come on with me," he said.

I got up and went with him out of the house. I was filled with wonder but, although he had suddenly become a stranger to me, I wasn't afraid.

Sherwood and his father walked through the rain to a pond, where his father told him to take off his clothes:

There was a flash of lightning and I saw that he was already naked.

And so naked we went into the pond. He did not speak or explain. Taking my hand he led me down to the pond's edge and pulled me in. It may be that I was too frightened, too full of the feeling of strangeness to speak. Before that night my father had never seemed to pay any attention to me. . . . It was as though the man, my father I had not wanted as a father, had suddenly got some kind of power over me.

This weird initiation rite welcomed Sherwood Anderson into the world of men. It transformed his relationship with himself and his father. The power of this kind of fatherhood lies in the fact that it beams down a series of jagged and discontinuous images that impress themselves on a boy's mind, giving him a sense of what he should be, an outline, but without filling it in with color and tone.

Anderson's story may seem to belong to another era but it is not, in essence, so different from Paul Atkinson's memory of his father in the 1950s. Atkinson was one of the first generation of men to come up against the expectations of feminism. Writing of a 1950s childhood (in Hoyland, 1992), he said:

> In the house, my father carried about him the mystery of another world. In the morning, he had gone before my day started. In the evening, he arrived like a stranger from an alien land. His body moved in an unfamiliar rhythm, carrying home the world outside. He smelt of somewhere else.

Atkinson also speaks of a moment of transformation: "When I was 12 or 13, my relationship with my father was transformed. He asked me one evening if I'd like to come out to work with him during my school holidays. I said yes, and entered his other world."

Nick Hornby's childhood, against the background of late 1960s liberalism, did not provide a closer vision of fatherhood but one that was even more remote. In 1968 he was eleven years old, his parents had just separated, and his father, desperate for a place other than the zoo to spend those bleak Saturday afternoons, took him to a soccer match. Nick's "initiation" was not into a relationship but into a package called masculinity, which he learned carefully and hung on to for dear life: "I remember the overwhelming maleness of it all—cigar and pipe smoke, foul language." For Nick and his dad, Saturday afternoon at the Arsenal soccer field became a substitute for real life.

Just how much could these men bring from their own memories of fatherhood to inform relationships with babies of their own? The need to identify with their fathers, to leave all the women's stuff behind, is almost palpable. The memories are, as a result, so clearly etched that they overshadow the memories of the earlier infant tie with their mothers. That has become the past, part of the world they have left behind, pushed down so far that, when the time comes to try to retrieve it, to try to find that softness that they need to care for their own small children, the memories don't seem to fit them anymore. They creak with disuse.

It is interesting in this context that in one of the few studies (by Kyle Pruett) of men who have taken the major role in the care of their babies, there turns out to be a "prevalence of absent grandfathers." I had noticed myself that the men who seem to be most involved with their children, and most able to allow their children to be part of the flow of their lives rather than a separate preoccupation, are often those men who have no memory of their fathers at all. Pruett suggests that for these men, nurturing behavior is "rooted in the father's identification with his mother, not his father." Perhaps without the overshadowing influence of a distant and somewhat awe-inspiring father to hold them back, these men find it easier to be uninhibited and available to their children.

Fatherlessness is certainly not the only route to involved fatherhood (nor are all fatherless men involved fathers themselves). Feminists always held out the hope that men would be able to challenge their own inhibitions in the home in the same way that women were taking on the challenge of the workplace. Since the publication of *Who Cares?* in 1979, there has been an unprecedented movement of women into the labor market. That year less than 5 percent of mothers (in the U.K.) returned to full-time work after maternity leave. Over the next decade, the numbers of women returning to work in the nine months after a birth almost doubled, from 24 percent to 44 percent, and those returning to full-time work tripled.

If men had applied themselves to fathering with the same diligence as women moved into the world of work, we would be
well on the way to producing a generation of young men and
women with a rich reservoir of useful early memories to draw on
for images of father love. However, even if the women were
ignoring Leach's words, their partners seemed to have learned
them by heart. The father who recognizes that equality in the
workplace must be balanced by equality in the home is rare
indeed.

A study in 1990 of families in which both parents worked full-
time found that in 60 percent of homes the fathers worked longer
hours than the mothers, and in 71 percent the fathers also worked
at least one weekend a month. When mothers worked longer
hours than the average, fathers tended to work longer still. Nevertheless, employed mothers tended to get up earlier in the morning,
not to go to work early but to do the housework before they left
for work. On average, full-time working mothers spent twenty-
eight hours alone with their children each week, while their partners managed only six (Brannen and Moss, 1991).

Some men seem genuinely to believe that sex equality is merely
a matter of maximizing family income. I will never forget the letter
from a *Cosmopolitan* magazine reader who said:

My husband believes in equality. He feels that we should
each contribute half the money. My problem is that I feel so
tired all the time and I am worried about our baby. I've
asked him to change his hours a bit so that he can help with
picking her up and taking her but he won't do that. Now
I've decided that I will have to drop back to part-time
because I just can't cope with it all. The trouble is that he
says if I do that he isn't going to subsidize me. I won't be
able to manage my half of the money if I work part-time but
I just don't think I can go on like this.

This level of mind-boggling selfishness is not (I hope) the norm. I suspect that for many men, the withdrawal from child care feels more like exclusion. In the early stages of adult relationships they have been able to recapture, briefly, the intensity of the one-to-one bond that they would have had with their mothers back there before the doors closed and they had to become men. For some men this return to a twosome feels like the discovery of a lost Eden. For others it feels more like being trapped in a hot, steamy kitchen. Some want in forever, others want out right away. Those who stay in long enough then find that the twosome is rudely interrupted.

Unresolved feelings of jealousy are certainly not unique to men, but when a baby is born it is usually the man, not the woman, who stands on the outside. His own baby is now interrupting his relationship with his partner, just as, many years ago, his father (or a sibling) interrupted the blissful union of his relationship with his mother. A grown man who loves his partner, and feels that he is a responsible adult, may not be able to understand the sudden rage he feels when the baby arrives.

It would, of course, be hard to get sympathy at this moment, even if he could understand why he feels so low, because the person he turns to for sympathy feels that this time she is the one needing to lean. So what many men do, at this crucial moment, is withdraw emotionally—not the action most likely to elicit sympathy from an exhausted new mother. However, it does create a situation that the man can more clearly understand. Instead of trying to deal with his own unrecognizable feelings of anger, he can now deal with his wife's anger. Now he feels that his misery is justified. She has caused it.

One father said: "I just couldn't see a way in. There was no entry. It felt like a journey inland. You feel helpful, full of goodwill, but not really there. I felt completely detached, cut out. My daughter's whole life was being lived while I was away." Some men react by sinking into depression; others by becoming, as one person put it, "unbearably joyful"; very large numbers indeed cope by withdrawing into the predictable, rule-bound, emotion-free world of work. Perhaps they think they are fleeing the emotional atmosphere at home. What they are often trying to run away from is the emotional maelstrom inside:

> I just got sucked into the male world of hanging around after work, so I was never there in the evenings when she went to bed. I was always too late. I couldn't sort out my own needs with the demands of this new life. I couldn't see how I could coordinate caring for a child with the things I needed to do, like climbing a mountain or playing cricket. I couldn't see how to organize things so that doing the things I wanted to do was not an act of betrayal. Whenever I tried to be an individual, it was seen as a hostile act, an act of rejection. We couldn't find a way of being separate as well as together.

Two years later, now separated from his wife, this father said: "I know what I do. As soon as I get close, I behave badly so that the woman will attack and undermine me. Then I can say to myself: 'You are just like my mother' and walk away."

Those men who avoid feelings of jealousy (or successfully repress them) may find themselves up against another unexpected problem. The big shock, for men in particular, is the fact that caring for babies is not something that comes easily to them. This is not a matter of prejudice but of observation. However, unlike Penelope Leach, I do not believe that just because men find baby care hard, they should leave it all to women. There are lots of things about the world of men that women find hard. Some give up and go home, some put energy into finding out how to be like men, and some have found ways of getting the male world to adapt to their needs. Few people would dare to suggest that women are biologically unfit for these jobs.

Michael Lamb, editor of *The Role of the Father in Child Development,* has this to say on the subject of biological fitness:

> Most biological predispositions are biases or tendencies, rather than imperatives. The biological tendencies are such that they would be trivial if not supplemented by social forces; they would be reversed readily if they were contradicted rather than reinforced by cultural influences.

Even given the powerful cultural influences against them, there is no evidence to show that men who do end up holding the baby do it any damage but, given the nature of our culture and the way we socialize boys, it is not surprising that a great many men feel at a disadvantage. Perhaps if women were less self-denigrating and more aware of the skills involved in mothering, they would have more patience with their partners when they do not show instant aptitude and infinite patience. After all, most boys have spent the greater part of their childhoods learning to suppress that part of their nature that they will most need to use when faced with a newborn infant: the tenderness and emotional responsiveness they experienced in infancy from their mothers.

Babies trigger emotions so deep that many of us never knew we could feel them. They produce extraordinary sensations of tenderness and fear. The tears that so many women weep in the first weeks of motherhood are not only about feeling tired and overwhelmed; they are also the outer manifestation of a process in which the mother opens herself up emotionally to a new human being. This is how a sixteen-year-old girl explained the feeling:

> Me mates used to knock on the door and say come out with us. They couldn't understand why I couldn't go. They thought I could just leave him with me Mam. They just didn't understand that when it is your baby, you can't just leave them. I felt dead guilty just leaving him for five minutes. It

didn't feel right knocking around with them. I would be thinking about him all the time I'm out.

This extraordinary emotional change is not exclusive to women. All of us are programmed to respond to small, vulnerable creatures. (It isn't only humans; animals are just as soppy. Have you ever observed a big ugly Tom cat sitting patiently while a kitten eats out of his bowl?) In the early days of new parenthood it isn't only mothers who are smitten. Fathers also walk around with idiotic smiles on their faces, expecting other parents to see that their child is undoubtedly the most fascinating and beautiful child in the world. But these sensations don't fit into the framework of masculinity that men have established; they are the very touchy-feely things that they have spent a lifetime learning how to avoid. Most mothers are used to responding to feelings, and most fathers are used to pushing them away.

A new father had this to say: "I never knew I could have this sort of feeling for another person, outside of love for your wife, you know. It's another kind of love, in fact, it's not physical love . . . it's love." Perhaps to some extent this hesitant attempt to describe his feelings betrays more than this man realized. The fact is that the love for a baby is very physical indeed.

Mothers respond to their babies through their whole bodies: their ears, their breasts, and their skin—just as they remember their mothers responding to them. Men have often learned to equate physicality only with fighting or sex, neither of which is appropriate for a relationship with a baby. Several men I have spoken to talked about their fear of hurting the baby. One very loving father said: "When they are newborn they seem to be in the balance between life and death. I feel happier when they are a little bit bigger and more robust."

Today the pervasive fear of sexual abuse may be making it even harder for men to see that a physical, sensual, and loving relationship with children is not only appropriate but necessary to the child's healthy development. With the frightening messages that men constantly receive about the essentially evil nature of physical feeling, it is hardly surprising that so many men feel awkward and uneasy with babies and small children.

The physical engagement that comes easily to most (though by no means all) mothers is only part of the story. The skills learned from the myriad, face-to-face playground relationships can now be used to understand the moods of their child. They learn to preempt a cry by providing what their child needs before it has even felt the urgency of that need. All those years when girls have been learning and processing information about relationships, very many of their male contemporaries have been learning to protect themselves by communicating via objects (such as baseballs or computers) and organizing themselves according to the rules of games and the pecking order of hierarchies. There is no intermediary with a baby; there are no rules and no hierarchies.

Just as women, without all this early training, find it hard to operate within the unwritten rules of a masculine workplace hierarchy (see chapter 13), men often feel lost inside the boundaryless, ruleless world of the baby. For women one of the greatest traps of motherhood is the ease with which they lose their boundaries and merge with their children, becoming unable to see where they end and their children begin. For men the problem is that their boundaries are often built too high and too thick to be breached. Sheila Kitzinger interviewed parents of persistently crying babies and found:

> Fathers help on and off but, on the whole, they think of it as the woman's job to look after the baby. Two-thirds of fathers of crying babies give a hand when they can, as assistants rather than main caregivers. They do this so that the woman can perform other chores. They hold the baby or give a bottle while she prepares the meal, for example. More concentrated baby-care—really taking over—is restricted to those times when they realize that the woman is at the end of her

tether because she is crying or in a state of physical collapse. Even then, some men manage never to notice that a woman is desperately in need of help.

These men withdraw from an emotionally highly charged situation with which they are entirely unequipped to cope. They are the men who are also likely to seek solace with another woman in order to escape having to confront the ghost of their own feelings suppressed so long ago. So much easier to hide your face in another warm breast and return to your own childhood rather than confront the reality of the fear, and anger mixed with love, that come ready packaged with a new infant.

Of course, there are men who don't run and hide, don't build the walls up thicker, but try to understand what is happening. Here is one of the men Kitzinger interviewed:

> At first I tried to grasp everything with logic. I would go through a mental checklist to see if the baby had everything, and failed to understand why she went on crying. Then I began to try different kinds of behaviour, approaching my child with feelings, and then I began to understand her. Suddenly there are no more rules. What calms today may not work tomorrow. You learn to become softer and mentally more generous. You throw away inflexible ideas out of the window.

This man discovered that the rules he had learned to govern his life would simply not work here, and he had the confidence to disregard them. The sheer difficulty of coping with a persistently crying baby had forced him to reevaluate all his early gender training and come up with the answer that worked: to throw away the rulebook and act on his feelings.

Such men have, in a sense, an advantage. They were driven by the crisis of a distressed child and distraught partner into inventing their own methods of coping with the baby. In less difficult circumstances, where mother and child are doing fine, a father may have to make a much more determined effort to involve himself. These men are having to dismantle the barriers that masculinity has erected for them and find a way of relating to their babies while their partners are looking on. Many men can testify to the difficulty of handling a baby, perhaps clumsily at first, with their lovers' eyes boring into their backs. There is no harsher critic of a clumsy father than the doting mother of his child.

For the boy on the playground that still lurks inside every man, one of the worst things that life has to offer is being "shown up." Every masculine subculture has a word for the jeering and jockeying teasing that boys employ to undermine each other. The verbal put-downs are part and parcel of the pain every boy goes through on the way to becoming a man. Men fear being laughed at more than they fear being physically attacked. One father told me: "I was very clumsy the first time I changed a diaper. If she had intervened, that would have been it. I would never have done it again."

Researchers have noticed that almost any woman with a baby (not necessarily her own) will bring the baby face to face, talk with a higher pitch than usual, make exaggerated facial movements, and, more often than not, want to touch and hold the baby close. Men, in private, will behave in much the same way, but most feel stupid if they do it in front of others. So one way in which some men overcome their fear of being shown up is by hiding away and looking after the baby on their own. Two fathers I interviewed talked to me about the importance of getting to know their babies away from the intrusion and disapproval of their partners.

One remembers: "I would feed her in the middle of the night. It was so nice being on my own with her, being in control, not being threatened or accused, or told I was doing it all wrong. When the others were there I wasn't allowed to be capable." Said another: "In the end her mother had her at night and I took over when she woke up at five or six A.M. It was wonderful to have a discrete and valuable role. It was a time when I could be alone with her, with her mother out of the way, not interfering. I remember those early mornings with such warmth. That's when I really started to feel crazy about her."

While these two men saw their partners as the major obstacle to real, involved relationships with their babies, it seems just as likely that they actually needed the cover of night and absolute privacy to allow themselves to let down the guard that they had built up so effectively. Being a softie, allowing your feelings to surface and using them, is something men find hard, and harder still in public.

Listening to an early edition of the radio program "The Locker Room," I was struck by a conversation between three men in which they all admitted to allowing themselves to cry freely while listening to sentimental music, but only when they were alone, in a fast car, driving down a highway (a pretty dangerous affliction, by the sound of it).

Men in the 1990s know about feelings. They know that they are now under a moral obligation to get in touch with these feelings. However, finding a path back to one's feelings means dismantling the barriers that have been stacked up in the way. Men have not erected the barriers in a perverse conspiracy to absent themselves from child care. They were erected because, at the time, they were needed, and they have been kept in place because they turned out to be useful in allowing men to function efficiently in a hostile world. The barriers will be lowered only when men themselves see that there is a positive value in doing so.

For some men, an intimate relationship with a baby may be the turning point, the moment at which the barriers start to come down. It is a moment that, for many men, won't arrive unless their partners have the courage to make a space in which it can happen. Asking a woman to stand back a little from the most intense emotional experience of her life is asking a great deal. She also needs to know that it is worth it. The reward may not seem very obvious at first, but it is the only way I can see to break the cycle of father deprivation for our own children and the generations to come.

9

Good Enough Fathers

For a woman, pregnancy and childbirth are major initiation rites, processes that will irreversibly change her life. A man may not even know that his child has been born. If a woman abandons her baby at birth, there will be messages on television and a police hunt to find her. If she wants to relinquish the care of her child, she can do so only through a legal process. Men abandon their babies every day and nobody even asks why. So what is it that turns the act of fertilization into the role of father?

In hunter-gatherer societies it seems unlikely that fathers had a distinct role in the family unit at all, other than that of jointly defending their own group against attack from animals—and other men. Women provided most of the food for themselves and their children. It wasn't until people learned the link between sex and conception that fatherhood started to evolve as a social institution.

Men joined themselves to the family unit through marriage and upheld their rights through superior strength. This then allowed them to control the labor and loyalty of a woman (or women) and, through her, their own offspring. For many fathers, proximity leads to affection (for both children and wives), but this was not necessarily expected. Marriage was primarily the means by which the rich and powerful could consolidate their wealth and influence and group leaders could organize the behavior of the group. (Marriage has never had quite the same importance for those people without wealth or property to secure.) In other words, fatherhood evolved for the benefit of men, not for the sake of children.

From the institution of marriage and fatherhood, men collectively built institutions of power that totally excluded women and a legal system that gave them control over their children while their wives cared for them. It wasn't until this century that the power base that men had won in the family, by binding women to them through marriage and financial dependence, has started to crumble. The first change has been the growing independence of women. Women have found that they can manage alone; they don't need to depend on men for economic support.

The second change sprang from the growing interest in psychology. Children became objects of concern in a new way. The assumption of paternal ownership gave way to a new family doctrine, which put the needs of children first. The judicial system followed the trend and decided that, when a marriage ended, custody and control would no longer go automatically to the father. Children's interests should be served first, and that usually meant staying with their mothers. The whole basis on which marriage had been erected started to fall apart. Women no longer had to stay inside unhappy marriages in order to keep their children. For the first time since marriage was invented, they found themselves free to leave. Seventy percent of marriages are now ended by wives, and a third of all children in the United Kingdom are born outside marriage.

But if a man is not necessary to the economic support of his family, and is not necessary for the physical care of children, then what is a father for? Listening to the stories of fathers who lose contact with their children after divorce, one may perhaps not find it surprising that so many of them feel redundant. They see that their ex-partners can cope with everything: they earn, feed, clothe, love, and discipline their children. They see that their children are upset by access visits. They find the visits awkward and embarrassing and, as psychologist Charlie Lewis puts it, "gradually become opaque and vanish." Within two years, around 50 percent of divorced men have lost contact with their children.

According to Mavis MacLean, who has spent many years researching fathers and divorce, many of these men just found it impossibly difficult to relate to their children from outside a family unit without the help of partners through whom they have conducted their relationship in the past. Some fathers are deeply upset at the loss of their children but feel that they are doing them a favor by making a "clean break." Some put themselves first and feel that they have a right to a new start, that somehow they can wipe the slate of their lives clean and begin again. Some mothers, eager to rid themselves entirely of men who have been violent, or with whom they feel angry, help the process of detachment by making it difficult for partners to keep contact with their children.

Although the relative lack of emotional connection between men and their children is at its clearest after separation, the roots of that disengagement lie in the deep-seated inequality between mothers and fathers during marriage. Most fathers who embark on family life believe that they really do want to be involved with their children, but it is hard to build a deep emotional attachment if you spend three weekends out of four at work, and arrive home every evening after bedtime. The reality is that many fathers have no idea what it means to be a parent, and they live in a culture that gives them very little help.

This book is about the current uncertainty in the construction of masculinity, and perhaps this question is central to it. If a man does not see that he has a place in the family unit, how is he to grow up? What is he for? Why should he jump through the hoops that his education sets up for him? Is there any reason why he should stop playing games and become an adult? Some men are beginning to realize that making themselves important to children is the way to find themselves a secure place in the family again.

Fortunately there is nothing easier in the world than making yourself important to children. The construction of fathering, looked at from an adult point of view, may well be detached and remote. Looked at from a child's point of view, it is a very different thing indeed. For a child, the father matters, whether he is there or not. His presence and his absence will both have an effect. A father may leave his children, but a child can never totally leave his father. He will always carry him around in his heart. He may carry hidden anger at his father's absence, or just curiosity, but his influence will always be felt.

The fact that fathers are losing their power base within the family gives them an opportunity to move forward and to explore their real importance, alongside mothers and children, rather than in domination over them. Fathers cannot connect to new life by having babies, but they can maximize their importance to the psychological growth of their children. They can do that by recognizing that the people who are emotionally close to a child in its early years provide that child with the mental matter for adult life, just as surely as those who shared the moment of conception provided the physical matter.

BEING THERE

Psychologists over the last twenty years have started to wake up to the need for detailed study of the ways in which a father contributes to the psychological growth of his children. Not that their task has been easy. Fathers spend little time alone with their children, and it is therefore difficult to set up a research project that looks at this interaction. Much of the available information is taken from studies of the development of children with and without fathers. It assumes the difference between the two to be the equivalent of the father's influence. However, it is not a simple equation. Children are without fathers for many different reasons: death, separation, economic necessity, illness, violence. A growing number have never had a father participating in their lives at all, and many children with divorced parents see more of their fathers than those living in intact families.

The trauma attached to the loss of a loved person will inevitably affect children, and it is clear that the age at which separation takes place, and the amount of contact afterward, will also have an effect. The same trauma is not experienced, for example, by the children of lesbians who have conceived without any intention of involving the father at all. These children also have no fathers, but they have not experienced the trauma of loss. There is a similar gulf between the experience of a child who loses, through death, a father who loved him and the child whose father has made a decision to abandon him.

However, in spite of these difficulties, research is beginning to show that fathers do bring something distinct to the lives of their children. The father's influence starts very early. Indeed, most research shows that the first three years have the most impact. A boy whose father is not available in the first three years tends to be less stereotypically masculine. A boy who loses a father after the age of five will already have learned what it means to be male. For better or worse the father, in these early years, has a tremendous influence.

There is nothing biological, or fixed, about this influence; it is probable that it would vary dramatically from one culture to another, and it will inevitably shift as wider social change dictates an adjustment in the way in which men are expected to behave. However, as things stand within Western society at the end of the twentieth century, the major cultural function of the father seems to lie in shaping his children into the place society assigns for their gender.

As the major influence in creating gender difference, fathers can, and often do, reproduce a form of masculinity in their sons that is reactionary and violent. However, they also have the power to pass on to their sons a masculinity that breaks with traditions of dominance. Fathers who recognize their power and use it wisely have a vital role to play in bringing up children. A boy will learn more surely from the father he seeks to emulate than from the mother from whom he is struggling to separate, but even then the influence is not a simple one. There is no simple equation in which a gentle, nurturing father produces a gentle son. Children react to parental influence in varied and complex ways.

Studies of two-parent families show that children between ten and eighteen months identify their father as a source of stimulation and respond actively. The same children, given a choice of parents, turn to their mothers for comfort and their fathers for fun. During the second year, while boys start to show a stronger preference for their fathers, girls shift attention away from their fathers and back to their mothers. According to psychologist Michael Lamb, "the preference seems to be caused by the father's greater interest in sons than in daughters." (Fathers who don't discriminate against girls have a very important part to play in their lives, though that is not a matter for this book.)

Fathers tend to play rough-and-tumble games more with boys than with girls, encouraging mock fights and tests of strength. Henry Biller, a psychologist with a particular interest in fatherhood (Lamb, 1981), found that eight-year-old boys who had been separated from their fathers for the first two years of their lives were regarded by their fathers as "sissies." These boys were also judged by psychologists to be "less masculine." Boys without fathers in these early years tend to be less aggressive than those with a father around (although mothers who treat their sons aggressively will also encourage them to be aggressive to others). Those who lose their fathers after the age of five tend to have learned already how to behave aggressively. Researchers came to the conclusion that what they regarded as the stuff of masculinity must be imparted in the first two or three years of life.

There seems to be some confusion over what researchers mean by *aggressive*. Sometimes it is taken to mean that children are more prone to fight and to play out aggressive scenarios with dolls. Sometimes it seems to have been confused with the idea of assertiveness: standing up for himself rather than being the person who always gets his toys snatched. Nevertheless, there is a message here for fathers. If your idea of masculinity is a boy who can hold his own in playground brawls, then you had better be sure to be around to teach him the techniques in the first three years of his life. Without the encouragement of macho masculinity, boys do not seem to have any more natural predilection for aggression than girls. They learn it—first from their fathers and then from their peers. However, they could also learn from their fathers how to use their strength and vitality to make them confident rather than aggressive.

Clearly, if these lessons are learned before the age of three, it is not because, at this stage, the son is looking to his father for a model of masculinity; rather, the father recognizes in his son someone who is "like" him, just as the mother recognizes the similarity of her daughter. Fathers pay more attention to their sons, talk to them more, and are more likely to keep in touch with sons than with daughters if a partnership ends. While the mother loves her children and binds both of them to her, the father makes positive efforts to entice the son away. Even before he understands what gender really is, the recognition of likeness on his father's face will not only tell the boy that he has done well; it will also reflect back to him a mirror image of himself and tell him what it is to be male.

One father I talked to has three children, the youngest a daughter. His description of the difference between his relationship with his sons and his daughter had clear echoes of similar remarks made to me by mothers who find it much easier to relate to their daughters than their sons. He told me:

I suppose I am more engaged with the boys. Jane seems more fickle; things aren't so constant with her. You won't always get the same reaction. With the boys I know what response I am going to get. In a way, that makes Jane more intriguing, but I find I am planning moves with her rather than just reacting to events. There is more going on with her. She has made up her mind what she is going to do. I have to steer around that, rather than the other way around.

A parent cannot easily reflect back to a child those things about him or her that the parent doesn't understand or value. A boy who greets his father with a playful punch in the stomach, and is rewarded by being hoisted in the air, will get a very different reception if he tries similar tactics with his mother. And if he tries it with another child, he will almost certainly be firmly told off. He is learning that some things are OK only with Dad. Some forms of behavior are labeled masculine. That binds him even more closely to his father, who appreciates his difference and rewards him for it, and starts to separate him from his mother, who feels anxious about his difference and tries to suppress it.

However, this father/son connection is not straightforward. A parent who finds a child's behavior puzzling or worrying may not be able to reflect to him a sense that he is fundamentally OK. A man who feels anxious and uncertain about his own masculinity, or remembers his childhood as a time when he felt afraid, may reflect that anxiety back to his son when he sees him starting on the same journey. A father who is remote or ambivalent may join in rough-and-tumble play occasionally and then, when the child gets excited, withdraw abruptly, leaving the boy anxious and uncertain about himself, his relationship with his father, and what is right and wrong. If the child doesn't respond in a way the father finds appropriate, his father may also withdraw. Psychologist Richard Green discovered that fathers tend to spend less time with their sons if they consider them to be "effeminate" (Green, 1987).

This mirroring, then, is a two-way process. The father doesn't wait for the son to attract his attention, but positively seeks his interest. The father who is emotionally engaged and supportive will effortlessly reflect to his son not only a sense that he is male but also that being male is good. He may at the same time encourage his son to fight, to be disparaging toward women, and to seek social acceptance through domination. Or he can transmit to his son the kind of confidence in his own strength that will ensure he doesn't need to use it in order to dominate others.

A father doesn't have to be available all the time to act as a mirror to his son, any more than a mother must be there all the time to provide the same service to her daughter. However, he does have to be there long enough to have an impact. Henry Biller (Lamb, 1981) looked at the amount of time fathers spend with their children and the impact that had on their children's achievement. He discovered that boys who spend an average of two hours a day or more with their fathers tend to be high achievers. The same study showed that fathers who spend less than six hours a week with their children (the average time recorded for fathers in the Brannen and Moss study of two-career families, 1991) have no more impact on their children's achievement than they would have if they were not there at all.

Of course, a child doesn't have to have a father in order to see a positive reflection of himself in his parents' eyes. Nor is a child in a two-parent family mirrored only by his same-sex parent. His mother will continue to reinforce in him those parts of his personality that she feels especially drawn to. In a family in which both parents are involved in caring for their children, and both have a positive sense of themselves and their children, traditionally masculine and feminine qualities from both parents will be reflected and reinforced in both boys and girls, so that they take on a sense of themselves that is flexible and whole. Male and female children both need a background of physical care and stimulation, laced with the intoxicating pleasure of the passionate devotion of someone who thinks they are the bee's knees, the cat's pajamas, or the best thing since sliced bread.

PARTING IS SUCH SWEET SORROW

Tossing a giggling infant in the air, rolling around on the floor, or soaping him in the bath may seem like loads of fun in the first two years. Then the child starts to assert his own identity, tests his wings, and starts the process of moving away from his mother. At first this may show itself as a determination not to do anything she asks. In earlier chapters I have described this process from the mother's point of view. Mothers are often desperately anxious about their sons' apparently impossible behavior at this stage. They are not helped by the sense of disapproval from other parents with which they so often have to contend while they are struggling to cope with a recalcitrant child.

Fathers can do a great deal to ease this change just by being available to their sons; taking the time to let their sons know that they see them, hear them, understand them, and know that they are indeed growing up to be a man. All too often fathers fail to notice that they are needed. The problem appears to be between mother and son. It takes a leap of imagination to see that it is even more about father and son, and it is tempting for the father, already fairly marginal, to withdraw further away.

Offices and bars are full of fathers looking for ways to avoid the uncomfortable daily confrontation with the children they are supposed to love—fathers who cannot cope with the overwhelmingly physical nature of their child's feelings. Perhaps they don't understand that a child who greets them with joy and then has an instant temper tantrum is not expressing hate but is telling his dad that he has been missed. Or perhaps they are remembering the pain and confusion of their own early years, when they had to come to terms with being not Mommy's boy but Daddy's boy—and Daddy wasn't there.

A father who comes home reluctantly, tense in anticipation of arguments, may in fact be more use in the bar. His son will probably feel more rejected by a father who is there in body but absent in spirit than he will by a father who is physically absent but, in his son's imagination at least, looking forward to spending time with him. Henry Biller, researching father/child interactions (Lamb, 1981, p. 515), came to this conclusion: "The child with a non-nurturant father may be better off if the father is not very available."

A son who feels that he cannot attract enough of his father's attention may become more irritable and anxious. He wants to feel that he is reflected in his father's smile but, if he can't get that, he just wants to be noticed. He will prevent his parents from talking to each other; jump into bed with them—not to cuddle but to stop them from cuddling each other; cause diversions and distractions, and shout from the rooftops: "I exist, look at me, notice me, play with me."

The father who reacts with irritation or anger may stop his child from behaving badly—but only by making him afraid. The boy's fear of his father will become part of the way he looks at the world of men. He will, in the end, learn either to avoid his father or to imitate him and seek praise that way. Or the irritated father will cause another reaction—in the mother. One mother said:

When he was in the house I was always tense and worried. I was afraid that he would shout at my son, or even hit him (in fact he never did). I felt that I had to be eternally vigilant to protect my child from his own father. As a result I never let them get close at all. I always stood between them—watching.

Some fathers withdraw because they are afraid of the power of the anger they have spent all their lives learning to suppress. They are afraid that they will hurt their children, and so they hurt them by staying away. The father who is unable to deal with his own feelings and withdraws from the whirlwind of demand is opting out of his responsibility as a parent. The father who assumes it is his partner's fault and criticizes her for her bad handling of her son is undermining her and making it even harder for her to get things back on an even keel. The father who shows affection to his partner and backs her up as well as being available for his son is telling him two things: "I love you and I love your mother. If you want my good opinion, you will be good to the person whom I love."

For the child who is facing separation from his primary love (his mother), both kinds of reassurance are important. A boy who wants to be like Dad will find it easier to let go of Mom a little if he knows that Dad loves her too. The transfer of identification will be far less painful. The child will feel more able to hold on to the parts of himself that his mother loves at the same time as taking on the parts of himself that he wants his father to love.

In an earlier chapter I talked about Pat, who was unable to cope with her son's disruptive behavior until she heard her partner tell her that he admired her patience. The father still paid little attention to the care of his son but, by supporting her, he enabled her to reflect something positive to her son about his own goodness. The confidence that his parents then felt in each other was in turn reflected in their child.

Two sons I mentioned in the last section found different ways of handling the move from mother to father. Both are now seven years old. One ended up in violent confrontation with his mother at the age of five. He had to wrench himself from her world. In spite of the fact that he spends most of his life in an all-female household, he has become a little macho man. His voice is gruff, he speaks only in short spurts, he has rejected all the pastimes that could conceivably be considered feminine. He is contemptuous of girls but has achieved a level of popularity bordering on hero worship among the boys. The other wanted only to get his hair cut "like Dad." He is warm and open and seems enormously self-confident, but is exceptional in that he is a favorite with both the boys and the girls in his class.

Both these boys have good relationships with their fathers. The little macho man lived through his parents' divorce when he was two years old. He sees his father regularly but cannot have been unaware of the hostility between his parents, which, to their credit, they have made big efforts to overcome. The other child has parents who, in spite of the fact that the mother is the major caregiver, seem to move between male and female roles without effort: they both tend to wear jeans, they are both tall and slim, they are both designers, they both cook, and they spend much of the weekend in joint activities with their children.

This boy can emulate his father without letting go of the things his mother has given him because there is no big difference between them. Dad does what Mom does and Mom does what Dad does and they love each other. It would be impossible to reject the female parts of his psyche because femininity is not solely the property of his mother. He is noisy and boisterous, but he is not ashamed to be soft and thoughtful too. Nothing in his life experience tells him that is not a part of being male. His inner, earlier world is not in conflict with the person he wants to become. He is rarely seen without a broad grin on his face. He seems to be an exceptionally calm and happy child.

The importance of mutual support does not end when a relationship ends. One father I talked to has made a significant relationship with the son of an ex-lover, whom he has been able to steer through difficult times (this is discussed a little later), yet he feels worried about his own son, whom he describes as angry and lacking in confidence. He has also been separated from this boy's mother since his son was three, and the hostility he still feels toward her, thirteen years later, is instantly apparent. They have difficulty supporting each other's different ways of dealing with their son's problems, and the boy is clearly reflecting their confusion. The father told me: "There were two courses I might have taken as a divorced father. I could have put a lot of energy into resolving a relationship with his mother or I could work out how to take responsibility for being a parent." On the basis of all the evidence available, he made the wrong decision. A better relationship with his ex-wife would have provided a firm background for his efforts to be a good parent. A bad relationship will continually undermine it.

The importance of the relationship between parents, as well as the relationship between parents and children, cannot be underestimated. Boys who have mutually supportive parents will not only feel more confident of their own goodness; they will also feel more able to engage, emotionally, with other people. Children in divorced and nondivorced homes were compared in a study (Hetherington, Cox, and Cox, 1982, p. 277) that concluded:

> The most androgynous boys had fathers who themselves felt comfortable with an emotionally expressive role, who admired their wives and encouraged a warm relationship between the boy and his mother, who were warm but who also tended to be dominant and to play an active role in decision making and childcare.

One of the difficulties of research is the fact that terms such as *androgynous, masculine, feminine,* and *dominant* are open to very wide interpretation. The clear thread linking different pieces of research shows that warm and emotionally engaged fathers, who participate actively and make decisions alongside their partners rather than leaving their partners to be parents alone, have far more direct influence on their sons' lives than fathers who are distant or authoritarian. The desire to be "like" comes from mutual regard.

IMAGES AND INTIMACY

The boy who spends time with his father will be learning that his father likes his company; but in many families, that is about all he will learn. This eight-year-old was asked what his father did in the evenings: "He gets lots of work from the boss and then when he comes home most of his time he spends doing the work. I see him quite a lot but not so much talking to me 'cos he's normally doing his work—but I watch him."

Fathers and sons who do things together often choose activities that allow them to be together in silence: they play football, go fishing, play with computers. All these activities have a place but they are not enough. A child's identity is made up not only of images of male and female. It must be securely grounded in an intimate relationship. In most families this intimacy is supplied by the mother.

Men who have grown up learning to suppress their emotions often have difficulty being emotionally open with their children. The common fear of the power of male sexuality may also get in the way of physical intimacy. They may be afraid that cuddling a daughter may arouse inappropriate sexual feelings or that cuddling a son may awaken deeply repressed homosexual feelings, which many men regard as even more frightening. In fact, Jungian psychoanalyst Guy Corneau feels that for some men homosexuality is a late attempt to get from other men the thing that their own fathers denied them: a sense that their bodies are beautiful.

Indeed, boys often suffer from physical separation too early just because their fathers feel unable to cuddle them and boys feel that it is babyish to cuddle their mothers. Of course, in many families, covert cuddling goes on throughout childhood until, as a boy reaches adolescence, his mother, feeling her son's growing sexuality, finds it necessary to make a distance between them. A girl with loving parents will have a constant reinforcement of the beauty and desirability of her body (indeed, she may have little else) until she reaches an age when she rejects them. A boy may be cut off from any confirmation of his own desirability by the time he starts school.

Body intimacy is not just about comfort and pleasure (though that is plenty in itself). It is also a vital part of a child's self-image. A father who is incapable of intimacy with his son may be able to provide him with an image of masculinity, but he won't be able to make him feel like a good person, at home in his body and happy with the person he is. A man who is afraid to touch his son, afraid to admire his body, anxious about physical intimacy, is telling his son that bodies are bad and dangerous things, not to be admired, not a source of pleasure, but more a thing to be tamed, to be exercised and trained into hardness. Body confidence needs to be rooted in a secure, warm, and intimate relationship.

Two different pieces of research into custody arrangements after divorce came up with some interesting information about the ways in which gender identity and intimacy interact and overlap. Psychologists Santrock and Warshak in the early 1980s came up with evidence that boys seemed to be doing better after divorce if they stayed with their fathers. These were children from families in which custody arrangements had been arrived at without bitterness and the children continued to have a good relationship with their mothers. Under these rather favorable conditions these boys seemed to be remarkably free of the kinds of difficulties that boys in single-mother households face. Compared to boys in mother custody, these children were rated "more mature, sociable, cooperative and dependent. They were less anxious, less demanding and had more self-esteem."

Clearly these boys were thriving in a setting in which they had warm emotional support as well as a multidimensional male role model. However, these were self-evidently fathers who had chosen custody. They were (though this was not part of the study) almost certainly fathers who already had a warm, engaged relationship with their sons and, since the boys had good relationships with their mothers too, they had none of the feelings of abandonment that so many sons feel when their fathers leave.

The children in the Santrock and Warshak studies were only just arriving at puberty. Those studied by Eleanor Maccoby (1992) had already reached adolescence when, so to speak, the pudding of child rearing is ready for the eating. Maccoby's research did not look specifically at fathers who had chosen custody but at those, in a large sample, who had ended up, one way or another, taking care of the children. In her survey, overall, the children seemed to be doing worse with their fathers.

Maccoby and the other researchers in this study put their results down partly to the level of hostility shown to ex-partners by fathers with custody, and partly to the fact that "fathers in sole residence were less likely than other residential parents to have intimate and open relationships with adolescents in their care"; this, in turn, made it harder for the fathers to keep track of their children's movements. The girls in father custody, in both studies, were doing particularly badly and having enormous difficulties with adjustment.

Looked at together, these studies seem to indicate that, while it is clearly an advantage for a growing child to have a close relationship with an adult of the same gender, that is not as important in the long run as a relationship with a parent who loves him and isn't afraid to show it. Gender identity is important but it can be gotten from any man who takes the trouble to show a real interest. In the last chapter, a single mother talked with great warmth about an ex-lover of hers who had taken the trouble to keep up his relationship with her son. Her son said of him: "He was the mover and shaker in my life. When I felt out on a limb at home, I talked to him."

This man himself said: "I was one of a succession of men who, as he saw it, had rejected his mother. I suppose I realized that some man had to stick around for him. I don't think that I contributed much to his life until the point when he came into conflict with his mother. I felt he needed me to reinforce his sense of his own needs."

His intervention worked because he showed his respect for both son and mother. He was therefore able to provide a way for this young man to move away from his mother without undermining her. Intimate, loving engagement is something special and hard to replace. This boy was able to hold on to the intimate relationship that he needed without feeling he would be suffocated by it.

A child who has an intimate relationship with two parents may have an advantage, but the child who has it from only one parent has an advantage over those who don't have it at all.

FULL-TIME FATHERS

One might imagine, then, that the father who is there all the time, and takes the major role in child care, must have an even more important influence than fathers who spend a couple of hours a day with their sons. If boys copy their fathers, then these men should also have gentle and emotionally responsive sons. There are few families in which the father is the major caregiver, so very little research has been done. And it would be difficult in any case to isolate the effects of having a father home full-time from the reasons why the father had taken this unusual course of action. Few men are thrust into this position by chance—in families where male unemployment is prolonged, the more usual course of action is for his partner to stop work as well. When families break up, fathers rarely end up caring for the children.

One clear picture that emerges is that full-time child-caring fathers are not the same as mothers. They still behave the way they would if they were providing secondary backup. Where mothers tend to treat their children as a part of their lives—continuing with socializing and housework at the same time—fathers seem to treat their babies as a project: a job to be done. They are far more task-oriented with their children. Play is central. They tend to do more with their children, and their houses are filled with projects and collections of objects and board games.

Most fathers I have spoken to tell me that they rarely do any housework while the children are with them. They wait for them to go to sleep or do it at night. The exception is cooking, and that becomes play as well. According to Kyle Pruett (1983), who has studied a few of these families, "the expectation that time together would be full, complete, fun, stimulating and jocular, if a bit chaotic and disorganized, seemed to pervade much of their play."

At the eighteen-month check, Pruett noted that all this stimulation was having a positive effect on the children's development: they were all well ahead of their peers. By four years old the development had leveled off. Pruett suggests that paternal enthusiasm had merely triggered certain aspects of development a little earlier than would otherwise have happened. One thing these children were not getting was the opportunity, typical of girls brought up by mothers, to watch their dads just doing what dads do. They don't indulge in imitative play because they don't see anything to imitate. The things Dad does he does for them; they are not actually learning about an adult role.

One seven-year-old child whose father has brought him up spends hours playing imaginary games, often all by himself. Most of the little girls of my acquaintance do this too, but where girls' play revolves around the domestic world of adult women (albeit princesses), this boy involved himself in games of fighting and monsters. His make-believe world still comes from the television, because you cannot easily imitate someone whose only function is to play with you.

At school, far from being more secure about their masculinity, these boys may actually appear to be more confused. They are confronted with male peers who reject girls because "girls can't do the things boys do," and they become aware of a man's world, which all these boys aspire to. How does this square with this boy's own world, in which it is the woman who goes out and does the interesting stuff while Dad stays home?

Pruett noticed that, at four to six years old, the boys in his study were not doing as well as the girls. They seemed flatter, less effervescent, than the girls. In fact, they seemed to behave in a similar way to girls who have been kept at home full-time with their mothers and have not had the opportunity to imagine for themselves a role in the outside world. (All studies show that girls with working mothers are more assertive than those whose mothers stay home with them full-time.)

These boys are not experiencing the triangle that Freud describes, in which the boy separates from his mother to join his father's world. Freud didn't conceive of a world in which a boy's primary relationship could be with his father. Nor are they developing in the same way as girls would if cared for by their mothers, because they are not only dealing with the internal world; they are reacting to the external organization of society too. A girl brought up by her mother is not forced, by the society she enters, to reevaluate her relationship with her mother. For a girl, nurturing behavior is considered normal. She may be a little passive, but there is no stigma attached to passivity in a girl. She can grow up in her mother's image.

For a boy, having a father who is a housewife, however much he is loved, is not having a father who matches up to the macho-speak of the playground. In an early chapter I described an incident in which a boy, cared for mainly by his father, brought some friends home from nursery school. Together they played with the doll's house but when this child put the Daddy doll in the kitchen to make supper, the other boys mocked him, telling him that Daddies don't cook. This child stuck by his father, insisting that his daddy did cook, but he never played with the doll's house again. He was beginning to learn that the things his daddy did were not things that the other boys respected. He needed to identify with these boys, and he loved his dad. He experienced an agony of indecision. Must he reject his father in order to establish his own image of himself as a boy?

These boys have emotionally close relationships with their fathers but, in those crucial years between three and ten, they find that the image of masculinity in front of them is seriously at odds with the image of masculinity that is recognized by their friends at school. One full-time caring father of a seven-year-old boy said of his son:

He has always been a bit shy outside, surly and uncommunicative, but boisterous at home. Lately there's been a change. I think he wants to find himself rather than be part of his mother and me. For instance, he will still automatically hold my hand, but then as soon as he is aware of it he will pull away. I still kiss him goodbye but he often runs off before I can do it. Now lately he has started making comments about me, that I am not a real man, that men don't do this sort of thing.

His father has explained that the job he does is taking care of children and that this is just as important as anything else he could be doing. His son is not convinced. He loves his father but feels angry with him because he embodies everything that he now learns is associated with being a sissy. He has few friends and he knows he is out of step with the others. He is beginning to suspect that the father he loves may be not man enough for him to emulate.

This boy's best friend had always been a girl, someone he could share his imaginary world with. He has a little sister, whom his father describes as a bit of a Daddy's girl, and he has a mother who blows in at bedtime bringing him a glimpse of the outside world. In his world women are fascinating and powerful people. In the world of school the girls don't want to play with boys and the boys don't want to play with sissies. So he is trying to be like a boy, like the kind of boy they recognize as a boy. His dad says: "He doesn't know how to communicate with them so instead of talking he will hit someone, or bump into them deliberately to attract attention."

His parents are baffled by his behavior. They interpret it, as the world almost certainly will too, as aggressive and macho, and his father tries to talk him out of it: to explain to him that he won't make friends if he keeps hitting people. His father cannot retrieve the situation by telling his son that he is wrong and that child care is valuable. His son now has his own view of reality, and it is shaped by his peer group. The overwhelming message he receives at school is that people who stay home with their own children are of less importance in the world than those who go out to work; taking care of children is something that only women do. And these days, even the girls want to be doing something exciting as well as caring for babies.

No wonder his parents are worried about him. His behavior will make him few friends. This boy's difficulties are similar to those faced by many boys from single-mother families. They find that the world they are expected to fit into doesn't have any holes that are the right shape.

The way parents react to a child's attempts to fit in is very important. If they are uncomprehending and negative about his dilemma, they will just reinforce his dawning belief that they don't really understand what the world is like. He will feel even more isolated, search anxiously for the key to being a real boy, and reject their attempts to reason with him. What he wants is to be told that, yes, he is a boy, and that being a boy is good, and that he can trust his parents' positive estimation of the person he is.

In another family in which the father was the main caregiver until the youngest child started school, there are two sons. The experience of the older child was quite similar to the child described above. He had a female best friend with whom he shared many interests, but on starting school he gradually gave in to "an overwhelming barrage of taboos expressed by his peers regarding gender activities." By the age of seven this firm friendship had dissolved.

This child also found the expectations of school very hard to cope with. He would escape from the classroom and go to play in the nursery. His parents were totally supportive of him and felt angry and betrayed by the school which, they believe, "thought a boy showing emotion at school needed to be repressed." They changed schools at one point and then found that he was being bullied. They considered changing schools again but decided against it: "He had some good friends, so we decided to support him as best we could. We emphasize his strengths, how he is different from some others, how he is special."

Now he is at secondary school. His parents still worry about him, but they feel reassured that he is making friends. He has begun to find a way of holding together the male and female parts of himself. He is a typically uncommunicative adolescent on the surface, but has held on to his ability to feel and to talk about the way he feels. His younger brother has had no similar problems. He found entering the world of school much easier because he had already been introduced to it through his elder brother. Indeed, the family has become overwhelmingly male, and ball games and computers dominate. But these boys know that men cook and clean and care for children as well as kicking balls around in the mud. Their mother says: "They have bits of both of us, both masculine and feminine."

Perhaps the most important thing this couple has done for their children is to give each other support to be themselves as well as being parents of their children. As soon as the children stopped needing full-time care, their father returned to work. Now these boys see two parents who share the caring, the loving, and the earning. Just as, in a conventional family, the support of the father strengthens the mother in the eyes of their children, so in a family in which the father takes on the nurturing role, the unambivalent support of the mother must strengthen him.

Modern feminism grew out of the frustration of women who were "kept" in a minor role while their husbands went out into the world. Men taking on the housewife role often romanticize it and fail even to identify, let alone articulate, the frustration they feel. Children learn strength and confidence from parents who feel strong and confident in their roles. A father who is given no respite from parenting to develop as an individual will find it as hard to reflect a whole, and complex, role to his sons as a full-time mother does for her daughters.

10

Fathers Holding Cracked Mirrors

It is a truism that any agent powerful enough to have an effect on the human body is also powerful enough to have a negative effect. The same thing is true of minds. If a loving father who is available and engaged can enrich his children's lives, an angry father who is rejecting and cruel can be equally effective in impoverishing them; and a father who is weak and disengaged may simply be rejected as a model, leaving his son with a vacuum to be filled elsewhere. This is why the current gung-ho enthusiasm for putting fathers, willy-nilly, back into families is not only misconceived but positively dangerous.

VIOLENT FATHERS

It is clear that a boy whose father is violent to him will be affected by that violence, but the effect is not straightforward. He may be so frightened of his father that he fails to identify with him at all as a child, remaining closely involved with his mother, as well as passive and fearful. He may be so afraid of attracting his father's fury that he creeps around, keeping a low profile and swallowing his own anger. He may grow up as an apparently gentle and passive man, looking for a loving woman to protect him just as his mother did. It may not be until his own child is born, and he finds himself pushed away from the warmth of his wife's protection, that all the buried anger surfaces and he finds that he is turning into the father he rejected and hid from so long ago.

He may, on the other hand, learn to identify with his father, in the classic way in which Freud described, on the grounds that it is safer to be with him than against him. This boy will take on the behavior of his father and become aggressive in his own dealings with other people. He will be the child who learns at an early age that it is better to be top dog. He will be the man with a short fuse who always hits out first, never waiting to find out whether the other person really means him any harm.

The boy with a father who is violent to his mother will also be indirectly affected, even if he is not a victim of that violence (though 50 percent of men who beat their wives also beat their children). One woman I talked to had worked for many years in a women's shelter. She told me: "The little boys were horrible to their mothers from a very early age. They treated their mothers with contempt and lack of affection."

A man who feels that he is due respect from his woman, because he is a man and a wage earner, is likely to instill the same thoughts into the head of his son who watches, reveres, and emulates him. If that man then finds that he cannot earn a living and that the basis on which he expects respect no longer exists, his arrogant assumptions of superiority are very likely to be replaced either by anger or despair.

In chapter 1, I mentioned talking to a woman living in a housing project. She said of her husband:

I recognize the pain he felt at losing his job. I would support him to the death if he didn't turn on me. He seems to think that everything bad that has happened to him is my fault. He calls me a cunt and a whore. I really worry about the way he puts me down in front of the boys, so I am constantly trying to keep a low profile and not antagonize him.

This woman decided to leave her husband in order to protect her children from his influence.

AN ABSENT PRESENCE

However, it isn't only violent fathers who teach their sons violence. A father can have the same effect by failing to teach his son anything useful at all and leaving him to find his own version of masculinity with which to fill the gap. John McVicar has made his name writing about the criminal society of the East End of London, from firsthand experience. Writing about his father (in Hoyland, 1992), he said: "The abiding image I have of him is the smell of whisky, which even now makes me gag."

McVicar's family was not one that, from the outside at least, should have made a criminal of him. Had researchers probed his home for signs of deprivation, they would have found little. He had two parents: his mother, by his own account, strong, warm, and protective; and his father, weak and ineffectual but rarely absent. They ran a shop and were very slightly better off than the working-class East End community they lived within.

The overwhelming feeling that McVicar conveys for his father is contempt: contempt for his drinking, but even more for his ineffectiveness. He can time the moment when he first started to despise his dad quite accurately. He was six years old. His father was taking him and his sister to a Christmas pageant:

My father slipped and fell into the gutter. A couple who were coming the other way came to his assistance. As the man reached out to my father, his wife, or whatever was her

relationship to him, shrilled disapprovingly, "He's drunk."
Her face was pinched in outrage. I felt my father's shame
and humiliation, but not because I was part of him, because
he was my father, but because I felt sorry for him as a person
and wanted to protect him from public disgrace.

McVicar didn't want to discuss his childhood with me, on the
grounds that "I am so resistant to anyone who wants to talk about
'feelings.' Indeed I am virtually allergic to the 'feelie' brigade." He
did tell me that he considers masculinity to be biologically based
and that, though culture might have an effect, "it is clearly subor-
dinate to the higher socio-political-economic institutions of society."

However, reading his own writing, I find it clear that McVicar's
particular kind of masculinity was at least partly shaped by his
individual circumstances. According to Biller (Lamb, 1981), children in families without fathers, who have a positive relationship
with a highly competent mother, are less likely to become delinquent than children in families with present, but inadequate,
fathers. If the father is perceived as weak and ineffectual in comparison to the mother, the boy is likely first to model himself on
his mother and then on his peers, bypassing his father completely.

In homes where fathers are unemployed, this is far more likely
to be the pattern. The mother, with the job of caring for children
and home, is relatively unaffected. She may be anxious or angry
about the loss of income, but it is not her own self-image that is at
risk. Whether or not she works for money she is still occupied, she
is still important, she still has a place. Her husband, without his
role as income provider, may feel that he has been stripped not
only of self-respect but of his place in the family. He actually has
no function at all.

Without direct access to a supply of money his wife may then
turn on him, accusing him of being useless, incapable, and incompetent. He is reduced to the status of child in the home in which

he believed he would be king. The image these children are absorbing of their father is far from an attractive model. Elder and Rockwell (quoted in Lamb, 1981) studied two groups of young men whose fathers had suffered unemployment during the Great Depression. One group had been under the age of five during this period, the other group eight years older. The younger group suffered low aspirations as young adults, whereas those who were older when their fathers became unemployed were highly motivated. The authors conclude that the fathers of the younger boys had been "less attractive role models at a more critical stage of their development."

Of course, there are many men and women who survive unemployment by supporting each other and finding ways of engaging themselves actively in their own lives and the lives of their children. But in those families where depression and hopelessness take over, young boys may find themselves learning to despise their fathers at the very moment in their lives when they would have been starting to emulate them.

The children who were older when unemployment struck had already absorbed a model of their fathers as competent and strong at the time when they were learning what it meant to be male. The disaster of unemployment was seen as a blow struck from the outside. These boys grew into adults who were determined to fight against adversity, rather than destroying themselves.

Clearly a child doesn't only model himself on his parents; he also reacts against them. A father whose son perceives him as weak cannot teach gentleness, because his son will copy his behavior only if he wants to emulate him. If he feels that his father is not a useful model he will look elsewhere, and the references for masculinity that surround him are all about aggression and dominance. In rejecting what he sees as his femininity, he will suppress most of what he is, and adopt instead a macho veneer.

McVicar remembers: "When I was eleven I went to secondary school; there I spent about a year of being a proper schoolboy before being swept into the maelstrom of staking out an adult identity. For me this was established by bucking the system, then crime." According to Guy Corneau, in his book *Absent Fathers, Lost Sons,* the lack of a usable father image leaves a boy without any internal sense of who he is. Without any internal structure on which to build his sense of himself, he looks around desperately for external order.

McVicar found order in defiance and an identity as a Bad Guy. Once in prison, he found a different set of rules with which to run his life, but throughout he has retained his absolute terror of looking at the gray mess he keeps deep inside. He found nothing to replace the father he (effectively) never had. Others become easy fodder for tightly organized fascist groups, get hooked on computer games, join religious cults, or become addicted to body building.

THE LOOMING SHADOW

Inadequate fathers don't have to be drunk, or unemployed, or violent. They can do a pretty thorough job by being overbearing and critical and stamping on any attempts their sons make to be independent.

One of the built-in advantages of the way masculinity is constructed is the way boys learn to admire men. Mothers suffer from the old problem of familiarity breeding contempt. Fathers who retain their difference, their separation, easily become idealized objects of admiration. The advantage lies in the ease with which men are able to set up hierarchies and establish heroes. The difficulty lies in the trouble so many boys have in living up to the image of their fathers.

If the father is too big, too clever, too successful, how can the son cope? How can he bridge the gap between being a little boy who knows nothing and a man who knows everything? Unlike his sister, who can practice every day being a mother, dressing up, cooking, and going out to work, he has no small steps to take on the way to becoming a man. He doesn't even know what his father actually does. The chances of falling into the abyss of failure seem far too great. No wonder so many boys seem simply to stop trying.

Fathers who respond by attacking their sons, or showing an overanxious interest in their activities, will make the situation worse. They are not closing the gap between their own achievements and their son's abilities; they are making it even greater. Andy, now in his thirties, is a pleasant, easygoing man who drifts through life without ever sticking to anything or anyone. He felt happiest and most secure when briefly involved in a mystical movement under the instruction of a male guru.

Andy's father was often away from home working. He kept in contact with his children, but Andy was conscious that the family life he experienced was "very ritualized." It was built to look like a happy family but it was empty inside. His parents, he has since discovered, did not really love each other; they had been pretending, in order to keep up the facade. In fact, his relationship with his father was based mostly on anxiety and pretense: "I was quite frightened of him. He was sarcastic and I remember once, when I was about six or seven, I was really excited about something and telling him about it and he just pushed me away. I was so hurt. I felt as though I had been swatted."

When Andy was older, his father's interest became more focused: "He wanted us to go on fishing expeditions with him. I didn't really enjoy it. I felt I was having to live up to his image of fatherhood. I was afraid of letting him down." It was the same with schoolwork: "We'd be called into his room one by one. He would look at my school report and say, 'I'm not angry with you, just disappointed.' I would rather he had got angry. I couldn't cope with his disappointment."

Andy's father had had no father of his own, and his mother's way of coping was to send him to a boarding school. He grew up without ever being able to feel, and then found a career in which he always had to work within rigid guidelines, with no room for imagination or creativity. He was a man who desperately wanted to be part of a family, so he did everything he could to create a family for himself—but he didn't know what a family felt like, so all he could create was its shell. His children knew how much he wanted them to be a family, so they all conspired with him. They all pretended to be happy.

Andy's father did not set out to frighten his children, quite the contrary. He just didn't know how to be warm and open with them, so they found his interest intimidating. Norma Radin, writing an overview of the role of the father in cognitive and intellectual ability (Lamb, 1981), points out the importance of the quality of a father's interest in his children. Fathers who try to help their children with schoolwork by standing over them, rather than encouraging them and then leaving them free to make mistakes, actually interfere with their intellectual ability, and authoritarian fathers reduce academic competence for both boys and girls. In fact, fathers who frighten their children actually impede their ability to think at all.

Radin quotes a study of three-year-old middle-class boys. The children were given puzzles to do in which there was more than one possible answer. The children with fathers whom the researchers rated to be impatient, authoritarian, unspontaneous, and unable to express emotion did not do well. They seemed unable to tolerate ambiguity. She concluded: "The father who is perceived as competent and strong but who permits his son to master tasks and solve problems independently provides the most fertile background for the youngster's intellectual growth."

A man a little older than Andy at first seems to share many of his characteristics. He looks a little like a hippy, is always into new ideas, interested in new schemes, prefers smoking dope to sipping whisky. He has all the outward appearance of the rolling stone but in fact his tastes, ideas, and involvements stem not from an inability to decide what to do but from a genuine delight in life's variety.

This man talks about a very different father: "We would make things together in his workshop and he would take me to exhibitions. My earliest memories are as much of my dad as my mom." While never aggressive, he was by his own account determined to defy convention. His parents worried about him but: "They decided that trying to make me conform was a lost cause, so they let me go my own way." His nonconformity is not a protest against conventional life at all; it is a choice of the life style that suits him and makes him happy. Within its limits he is extremely conventional. Few people manage to make such choices.

Fathers who are warm and close are not the same as fathers who loom over their children, anxious to mold them in their own image. A child who operates out of fear of getting it wrong, rather than interest in getting it right, is afraid to make mistakes. He becomes literally rigid with fear. Rigid patterns of thought do not allow creativity. These children are afraid to think for themselves. They are listening to their fathers' voices in their heads and worrying about getting things right.

Girls will also be affected by their fathers' criticism, but they can also take refuge in their female identity, and side with their mothers. A boy with a hostile, critical, or aggressive father has to negotiate a gender identity around him. He may well try to stop thinking at all, lest he think something wrong, take refuge in rules to protect him from the possibility of a mistake, and take his rigid thinking into adult life, applying regulations and restrictions where none are needed. He is the man who is afraid to be intuitive, afraid of being outwitted, and who protects himself from his own fear by building an aggressive shell of his own to hide in.

Clearly, then, there are many boys who, to quote Biller again, "may be better off if the father is not very available." As things stand, there is an increasing likelihood that fathers like these will be dispensed with altogether. Dennis and Erdos (1992) argue that this growing lack of fathers in families is the reason for lawlessness and rioting among today's young men. Interestingly, however, their statistics provide the best possible reasons why shoring up the family as an institution in which men dominate, rather than participating equally, would be unhelpful.

The English study they refer to was carried out in 1979 at the University of Newcastle, under Professor Israel Kolvin. Families were rated on their level of deprivation. The researchers used a number of criteria to assess the families' level of deprivation, so not all people living in poverty would have come into the multi-deprived group—only those who were least able to cope with life. Some criteria dealt with the competence of the mother, some with economic circumstances. The researchers came to the not very surprising conclusion that the sons of inadequate mothers, living debt-ridden lives of poverty, were four times as likely to have criminal records as those living in happier circumstances.

The research also showed that nearly half of these mothers were single parents, and on the basis of this the authors conclude that the delinquency of the sons was due to the absence of fathers. The same study also showed, however, that in the half of the multi-deprived families that did have resident fathers, only 7 percent were rated "effective, kind and considerate" and two-thirds did not participate in household tasks. These men clearly made no useful impact on the lives of their children, so it is very hard indeed to see how adding similar men to the lives of the other single mothers could have helped. The difficulties faced by these families cannot be reduced to anything that simple.

The most important information in the survey indicates that, among deprived males, one of the six most important factors protecting against a child becoming delinquent is the rare possibility of having a father with an "effective personality." If we are concerned about delinquency, what we need is effective parents. Simply gluing inadequate fathers back on to unstuck families will not help one bit.

WHEN THERE IS NO FATHER TO HOLD
THE MIRROR

Just as a child's experience of fathering depends on the kind of father he has, so a child's experience of having no father will depend on many things other than the lack of a father. According to numerous research studies, boys born without fathers (or who are fatherless before the age of five) tend, by eight or nine years old, to be rated more dependent on peers, less aggressive, having less interest in contact sports, and more likely to underachieve. In other words, they share a lot of characteristics with girls.

Leaving aside the fact that the world might be a better place if it contained more boys who were dependent on peers, unaggressive, and lousy at football, the results contain an interesting class bias. Middle-class boys deprived of a father in the first two or three years of life are far less likely to underachieve than are working-class boys in the same circumstances. Indeed, a number of studies mentioned in a review by Henry Biller (in Lamb, 1981) indicate that middle-class, father-absent boys may be highly successful academically. One study (Santrock, 1972) noted that sons of fathers who died before the boys reached the age of two tended to have a superior IQ to their peers. These boys also tend to be better in verbal skills than in mathematics (a pattern that is more common for girls).

It is working-class boys, particularly those from cultures in which men tend to be dominant, whose achievement in school is most likely to be adversely affected by father absence. In these families, physical prowess is particularly highly rated, and boys who can perform well physically attract the admiration of their peers. On the other hand, boys who have not learned, by the age of seven at the latest, how to handle themselves on the soccer field are likely to find themselves socially marginalized. A child who feels insecure will have difficulty learning.

These boys are subjected to the expectations of children who believe that to be male means learning to fight and protect your territory. Having lived alone with Mom, and loved her, these children will not yet know that they are deficient males. They won't find out until they are told—and that won't take long. They may then react either by copying the most masculine of the boys they see, or by withdrawing and quite possibly suffering bullying as a consequence. They may oscillate between the two, attempting to build up their confidence and prestige by bullying children whom they perceive to be weaker than they are. Without a confident position in the social world, they will be more easily sucked into the antisocial, anti-intellectual groups that seem outwardly to be ultramasculine.

African-American educationalist Jawanza Kunjufu describes this as "fourth-grade failure syndrome," because it is in fourth grade (at nine or ten years old) that so many black boys start to slide into underachievement, getting sucked into what he describes as the Street Institution: "He becomes a student of the 'asphalt jungle' because that is where he can learn the skills he needs." Kunjufu points out that these boys rarely see a man with whom they can identify unless he has a basketball under his arm. There are few role models of academic achievement for black boys.

Sometimes mothers, anxious to counteract any sign of femininity in their sons, push them into adopting a kind of hyper-masculinity. These are the mothers who call their two-year-olds "little men," encourage them to fight back whenever anyone teases them, and generally nudge them out of the motherly nest as fast as they possibly can. These boys may be dressed in tiny replicas of whatever is the male fashion of the moment and encouraged to walk tall with a masculine swagger, but at the same time they are learning not to cry, to manage without the cuddles and caresses that tell them they are lovable and cared for. They learn to stop feeling.

The boy who does not have a father and yet survives his encounter with school, without adopting an ultramasculine veneer to cover his shame, will be the one who has internalized a strong enough sense of himself as good. If he is lucky he will have a mother who makes him feel so good about the other parts of his identity that he won't experience fatherlessness as a lack. One man, now a successful writer and father of two sons of his own, said: "I never doubted for a moment that I was wanted. I lived more as a partner than a child. It was me and her against the world. There was no conflict between us; the conflict was with the rest of the world."

It is almost certainly significant that this man went to a school where, by the age of eight, most of the boys had left to go into private education. He passed the years of his life when many unaggressive boys suffer at the hands of their peers surrounded almost entirely by girls. He remembers: "I got on fine with them but I was a pretty solitary child: making models and writing stories. Solitary activity seemed natural to me." By the time he started secondary school he had built up a level of internal confidence that kept him safe: "I was small and had glasses and didn't play football. It ought to have been a problem but it wasn't. I was aware of the aggression around me but I wasn't affected by it."

Many of the studies of father absence in early life look at death, or separation due to wars, or the pattern of work. When children are studied after separation due to divorce, the story changes. Nursery school–age children were studied by Hetherington, Cox, and Cox at two months, one year, and two years after divorce. They were found at all three interviews to be less cooperative and more solitary than boys in nondivorced families. They were less likely to share and to help, and more likely to try to attract attention with negative behavior. They also had more difficulty adjusting to single-mother life than girls did.

These children seem to be significantly worse off. They seem to feel the loss of a father much more than those who are fatherless for other reasons, and far more than their sisters do. Clearly they had already started to attach themselves to their fathers and are reacting to that loss, but that doesn't explain why they are more hurt than boys of the same age whose fathers have died. The explanation (as I suggested in the last section) may well lie in the attitude of their mothers. A partnership that ends in divorce will leave a legacy of anger. The mother whose partner has died keeps a memory of love. Perhaps divorced mothers have a harder time telling their sons that it is good to be male. Perhaps these boys see only a negative image of the male when they look for a reflection of themselves in their mothers' eyes.

These young boys will try to find a more acceptable mirror. If their mothers find new partners while they are still young, they may well graft on gratefully as if desperate to find the missing piece in the jigsaw of their inner selves. If there is no male figure at home they may make desperate attempts to attract attention from male teachers (often attracting negative attention because they find it so hard to make the right approaches), and they may seek out older boys or men for attention. Sometimes this attention will be sexual. A boy who has never seen himself, as a boy, in a positive light is quite likely to turn to a man, who loves him as a body and as a boy—who brings the physical and the emotional sides of his life together again.

If these boys fail to make themselves attractive to their peers, fail to retain the warm and steady regard of their mothers, fail to make themselves attractive to another man who can act as the holder of the mirror, they are vulnerable. It takes enormous strength to hold on to a sense of yourself as good when the world is reflecting back to you an image of deficiency. If you cannot regard yourself as good, you may as well cut off the good parts of you and be bad.

Boys without fathers are less aggressive than boys with fathers, and yet studies of those children who do turn to crime and delinquency show that father-absent children are overrepresented.

(Though interestingly, according to Joe Whitty, governor of Feltham young-offenders unit, the overwhelming majority of those detained, as hard-core miscreant, do have resident fathers.) Just as the son of an inadequate father searches for images of masculinity, so will the son of a father who is absent.

John McVicar, whom I quoted writing about his father, has also written about his son, to whom he presented a very different father figure. The early years of his son's life he spent in prison, emerging as something of a celebrity: the reformed, self-educated ex-thug living life alone, training, writing, and indulging in brief, uninvolved relationships with young women.

Eighteen years later McVicar wrote about an encounter between his son, Ray, now twenty-eight years old, and a taxi driver he beat to a pulp for the crime of double-parking in front of his car. He was angry and upset by his son's behavior, and protests: "For years and years I've confronted, battled, and attacked his criminal beliefs but . . . these ideological showdowns only reinforce the psychological satisfaction he derives from being precisely what I was and now detest."

McVicar sees Ray's behavior as a kind of knee-jerk reaction: the son locked in a rivalrous battle with his father. His payoff: "I have failed with Ray, but on the grounds that my involvement in his condition only aggravates it, I've passed. He is no longer my problem." He dismisses the alternative explanation that his son's turn to crime was a way to get back at him "for being in prison while he grew up, rejecting his mother, and whatever else, emotionally, he resents me for."

For Ray, an absent father had exactly the same effect as a present but passive father did for John. Only in this case, instead of feeling contempt for his father, Ray clearly idolized him: a remote and glamorous figure who rejects close emotional attachments, exercises fanatically, gets him into clubs, buys him expensive meals, and allows him to make use of his apartment for sex with the "nubile young girls" he has picked up. Ray has learned from his father that men survive by cutting off their feelings at birth and being tough. So Ray is tough, just like Dad, and his father thinks that the only thing that will do him any good is a long stretch in prison.

If the only images available to people like Ray are of violence, aggression, and dominance, then in order to be male they will feel that it is necessary to become aggressive. The job of adults in society is to ensure that these boys can find some other way of achieving their aim of becoming men.

INITIATION RITES: THE QUICK FIX

Human beings have an overwhelming need to belong. For some people that sense of belonging is something they carry with them. It is a sense of internal order. They feel at ease because they know who they are. It is hard indeed for a boy to know who he is if he is uncertain of what it means to be male. Being male is a very important part of his identity. If it is missing he must make up the deficit elsewhere. He may make up for it by identifying instead with a group. The order of the group will provide him with the internal order he needs. He will absorb it and it will become part of him. The group will become the father he has missed.

All may seem to be well while that group provides him with a framework that works well with the rest of society. In cultures in which religious rituals are still part of the fabric of life, many young men will simply learn the religious rules, and use them to provide the inner structure they are missing. Many religions have a form of initiation ritual, filled with symbolism, during which a boy is taught the mysteries of the adult members of the group and learns that he is now expected to act responsibly. His behavior may be narrow, rigid, and ungenerous. He may use the rules to reject all possibility of change—as have, for example, those Angli-

can Christians who oppose the ordination of women—but since
he works within accepted parameters, he will be accepted as a
member of the group.

In a society in which religion plays little part, many men take
refuge in conformity and a life bounded by rules of games, rules of
hierarchies, rules of dress, and rules of behavior. Others have
decided that the way forward is simply to do what Mommy tells
them and be good boys. That way, at least, they can save themselves from the abyss of the unknown. They can avoid trying to
find out who they are and hang on to her version of what it means
to be male.

Poet Robert Bly described the dilemma of boys growing up
among women in the words of a young man's dream:

> He and a clan of she wolves moved fast through the forest,
> in formation, and eventually they all arrived at the river
> bank. Each she wolf looked into the water and saw her own
> face there. But when Keith looked in the water he saw no
> face at all.

A man who looks but does not see himself is not a man who can
be happy. He is missing something. He may even find that the
women he is seeking to please turn away from him because they
are also aware that something is missing. They can feel that he
doesn't know what he likes, or do what he likes; he is operating on
the basis of their needs, not his own. The missing part is his sense
of himself and his own needs. An equal relationship is based on a
partnership of two wholes, not one and a half.

One young man I talked to has an exceptionally good relationship with his mother, from whom he learned a view of the world
that set him apart from his school contemporaries. Her continued
determination and support for him ensured that he was free to be
highly successful in his chosen field, but he was conscious of
something missing. It started in his teens:

By the age of sixteen I began to see that there was no place for my mother's identity with my male identity. I had no way of operating around girls. I felt an acute irritation about missing out on the experience of irresponsible adolescence.

For this young man the problem was sex. He could talk to girls, in fact he got along well with them, but he didn't know how to shift gears, how to let a girl know that he wanted something more:

I had learned that the power was invested in the one who could say yes or no. That meant I would have to wait for someone to come to me, and I wasn't always sure when that was happening. I had a real problem with being an initiator. There were some boys for whom this didn't seem to be a problem; they seemed to have made the connection between sexuality, desire, and self-esteem.

The life in his head was working fine. He had achieved a level of accomplishment against many odds and clearly felt pleased with himself and his achievement. It was on the inside that he still felt confused, and at the center of that confusion was the view he had internalized that "male sexuality is represented as aggressive." It is a notion he found both repellent and exciting. In order to be a good boy he had to be passive sexually and "wait for someone to come to me," yet at the same time he fantasized about "depraved sex," the kind he believed his mother would disapprove of. She had taught him to respect the needs and desires of women, but he had missed out on any validation of his own needs and desires.

Perhaps the most important missing component for a boy brought up without an effective father, a man who touches him and makes him feel physically loved, is a sense of pride and pleasure in having a male body. (Women may also suffer in this way if their parents have treated their bodies as dirty and their growing up as something to be afraid of.) Our culture provides nothing to make up the lack. Male bodies are presented in two forms only: the flaccid couch potato who is an object of derision and the hard-bodied aggressor who fights and "takes" women. Where are male images of sensuality that could give young men a clue that their bodies can receive pleasure as well as give it?

I was struck by an article in *She* magazine (March 1993), in which writer Will Self said:

> Sometimes, during periods of celibacy, I have started to feel my own body becoming cloudy and diffuse, as if only physical contact with a woman could somehow paint-touch me back into corporeal sanity. This has been the terror of being without physical love for me: a very profound loss of bodily self-respect.

This sense that something is missing is the central theme of Robert Bly's book *Iron John*. In it he captures a clear sense of the unease felt by men as they sit at the top of the tree and watch women attempting to shake them off their perch. His book is powerful and compelling and it harks back to an older, golden age, in which boys had the guidance of initiation to teach them the mysteries of being male. Bly speaks of a powerful symbol that can be traced through much ancient literature, in which a pubescent boy receives a wound. According to Bly, this wound has a symbolic significance: "It hints at an initiatory ritual administered by old men which we have forgotten. Apparently a leg wound, when accomplished ritually, strengthened young men."

Few ancient religions provide initiation rituals for girls. Certainly there is the abhorrent act of female genital mutilation, but that is carried out at a very early age. It is not a means of initiating women but of serving them up as sacrifices to men. It seems to me likely that initiation rites for men evolved because nature had not supplied them with anything to equal the symbolic and actual power of menstruation and childbirth.

Certainly boys' bodies do change, but the changes are gradual. There is no sudden, single, and dramatic moment at which a boy becomes a man, capable of generating life. Yet, in their desire to seize power, men played down the "wound" of menstruation until it became a mark of shame and played up the artificial wound administered by old men on young boys as a symbol of strength. Where life supplied women with the trial of childbirth, men felt the need to undergo trials of their own, and many initiation rites force young men to undergo trials of strength or endure great physical hardship in order to become men.

Guy Corneau, in his book *Absent Fathers, Lost Sons,* is fascinated by the powerful imagery of initiation rites. He sees initiation not as synonymous with giving birth but as a symbolic second birth:

> Where a man's first birth is nourished by his mother's milk, his second is a birth nourished by his father's blood. The elders of the Kikuyu tribe in Africa take on the role of male wet-nurses: their boys sit in a circle with the tribal fathers, each of whom uses the same carefully sharpened knife to make a small cut in his arm and let a bit of his blood drop into a bowl. By drinking this blood, the adolescents become men. Born in their mother's milk, they are now reborn in the father's blood. What an impressive way to be welcomed into the male community.

Yet, if we read these mysteries as the attempts by men to take for themselves the life-giving power assigned to women, then they lose their sense as a useful route to an understanding of masculinity. Masculinity that is rooted in jealousy of women cannot be the kind of masculinity needed for a society in which men and women are equals.

Initiation is used in societies in which children spend their early years exclusively with women. It is these societies that produce men who are most insecure about their masculinity and in which, after initiation, men are most divided from women. Initiation, and men-only groups, are a means by which individual men get their own back for the power that their mothers held over them, and men as a group get their own back for being deprived of the central role in life: childbearing.

While men fail to develop a sense of themselves from within, they will continue to find ways of structuring themselves from the outside, and initiation rites will continue to play a part. Those who say that we lack such rites are simply looking for them in the wrong place. Initiation rites in our society are not carried out in an ordered way, sanctioned by society; they are carried out by groups of young men who force conformity on their peers in an effort to ensure that they are all men together and that they all belong. It is the initiation of bike gangs in which the price of entry is evidence of a murder or rape; the membership of paramilitary groups in which belonging to a particular religious or national group provides the cloak of identity and initiation involves killing a member of the hated out-group; the beating and raping of young soldiers to give them a clear sense of the hierarchy they have attached themselves to.

Ritual initiation has little, or nothing, to offer us because it is essentially a means by which men separate from women. It is the obvious end-point of a version of masculinity in which to be male means only to be not-female. This is not to deny the pain and confusion that men feel as they are forced to reassess their place in society; the answer is not to take refuge by moving backward into the divisions of the past, but rather to move forward into a partnership of male and female.

For the young man I quoted earlier, the solution to becoming a man seemed to be getting a BMW and a big pair of speakers. Initiation rites without any cultural context are about as useful. They are just another form of "quick fix" for a pain that needs something more profound. There is a much simpler solution for young men, which doesn't sound trendy and doesn't have the resonance of initiation rites. Adult men could simply try a little harder to befriend young men.

When I look around me I see very little evidence of communication between adolescents and adult men. Mostly teenage boys are treated as a general nuisance to be swatted like flies. Men seeing a boy without a father do not think: here is a young man to talk to, to listen to, to make friends with. They think: here is a young man who lacks male discipline. They wade in with orders and instructions. Not surprisingly, these young men are not grateful. They walk away. Fatherless young men often grow up with a profound distrust of adult men and react badly to attempts at discipline.

Perhaps what they are saying, in that gruff and inarticulate way they have learned to cover up their soft insides, is that they don't want to be yelled at; they want to be listened to. Perhaps the answer to male adolescent rebellion lies in the friendship and understanding of adult men. Perhaps men, in general, need to take responsibility for boys, in general, and to start supplying them with real, three-dimensional images of what it means to be male.

Adolescent boys, whether they have a good enough father, an inadequate father, or no father at all, need the help of other adults to move away from the womblike security of home and to find their own place. It is not an easy task and it is one that will often involve a period of angry rejection of the father, just as, way back at the age of five, and again at the age of twelve, they fought for independence from their mothers.

Young men need the alternative voices of men who are not emotionally mixed up with them so that they can get their bearings, start to see their parents as real people rather than idealized figures, find the courage to make their own way in the world. They also need parents who have the courage to let go of them and give them the freedom to find their own way. This task would be a great deal easier if there were more men out there willing to act as guides and helpers to sons who are not their own.

Davy, at sixteen, stopped seeing his father regularly. They had arguments and Davy said: "I felt intimidated by his expectations of me. It came to a head when I dropped out of college and didn't tell him beforehand or involve him in the discussion. I knew he would have made me stay there. He would have gone on at me about self-discipline." Davy did talk to his mother, but found that the best way of dealing with how he was feeling was "playing tennis with John. It felt much better than trying to explain how I felt." John, a family friend, is reliable and interested, but not emotionally involved.

A year later Davy had reassessed his life, come to terms with the problems he had faced in his first term at college, and found the courage to try again. He needed distance from the parents whose anxiety made him unable to think clearly, and a steadying hand while he thought. He was lucky that he had someone around to help him make that journey. Those people who are so anxious to glue the family back together would perhaps do better if they looked around at the young men on the periphery of their own lives and asked themselves, When did I last give any of my time to listen to a young man who was not my own son?

V

THE POWER OF
PEERS

11

Into the Madding Crowd

So far I have looked at the development of boys from the point of view of their parents but, in spite of the powerful influence they exert, they cannot determine the people their children will grow into. All children need to discover their own identity and that means moving out into the world, measuring themselves against their peers, using what they know and what they see and the influences that bear on them to work out what kind of adult they will become.

For most children the first independent steps into the world will come between the ages of three and five when they move beyond a small-scale group, or individual care, into preschool and then kindergarten. For some the transition is smooth. They make friends easily and enjoy the stimulation of learning new things. Others feel overwhelmed and take time to adjust. All of them will be learning a great deal more than reading, writing, and arithmetic. They will be learning how to make relationships with other people and what, in their particular world, a boy or a girl should be.

Even a child who seems to have been well prepared may be shocked by the experience of a playground full of huge, rough children all screaming and running around. This may be the first experience of play that is not monitored by an adult. Up until now they have sought approval mainly from adults. Now they start to look for approval also from their peers, and all too often the criteria will be quite different. A boy who has learned to take pride in his cleverness at building Lego cars, riding a bicycle, or learning his letters may be completely floored by this alternative world in which alliances seem to be made by rolling around on the ground or chasing each other in confusing games of tag.

Some boys will already have a clear sense of what separates them from girls. Perhaps they have a father who encourages them to put up their fists in mock fights or takes them out for boys-only play sessions in the park; or siblings who have already passed on some of the boy lore; or perhaps they have already had more freedom to play in the street. These are the ones who lay down the guidelines of what a boy can do. The shy, the uncertain, the different, and the new ones will then be forced into the mold by the pushing and prodding of peer pressure.

For Graham, "school was just an extension of what happened in the projects. If you didn't want to be pushed around, you had to defend yourself." This is how Dan remembers it:

> I still remember the first day. I cried and clung on to the bars and didn't want to go in. It was tough. I had to deal with kids who were used to being rougher than I was. I got teased because I didn't fight, and if someone teased me I would just cry. Adults said I should learn not to react to the teasing but my first reaction was to cry. I hated it there.

For Dan, elementary school was about learning "to feel confident, learning not to react." Graham, the more confident child, enjoyed school, rarely got into fights, was never teased, and had plenty of friends, but his confidence was built on learning the same lessons a lot earlier: "I used to cry a lot but crying wasn't encouraged at home or school. It was seen as a sign of weakness, so you learned to internalize it."

Girls will also be exposed to behavior they find bewildering and frightening, but, though they may be alarmed by rough boys, they are not obliged to try to play with them. They can, to a large extent, ignore them. My seven-year-old daughter told me about a school assembly to discuss fighting on the playground. She was awestruck by the idea but totally unaware of any actual fighting that had taken place. It has nothing to do with her. For a boy, entry to the world of boys means finding the courage to join in or a strategy for avoiding trouble, without being seen as a sissy. It certainly can't be ignored.

Most girls arrive at school with a pretty well developed sense of what it means to be a girl. They have already internalized a sense of what constitutes gender-appropriate behavior. It is easy to make friendships because there is already a shared language. Girls' behavior does not change very much when girls move into a bigger group. They still put most of their efforts into developing and maintaining close friendships. They create a smaller-scale world in which they can operate safely.

Psychologist David Panter looked at the way in which girls and boys adapted to the transfer into school (1988). He found that although both boys and girls were aware of gender in preschool, girls had already internalized a clear sense of what that might mean in terms of behavior. Girls didn't want to play with a toy space station once they had put the space people to bed. The boys had not yet learned that playhouses are girls' toys and played with both.

The girls had also developed the cooperative "person-oriented" behavior that would characterize their interactions in later life. Pairs of girls would automatically share a task that was set for them, taking it in turns, scrupulously ensuring fairness, and jointly devising imaginative ways of extending the game. In boy pairs, one would always dominate and control the entire operation, and there was little attempt to use imaginative ways of extending a game. In mixed pairs, the girl adopted a teacher relationship, facilitating the boys and directing them.

In preschool, boys are living in a world that is much like an extension of home. The rules are social rules, there is very little structure, children are expected to play together and start learning to make relationships under the close observation of usually female workers. Entering school, these boys find themselves involved in a crash course in learning what it means to be a male—a course that entails close observation and rigid monitoring.

Studies of boys' behavior in school reveal that they are more susceptible to peer pressure than girls are, and it is through rigid peer monitoring that they learn what is considered gender-appropriate behavior. In one study (Green, 1987), four-year-old boys and girls were involved in play more usually associated with the opposite sex. The boys quickly stopped what they were doing in response to negative comments from other boys, whereas girls relied more on their own judgment and were much slower to respond to negative remarks from other girls.

A study of the behavior of four- to six-year-old children (Hetherington, Cox, and Cox, 1982) found that immediately after divorce both boys and girls were more likely to indulge in bursts of immature, unprovoked, and ineffective aggression. A year later the girls' behavior had improved but the boys were still more likely to behave this way. By two years after the divorce researchers found that the boys' behavior had improved. Yet, at this point, male peers still rated their behavior as aggressive, and "rather than becoming more accepted these boys appeared to be more socially isolated relative to their male peers."

Mavis Hetherington considered the impact of negative peer attitudes so important that she was moved to recommend that parents should seriously consider the advantages of moving children to a new school if the impact of a divorce has had a particularly negative effect on their behavior. She points out: "Boys who were shifted from one school to another between the first- and second-year assessments were perceived and responded to more positively by both peers and teachers."

This tendency of children to pick on classmates who are vulnerable is well documented. Episodes of bullying often follow a
trauma such as the death of a parent or divorce, but children may
also be picked on for some other reason such as race, dress, or dis-
ability. Children who are developing a sense of self want as many
other people as possible to be like them. Deviation makes them
feel anxious because it threatens their fragile sense of identity. In
an insecure world, what they want above all is continuing evidence
that they are the model and the others the deviation.

Girls also victimize other children for their difference but they
are not as unforgiving as boys. Hetherington noted that, while
girls accurately observe the deteriorating behavior of classmates
immediately after divorce, at the two-year follow-up there was no
difference in behavior toward girls of divorced parents and others
in their peer group.

Perhaps this difference is also a product of the girls' greater
confidence in what constitutes appropriate behavior. They know
what a girl should do and therefore feel secure in trying out different kinds of behavior without feeling that their status as a female is
threatened. Greater confidence about their own status may in turn
allow them to be more generous in their assessment of others.
Small girls can be buddies one day, hate each other the next day,
and then be pals again by evening. They seem less likely (at least in
these early years) to fear that being nice to a child who is unhappy
will reflect badly on them and affect their own status in the group.
(This kind of behavior does happen later, as girls enter puberty
and become less secure about their role.)

I asked some six-year-olds: "Who are the naughty children in
this class?" There were six children at the table, three boys, three
girls. The boys nominated three classmates. The girls agreed with
two of them but said of the third: "No, not Robert. He's trying to
be good." I wondered if this was a freak result, but I found on further inquiries that the more vocal girls in the class had seen, and
appreciated, the strenuous efforts of this child to change his ways.

They were ready to give him another chance. His male peers had written him off.

The effect of being "written off" can last for a considerable time and may affect many different aspects of a child's behavior. The same research (Hetherington, Cox, and Cox, 1982) points out that in the two years after divorce, boys are "more solitary and spend an increasing amount of time playing with younger children or with girls." This evidence is usually interpreted as showing that the lack of a father's input accounts for their "more feminine" behavior. It seems as likely (probably more likely) that these boys are suffering from the behavior of their peers, who simply shut them out. In later research Hetherington discovered that boys who were seen as socially unskilled and incompetent in preschool were likely to be less competent and more antisocial at the age of ten. Early social ineptness among girls did not indicate future problems with relationships.

This research coincided with the early years of school life. The ostracism of their peers ensured that these unhappy boys were never really given a chance to find their feet. They were relegated to the fringe, where there were two options: they could live life flattened against the playground fence or fight for recognition.

If a boy is unable to learn self-confidence in the early years of school life, he will be vulnerable. He is more likely to be victimized just because his unhappiness makes him less capable of responding cheerfully to playground teasing. This early incompetence means that within the first couple of years, he will have been relegated to a place far down in the pecking order of school life and, without support and reassurance, he may stay there.

Periods of free play may seem to last forever to a child who is desperately trying to be included in someone else's game. Some may resort to aggression in their frustration at being left out. Others may never find the courage to intervene. Insecurity on the playground cannot be entirely shaken off, but the classroom will almost certainly feel like a safer place for those who are finding this new world hard to come to terms with.

Much of the misery that some children experience entering elementary school could be dealt with by providing a far higher level of supervision at free play times and designing playgrounds so that both energetic and more sedentary activities can coexist. Sadly, play supervisors are always the first to go when spending is tight.

In classrooms teachers could also be more aware that when children are encouraged to form their own pairs, or groups, for cooperative work, the most socially inept will always be made aware of their deficiency. Many adults carry with them vivid and painful memories of being the last person to be picked for the team. Friendship need not be the only basis for cooperative work in class.

Parents can provide support but they will need to be very sensitive in what they do. If the child feels that his parents are worried about his lack of friends, that may add to his feeling of anxiety. He may feel that he is failing in their eyes, and if he finds it hard to interact with others his anxiety may actually make him even more socially inept. It is probably better simply to reassure him that he is loved at home and that making friends, like reading and writing, is something that will come when the time is right.

A child who is having a hard time at school may turn inward and spend time developing his own resources, using his imagination to overcome his isolation. Or, as we have seen in early chapters, he may turn his feelings outward into difficult and demanding behavior, and if he is preoccupied with social relationships it will be much harder to start learning.

BOYS JUST WANT TO BE HEARD

In 1980 Dale Spender published *Learning to Lose,* a book that opened up the school world to feminist scrutiny and encouraged many teachers to start tackling sexism in schools. She was the first to point out that boys attract the lion's share of teacher attention, a finding that has been confirmed since by other research. In 1988 a review of research confirmed that boys get more teacher time "regardless of socio-economic status, ethnic origin, gender of teacher, age level of pupils, curriculum area, or country" (Kelly, 1988), and that much of the attention was directed at disruptive behavior.

David Panter (1988) observed the change in boys' behavior from preschool to kindergarten. In preschool the girls' ability to cooperate, without external rules and structures, served them particularly well. In kindergarten, however, "there was a complete immersion in a world of rules and structures. There were rules about play time, breaks, going to the toilets, eating." At this stage the boys also start policing gender roles and in many cases "use abuse as a way of asserting themselves against the girls. The boys came out of themselves and the girls became withdrawn."

Although Panter and the teachers judge the boys' noisy behavior as "more confident," I see no evidence that greater noise is the same as greater confidence—in fact, quite often the reverse is true. Indeed, had they listened more closely to the children, they might have made a different judgment. One child, Darren, had been very shy and withdrawn in preschool and, according to his teachers and parents, was "more cheeky and talkative" at school. He also started to do more "boys' things," played more with his older brothers, and was more inclined to stand up for himself. He was now behaving in what was considered by adults, siblings, and peers to be a more gender-appropriate way, but he was clearly not enjoying the learning process. Darren told the researchers that he did not like school, and his parents had difficulty getting him to go.

Although all the research confirms that boys are more attention seeking, none of it seems to ask why. Spender's conclusion is that boys make trouble because trouble gets results:

> If boys do not get what they want then many of them are likely to be uncooperative and in a sexist society their lack of cooperation is often expressed in sexist ways. In a society in

which males are expected to be aggressive, to be authoritative, forceful and masterful, then in many respects boys are
only doing what is expected of them if they act in an aggressive manner when registering their protests.

If this is the reason why boys make more trouble in class, then it
does not prove very efficient. Boys, as we saw in chapter 1, tend to
be less academically successful than girls, and there is certainly no
evidence that being a troublemaker leads to a better education.
Indeed, research by Croll (1985) found that it was pupils with
learning difficulties who attracted the most attention, and there
were twice as many boys with learning difficulties as girls (more in
other studies).

The behavior of disruptive children impedes education for all
the other children (not just the girls); however, it is not very useful
to see this as simply a product of sexism. A child who is demanding attention usually has a reason. Ignoring the demand means
ignoring the reason, which will probably make the problem worse.
It seems to me unlikely that the boys' domination of the classroom
can be changed until we better understand why more boys than
girls seem to need so much attention.

Watching children make the transition out of preschool, I was
also conscious that, for some boys in particular, the increasing
structure is a welcome relief. However, the boys do not react uni-
formly. Some become calmer, happier, and more controlled in the
classroom, as though relieved that the responsibility for working
out how to behave has been temporarily lifted. Others, vaguely
conscious of the existence of rules and structures that are outside
them, respond by vocally denouncing anything or anyone that
seems to spell a deviation from the rules. A minority seem unable
to connect rules (either explicit or implicit) with themselves at all.
Until they see the need to relate to others, they will continue to be
almost impossible to contain and direct.

In classrooms where teachers are very gender-aware, I watched and recorded the interaction between staff and five- and six-year-old children. Where groups of girls were working happily together, asking each other's advice on the task at hand, or just getting on with it, there would always be a number of boys who would be up and down every few minutes asking what to do. The girls were not being passive; they were being competent and co-operating in a way in which few of the boys could manage. One or two boys would inevitably start clowning around when the teacher's attention was off them. They seemed often to be looking for alternative activity because they were unable to concentrate on the job they had been set. There were also a couple of boys who simply gazed into space. They seemed to be unsure what they were doing unless they were reminded and encouraged.

I find it hard to believe that these children were simply acting out what they saw as their right to be "authoritative, forceful or masterful." The overwhelming sense I had was that they felt lost in this great big world with no Mommy figure to look after them. Some of the girls also felt lost but this usually led to some other, more competent girl taking them under her wing and mothering them.

One of the elementary-school teachers I talked to mentioned that the girls in his class would also extend their mothering behavior to boys, but that the girls are very selective about which boys they will mother. They have to be "cute." Sometimes the mothering behavior is so effective that a boy who is initially taken care of because he is cute will develop into the charismatic type who is chased and teased by the girls in a way that also enhances his status among the boys.

The girls also monitor the behavior of their peers. If a girl is unruly, the other girls will effectively pull her back into line. If a boy is neither cute nor charismatic but is miserable or demanding, there will be no attempt by his peer group to modify his behavior. He will be left alone.

This teacher defined a number of different groups of six-year-old boys:

There is always a bunch of them who are uncontrolled. I don't see them as naughty so much as immature. Then there are the ones who seem unable to do anything without being told what to do: "Should I lift my pen now?" Girls don't behave like that. At the moment I've got one boy who just seems to be lost. He behaves as though he is lost in a forest.

RULES AND REGULATIONS

What is actually going on? I suspect that the girls are continuing to benefit from their more secure gender conditioning, while the boys feel, as they start school, extremely anxious about their male identity because it is here that they meet the full onslaught of the male conditioning process. Girls don't need to be organized very much because they are internally directed. Boys, who so often lack any internal sense of identity, long for direction and clarity.

I watched a couple of five-year-old girls playing with a pair of scales. They were deeply involved in piling colored blocks onto the trays, but they were not even attempting to get the scales to balance. One girl was holding a tray level while the other continued to pile on bricks. A boy watched them for a minute and then started to complain loudly that they were "cheating."

The girls eyed him with amazement. I asked him why he was so upset about it, and he said that they weren't playing by the rules and that was wrong. This same boy had just, reluctantly, left the computer that he had been playing with for some time. Indeed, as others have noted, most of the boys gravitate to the computer, while most of the girls need to be persuaded to sit down and use the buttons to make things happen on the screen. The eight-year-old daughter of a friend, when asked if she would like to play on my son's computer, insisted on converting the joystick into a microphone and pretending that she was a flight attendant.

Is this, as we have been led to believe, because girls lack the

necessary technical skill? Clearly not; fewer girls than boys take
computer studies at sixteen but, of those who do, half get high
grades, compared to just over one-third of the boys. For small girls
the computer is boring because it tells them what to do, and they
would rather use their own imaginations. For many of the boys the
computer is a godsend just because it tells them what to do. They
are not expected to make any independent judgments—just to follow the rules. It makes them feel safe in this alien environment. It
can hardly be considered a scientific observation, but one of the
few little girls I have noticed spending a long time on the computer happens to have a particularly difficult home life and few
friends. For children who find social interaction difficult, the computer provides a world in which they can be intensely involved
without ever needing to speak to anyone.

Boys, I am told by elementary-school teachers, seem to respond
better to very clear instructions. They like to know exactly where
they stand or they feel anxious and run around. They need to
know who is in control. Girls, on the other hand, often feel mor-
tally offended if they are told off. They feel that they should be in
control of themselves; they don't want external control. They
expect to get by through collusion with teachers, not through
being ordered about. It was an eleven-year-old girl who pointed
out to me: "Boys aren't as grateful as girls, so they don't get as
much as girls do." While boys are still moaning and saying "it's
not fair," girls have already worked out that a big smile will win an
extra helping of dessert.

It may be that the greater passivity that Panter noticed among
the girls was not due to the behavior of the teachers (as he
assumed), but because of the way in which girls monitor themselves. Suddenly confronted with rules presented from the outside, they start to feel uncertain about the direction they have
always taken from the inside. They aren't used to being told what
to do, so they overadjust their behavior in order to avoid external
controls. The boys, on the other hand, are used to being externally

controlled—they may not like it, but they expect it. It doesn't make them feel quite so bad about themselves.

For some children the need for external control is solved by religion. A six-year-old Moslem boy who had just started going to Koran lessons became visibly calmer in school. He told me: "I must be good for Allah." He seemed very happy to have discovered a world in which everything had a reason and an order. The father of a particularly unruly five-year-old talked about the value of the religious community: "There is a network of people, a power beyond us that he has to respond to, and there are social rules: putting something on your head in synagogue, saying special words, special rituals and ways of behaving. It gives him a broader perspective."

However, religious dogma can also be used in a very negative way. Being good for the love of Allah is very different to being good because otherwise "Allah will burn me in the flames," as another child told me, wide-eyed with fright. Fear of hellfire and damnation may, like caning, be a way of controlling children's behavior, but it is not an effective means of helping them toward the inner resources that will allow them to direct their own behavior. A child who believes that he must be good to avoid punishment will have no reason to be good if he stops believing that there is a God. Or he may just look for some other structure to replace God: nationalism, racism, or some other kind of value system that will allow him to follow the rules whether he understands them or not.

TEACHER'S PETS

Girls tend not only to be more socially skilled and organized; they also take more easily to the work of elementary school. Perhaps they just have more energy left over for work because they are better organized in other ways, but there is also evidence that boys tend to develop the physical coordination necessary for writing a little later than girls. Of course, all boys don't have difficulties with writing—these skills develop at different rates in different children—but they are more likely to find writing hard. A boy may be bright, good at the computer, a whiz at number work, but, oh, the frustration when he tries to write things down.

The first few years of a child's life are all about learning from success. You try hard and you learn: to sit, to stand, to walk, to speak. Small children are geared to success. If they fail, some of them will just stop bothering altogether. Girls may cover up their deficiencies by working cooperatively, the stronger child doing the work for the weaker one until someone spots what is going on. Boys, in the early years, are less cooperative and more depen-dent on the individual praise of the teacher. Failure can be a ter-rible blow. Alistair said: "School started to get difficult after the first year. I've never been any good at writing. I was behind a lot of people. I really wanted to be ahead. I really liked the feeling of being ahead of everyone—and I wasn't. I liked to look at the others and think, 'ha, ha, I'm better than them.' I really wanted to be best."

This child gave up. Perhaps a similar feeling of failure lies behind the number of boys diagnosed as dyslexic. (Boys substan-tially outnumber girls among those children diagnosed as dyslexic.) Some of them are genuinely dyslexic but many others find that, when they are moved into a more intensive teaching situ-ation, in which they can struggle with the work in private, they can after all learn to write. For those whose parents cannot afford the necessary diagnostic tests and remedial work, the next few years may be frustrating.

If a child goes to school, he has to learn to write. A bright child does not like the daily reminder that, at the one thing that matters (writing it down), he is a failure. He may become thoroughly depressed by his failure or he may disrupt the class in order to cover his own confusion. In fact, he will almost certainly learn to write when he arrives at the time in his own development when the task will become easier. Sadly, by that time, he may well have been labeled as disruptive and possibly learning-disabled as well.

CREATIVE SPACE

The sheer difficulty of working out how to behave means that boys have to put more effort than girls into understanding their environment. In these early years girls, on the whole, find life so much easier that they are also more inclined to coast. Parents of girls who around the age of eight or nine can read, write, and perform effortlessly in class often notice that their children have stopped thinking. They complain that teachers seem unaware that, in spite of the production of competent work, their daughters are simply not trying very hard. This is when some of the boys start to edge ahead.

A boy who has to listen and ask questions and analyze and evaluate, just to work out how he is supposed to behave, will not stop with trying to work out who Joe Blow is. He also wants to know about the sun and the stars and how engines work and why the trees grow. Everything important in his world is hidden; everything that needs to be known must be discovered. No wonder so many little boys are so eager to ask questions. For them, the life of an adult man is no more comprehensible than a wizard or a dragon. For girls, the world seems to lie open and revealed. While girls are writing stories about mothers and daughters, boys, if they are writing at all, feature burglars and fire-eating dragons.

Perhaps creativity is the thing that happens in the space between children and the people they love. In research on child care in France, researchers noted that girls who had been in day care were more assertive, whereas those who had been full-time with their mothers were passive. Other evidence points to greater career success among girls whose mothers go out to work. Perhaps it is not just that they are following a role model, but that the gap between them and their mothers leaves room for their own thoughts. However, as I have pointed out in earlier chapters, the balance between security and distance is a fine one. A child who feels insecure will be unable to concentrate on anything but achieving security. A child who is firmly attached—but not too close—has the freedom to explore.

This feeling of distance and childrens' need to find out who they are may also be the reason for the gender difference in tests of what psychologists call "field dependency." In these tests children are asked to identify a shape that is embedded in a more complex pattern. The ability to pick out the shape (field independence) seems to be related to certain mathematical skills. Boys are more likely to be "field-independent" than girls are, but interestingly this is not a biological difference. Boys without fathers are, like girls, also less likely to be able to pick out the embedded pattern, and they are less good at math.

Boys who are good at math are not just those who have fathers, but also those who have fathers whom they don't see all that often. It seems that the effort of trying to relate to an important figure, who is usually just off-camera, develops mathematical skills, while the more comfortable relationship, with a figure who is accessible, develops empathy and verbal and listening skills (Radin, in Lamb, 1981).

In the process of discovering who they are, boys will inevitably find out that the world outside the home and school is one in which male people have a clearly defined place. A small boy has little idea of how this miraculous process will take place but he senses that now, at last, he has some weapons to use against the women and girls who have always been in charge.

EQUAL OPPORTUNITIES

Panter's observation that boys started to be abusive to girls once they started school is something that Dale Spender also picks up. The problem is that she usually fails to distinguish between the ages of the children she is describing. The behavior of five- and twelve-year-old children is different and needs to be addressed differently. A five-year-old boy who expresses hostility to girls is trying to assert himself within a female-dominated world, while a twelve-year-old, who has learned a thing or two, is operating from the safety of a male group, often within a male-dominated hierarchy, and has learned to employ the sexist assumptions of society.

Some of the antisexist work in school fails totally to address this issue. It is hard to explain to a nine-year-old boy why girls should have special "girls-only" soccer sessions while he has to get on with his work. For a little boy who sees that his home life is run by his mother, his school life is run by a female teacher, and that girls can read and write better than he can and are far less likely to get told off for their behavior, it is difficult to grasp the concept of female inequality.

What many women see as an expression of a boy's assumption of superiority could be seen as his attempt to assert that he has an existence at all. One teacher complained that, when she taught a class about space travel and described the people as space women, the boys were upset and all wrote about space men. She saw this as evidence of their inflexibility and refusal to take new ideas on board. However, this is actually no different from the behavior of four-year-old girls who absolutely refuse to let little boys cook in the playhouse. For little girls, the role of mother is huge and demanding and exciting, and they don't want to share it with boring, smelly boys. Small wonder, then, that when the boys finally discover that they have a world of their own out there, they also feel reluctant to share it.

Gradually girls learn that the jobs assigned to boys actually have more status. Some girls still don't want to take on anything that might reflect badly on their femininity but, as women's roles in society have changed, so has the range of possibilities for girls. A girl can now be good at math without feeling that she will lose status as a female. We have not yet come up with a similarly positive way of suggesting to boys that their definitions of gender could also be expanded. And, while we have recognized that girls occasionally need special lessons away from the domineering behavior of some boys, there is little recognition that there are areas in which boys lag behind girls and would also benefit from special attention.

Elementary schools could recognize that, while boys often lag in the skills needed for writing, they tend to be more advanced in work that requires spatial sense, such as model building. Girls, on the other hand, are often quite tentative about building in three dimensions and could use some encouragement.

An approach to equality that accepts that all children grow best through emphasizing success, rather than failure, should be aimed at valuing equally the skills acquired on the soccer field, the ability to make models, and skill in reading and writing. A feminist teacher with a son and a daughter told me what a hard time her son had in school because he wasn't any good at playing soccer. A year later her daughter (a wonderfully assertive and very physical child) started school and this mother told me that she wanted to start soccer training for girls. Why only for girls? I asked. Surely boys like her son had just as much need for soccer training? Positive action for girls needn't be designed in such a way that it seems to be biased against boys.

A fairer answer would be training sessions in soccer technique that both boys and girls could attend. This way all the children would get an opportunity to play, but the rough stuff would be kept out. Boys and girls who tend to opt out of informal games would have a chance to improve their skills, and the boys who normally dominate would learn that soccer is a game of skill, not aggression.

If we believe that boys should have the opportunity to grow up as rounded, whole, nonaggressive human beings, we have to show them that they are capable of being just that. Informing them, at age five, that they are too rough and aggressive to play soccer with girls is unlikely to bring out the cuddly side of their nature! We need to start separating the idea of rough and aggressive from the idea of male. Too often antisexist initiatives do the opposite and in so doing classify all boys as aggressive rather than recognizing, and respecting, the differences among them.

THE BOYS WHO WOULD BE KINGS

Boys who have been led to believe that part of being a boy is competing to be tougher and stronger than the other boys will start very early in their school careers to ensure that they have a dominant position on the playground. These boys are often popular and intelligent. Schools can intervene fairly successfully with this group if, at an early age, it is made clear that such behavior is not socially acceptable and peer pressure from other children is employed to reinforce this view.

More and more schools are now adopting antibullying initiatives, which include group discussions and sometimes drama to set the parameters of what is, and is not, acceptable behavior, reinforced by rules that children draw up themselves in class (children as young as six are perfectly capable of doing this) and clear sanctions for any breach of the rules. The value of this strategy lies in helping those children who find it hard to see each other's point of view, and hard to empathize with the feelings of their victims, to understand why certain types of behavior are not sanctioned by their peers. Anything that mobilizes peer pressure against bullying will be far more successful than efforts by adults to spot and deal with individual perpetrators.

The more fragile boys will positively benefit from this protection, and those casual bullies, who are already well accepted in the group, may start to see that popularity lies in conforming to the group norm rather than setting up an alternative pecking order backed up by physical toughness. Research into the behavior of those young people who end up in young-offender institutions has discovered that they tend to be impulsive and lacking in awareness of the feelings of others. Attempts to rehabilitate teenage offenders now include lessons in "thinking skills" to try to increase their awareness. This approach could usefully be started long before behavior patterns are firmly set.

The boys whose behavior may be hardest to modify are those who are most conscious of their deficiencies in the classroom and start to use those qualities they see as being "male" to control the only territory in which they are able to shine, by intimidation. A study by Lowenstein (1978) found that these bullies were not only academically less successful but also more likely to have difficulties at home. These children are in a tiny minority in any school: Lowenstein identified only 1.4 percent of boys aged seven to eleven as bullies (fewer among younger children and more among older ones), though there is certainly a much larger number of people, both boys and girls, who are affected as victims.

If a boy has no other stake in conforming, then it is hard to get him to understand that he has nothing to gain from intimidation. If he feels that he has no other means of getting attention, he will continue to use disruptive tactics and aggression. Some teachers try to find the time to help these children discover and develop more positive aspects of their personalities. If they are continually derided or physically abused at home, then it will be an uphill task.

While aggression needs to be controlled, schools need also clearly to differentiate between aggression and "horsing around" when they discipline children. A number of boys I have talked to complain that they are punished far more than girls are, and surveys indicate that female teachers treat boys' behavior more negatively than male teachers do. One female teacher said: "The naughty boys stick out more because they are more physical. I might say that the boys are all behaving badly, but in fact it's usually just a couple of them."

If teachers fail to treat children as individuals, they will be reinforcing the strength of the groups in which bullying thrives, and it is the most vulnerable members, on the fringe of the group, who will suffer most. Teachers who, for example, hesitate to tackle a bully because he is black are implying that blackness and bullying are synonymous. They may say that they are trying to avoid being racist, but they are guilty of racial stereotyping. In the same way, teachers who assume that all boys are naturally aggressive and all girls are naturally passive are providing aggressive boys with the label of normality and marginalizing the boys who don't conform. Tackling bad behavior, rather than bad boys, is not only fairer; it will also have a more far-reaching effect.

12

Secondary Pecking Orders

It is at secondary school that a boy learns to use his training in being male to lever himself up and out into a more powerful position in society. And it is here that, if he fails to find a place on the ladder toward success, he will start to show what it means to be marginal in a world in which men have been promised power.

The first two years are a consolidation period in which pecking orders and hierarchies are sorted out. A report from the National Foundation for Educational Research (1993) found that half of the schoolchildren surveyed reported bullying at eleven; two years later, the figure had dropped to a third. By the age of fourteen or fifteen, order will have been established. Most of the scuffling and fighting for position is over. Now when boys fight, it is deadly serious; when they work, that is serious too; and when they fail, the failure is often total.

It is an unusual boy who has gotten this far without closing down, or blocking off, that part of himself that allows him to express his feelings: happy or sad. In secondary school, feelings have to be tucked well out of sight, reserved only for examination at home with Mother (for those who still get along well enough with their mothers), or, in time, with a trusted female friend, rarely with another boy. An intimate detail to one boy is a sign of weakness to another.

During puberty the fear of exposure intensifies. Conversation that used to be about sports now extends to a similar "scorecard" approach to girls, who will be discussed in terms of their physical attributes much as an athlete is discussed in terms of his skills. The emphasis is on scoring points, either for wit or for prowess, the bantering tone designed more to ward off intimacy than to invite it. A fourteen-year-old said: "I'd rather go out with a girl no one knows so people can't talk about it. Then they can't do anything nasty. Every time I show any interest in a girl the others start criticizing her." One fifteen-year-old wrote: "There will always be showing off between boys who are developing, about how many hairs they have, and how big their dangly parts are. When one boy boasts about what he can do or what he has grown, the others in the circle of friends will feel like they have something wrong with them if they can't do it."

Another, writing anonymously and without hope of a reply, confided the fear that he wouldn't dare share with his friends: "One of the main things I worry about is masturbation. I've tried a few times but nothing has happened. I've read all about it in books and magazines and heard what it's like from colleagues. They say that they do it every night and that it's really good. I think that I am going through puberty too slowly, or something's wrong."

They are equally careful to avoid showing enjoyment of anything that is not sanctioned by the group. This is from a fourteen-year-old: "So far I've really enjoyed school this year but I don't show this to my friends because I've seen people who do and what they get called is not very nice." Things that boys can safely enjoy include crude jokes about "out-group" people. That may include racist remarks, mocking accents, commenting on appearance, and teasing each other, particularly those who are most likely to react. The boys may not really enjoy the teasing (they know how painful it feels to be teased) but while someone else is on the receiving end they, at least, are safe.

Sadness cannot be expressed publicly at all. It is seen as a sign of weakness and a reason for jeering and, by the age of thirteen, boys have usually managed to get their peers to conform to that most hallowed of rules: "Thou shalt not tell." However hard a school tries to reassure pupils that it is right to report bullying behavior, among the children "telling" is considered to be worse than bullying.

By the early teenage years, girls will also be aware of the pressure to conform to group norms. However, most girls will still have an intimate best friendship where they can talk about the changes they are going through. (Girls who are marginalized suffer no less than boys do.) With boys having no way of talking about things that worry them, it is perhaps not surprising that, as one perceptive eleven-year-old girl put it: "When there is a problem boys go straight into being aggressive."

For boys, anger expressed through tears is definitely out. One secondary-school boy said: "It's quite hard at my age trying to mix in with other boys because I cry easily. If this happens people bring it up all the time to embarrass me for not being manly enough." Anger expressed physically is accepted. It is a way of establishing hierarchies and settling scores that is inherently unemotional. It is better to fight than to show feeling, and the fighting serves also to cover up and distract from the feeling. A boy's willingness to stand up and be counted by fighting will almost certainly be tested in these early years. It takes a very particular level of self-confidence to avoid this testing entirely.

Teenage boys often behave as though they are on the verge of a volcanic eruption, not, I would suggest, because of the hormones surging through their bodies but because, on the pressure-cooker principle, steam that is held down for long enough will inevitably escape. Girls are far more likely to let off steam through tears (isn't that what they were meant for?) and with words (any parent of teenagers will confirm the fact that girls are more articulate and accurate in their abuse than boys are) and, if that doesn't work, through depression, which is just an extension of the behavior they have always used: being meek and mild and good and hoping that someone will feel sorry for them.

Some boys have undoubtedly learned that male aggression is natural, inevitable, and something they can and should use to "show who is boss." However, there is another group of boys who, in these more liberal times, have learned to regard male anger as unpredictable, violent, and a threat to all living creatures. These are the boys who grow up as men unable to identify the way they feel, let alone do anything to express it. They have learned to be so afraid of their own anger that they bottle it up behind a wall of silent menace. Psychologists call this passive aggression. I recognize it when I talk to men who say, "I have no problems with my ex-wife," without realizing that their teeth are clenched and they are starting to sweat.

SHEEP AND GOATS

By the age of eleven most boys will have learned how to create their own external rules to make up for the lack of internal ones. They will spend much of their free time in structured activities that provide a well-ordered way of relating. Says one young man of his sporting experience: "Sports is about technique, not brute force. At some point I realized that I had learned the intuitive rules of interpersonal relationships."

My first thought was that girls don't need sports to learn about interpersonal relationships, but, in fact, young men are learning a quite different form of communication. They have developed a form of interaction that rarely ruffles the surface but constantly oils it. Women are used to digging underneath. I suspect that this difference is one of the reasons why men feel uncomfortable around women at work. It's easier to be around other men because they understand the rules of engagement. Women tend to reveal their emotions and to stumble unsuspectingly onto emotional soft spots that the men have spent most of their youth learning to conceal.

The boys who have already learned the lessons of emotional detachment skate well in the world of secondary school. The more insulated they are from peer-group struggles, the easier they will find it both to dominate the group and to turn their back on it if need be. This ability to stand back, which women find so hurtful and baffling, is the means by which a boy floats free of playground rivalries and into a position from which he can make his way in the world.

This is what one (now adult) man had to say about secondary school:

> There were times when people were "in" and times when they were "out" but I don't recall being "out" very often. Friendships were quite easygoing. I suppose boys don't really play games which involve intense emotional relationships.
>
> There were the odd scuffles at school but I never felt under any pressure to join in. I was pretty contemptuous of fighting for its own sake. Though I must admit I admired some of the people who did it. People did get bullied a bit but I was never on the receiving end. I was occasionally on the other side. It wasn't physical but no less unpleasant for that.

He remains one of those men who float easily in male company but steer clear of women. Floating is useful but it helps also to find a niche where you will feel accepted. By secondary school, personal interests have started to intersect with social and cultural frameworks. Children have learned the social meanings that go along with differences in accent, color, dress, and behavior, and it is hard indeed to straddle two different niches without incurring the suspicion of one or the other of them.

There are a few boys who manage to learn the rules well enough to float in several streams. Keil by the age of eleven had become super cool. The only child of an actress, he was virtually brought up in the theater and seemed to have learned the facility of slipping from one role to another, developing a persona that provided him with an impenetrable shell of style:

I dealt with all that male aggression and challenging behavior by making the challenger see that my style is to be respected. It was saying to them: it's nice to have me on your team because you will have a stylish person on your team. I had this whole internal vision of the kind of soccer player I was, a cool, stylish player, stylish and slow.

I had two sets of friends. The inner circle of unsporty, quite effeminate people who sat around talking, and were unthreatening and mellow, and a whole other set of exclusively working-class friends who I knew from soccer and sports. I remember one boy commenting that I had a hairstyle like Jimmy Connors. He was trying to find an acceptable niche for me by identifying someone outside his particular sporting world and associating me with him. It was a way of letting me know I was acceptable even though I was clever. I felt very good about it.

Robert, now seventeen, had a difficult time at elementary school and that got him off to a very wobbly start when he arrived at secondary school. He found that the things his liberal parents had taught him seemed to be at odds with the world of the inner city in which he actually lived. He said:

I was taught not to fight and I believed it, but I found that at school you have to fight. You may only have to do it once but you have to prove that you can do it. I never did fight so people teased me. Now looking back, I think it would have

been different if I had. I mean, there were some kids who
everyone thought were puny but if they fought back once it
was OK. No one would mess with them again. You have to
kick someone when they are down so that you can stay up.

Instead of kicking back, Robert survived on rage. He believed in
his right to be an individual, to have opinions of his own, so he
shouted at the teachers, he argued with his parents, he raged at
himself, but he didn't allow himself to sink. By the time he was
fourteen he had found a way of fitting in. He still argues aggressively with people in authority, but the fierce questioning and the
anger have also allowed him to start paying attention to the person
he wants to be. When I talked to him he planned to travel to Eastern Europe in order to find out more about his personal history
and the person he really is. For Robert, confidence was hard-won;
his upbringing meant that he was at odds with the culture he
entered. Others are potentially similarly at risk but they have the
confidence of numbers.

Billy and George are brothers who were brought up in a commune in a rural area. They had been taught that fighting is wrong.
Billy, small and intense, started secondary school with only one
other child from the commune: "I was in a few fights. I hated it. I
couldn't understand why people did it, but once you show that
you won't react it gets better." By the time George started school
there was already a group of kids from the commune to move
around with. Tall, with a mop of blond hair and an amiable smile,
he has never had a fight in his life. Nor has he developed the competitive instinct that has gotten his brother a college degree in
technology. George left school at the earliest opportunity to work
as a blacksmith. He says: "I'm doing what I want and I feel fine."
George won't get rich but he will probably be happy.

For Roger (mentioned in an earlier chapter), confidence lay not
in conformity with male norms but in insulation from them. He had
never been through the mill of elementary-school peer pressure

because, at the school he attended, almost all the boys left at the age of seven or eight to go to private schools. In the years in which many a small, bespectacled, fatherless boy would have been teased into his place in the pecking order, Roger was playing with girls.

He got along well with the girls but, at the same time, learned the value of his own company. At the age of eleven, what he had lost in knowledge of how boys behave, he had gained in self-confidence. He had learned that he didn't need other people badly enough to be vulnerable to their teasing, and he had also learned the value of real friendship as opposed to the wary standoffs that substitute for friendship among insecure adolescents. On day one, he says: "I found another boy clinging to the fence and befriended him."

Davy kept out of the fray by a combination of wit and charm. He says:

> I wasn't into fighting and I never made any enemies. I was teased a bit because I've got big ears but I didn't go home and cry about it. I just didn't rub anyone the wrong way. I was very confident and I felt quite contemptuous of a lot of the stuff that goes on, so I could just cut in and out of it. It didn't get to me. I know there were people who resented me for being clever, but I never got bullied for it because I didn't rub anyone's nose in it. I had one friend who was bullied throughout his school life because he gave the impression of being arrogant. I felt a bit outside things but I got along with everyone.

FINDING A NICHE

Finding at least one other child who shares your niche is, for most eleven-year-olds, the overwhelming need of the first two years of secondary school. Where girls use a sort of emotional homing device to sort out who will be their best friend, boys still need to have a common interest as a defense against negative evaluation while pecking orders are being established. Nick Hornby, in his autobiographical novel *Fever Pitch,* explains it like this:

> Transferring to secondary school was rendered unimaginably easy. I was probably the smallest boy in the first year, but my size didn't matter . . . even the fact that I was one of only three boys wearing shorts wasn't as traumatic as it should have been. As long as you knew the name of the Burnley [soccer team] manager nobody much cared that you were an eleven-year-old dressed as a six-year-old.

His sartorial difficulties would probably count for more in the 1990s, but the sentiment still holds true. A boy who can swap information about sports has a ticket into virtually any social situation. Men can be at opposite ends of the political spectrum and still find common ground in a discussion about the World Series or the Super Bowl. A psychiatrist told me that sports chat provided an instant rapport with his mostly working-class male patients, even though he hasn't attended a game in years.

Sports provide, for the less confident, a ready-made slot to slide into. Boys who don't find their identification through ownership of the right sports equipment will need some other way of showing that they aren't to be messed with and won't submit to someone else's pecking order, an alternative world in which they can be safe. In schools that emphasize academic success, work may provide an escape from peer-group pressure and a means of making relationships. In schools where academic success is seen as slightly effete, art may provide an alternative outlet. Being able to draw is a very public accomplishment that wins admiration even from those who disdain any sign of bookishness. One adult man looking back says: "I was always drawing very complicated things in my textbooks and I used to make counterfeit money. I suppose that compensated a bit for the fact that I was so small." Another said: "I didn't get bullied, because I was clever and good at art. It depended what you were good at—some things had mystique."

For many others it is music. Roger remembers: "At about fourteen I discovered the guitar, that great democratizer of music, then I discovered jazz: nonverbal, obsessive, and very private." For Davy, music has also provided an alternative world:

I only had a couple of friends in my own class. I made all my other friends through music; it became very important. I had never done anything before but the school was very big on music and, in my second year, I just went along to the music block and got involved. It was an important binding factor, an independent social structure within the school.

Some try unsuccessfully to find a common denominator, a way out of their isolation. Tom said:

I couldn't stand elementary school. I hated it. I didn't have many friends. When I went to secondary school I thought it would help if I toughened myself up a bit, so I decided to join the cadets. There were some real nuts. Kids who said that their ambition was to kill somebody. It was during the Falklands War and we would get reports about what was happening. The others were really into the idea of winning, but nobody talked about why they should be fighting in the first place.

It is not a useful strategy because it alienates the quieter, more academic boys. It made Tom a target for attack by local gangs and failed to provide him any of the safety he sought because, he said: "Some of the kids were really violent. I've always been pretty timid and it began to get to me." In the end the aggression proved too much for him; he dropped out of school because he failed to find a niche and couldn't stand the feeling of alienation.

Samuel, like Tom, had been out of step when, a generation earlier, he came from a working-class home into a selective school. "I remember the trauma and the desperation to know everything like the others seemed to. There was a lot of bullying and I learned to join in. I was vile, hell on earth. I made myself look hard, but I also felt sorry for the people I was bullying. In the end, drugs seemed easier." Samuel nearly went under. He survived through luck and the help of a teacher who saw through the tough facade.

If a boy does find a shared interest in which he excels, it will often provide the structure that allows him, at last, to channel his energy. If he does well, the effect on his self-esteem may spill over into his other work too. Davy opted for a career in science, not music. Sports can have the same effect but only if there is a way of channeling self-esteem from one arena to another. Jawanza Kunjufu (1985) wrote:

> My transition from elementary school to high school was a rocky one. In my first semester, I received all D's and F's, after being an honor student at elementary school. My track coach inspired me to improve my grades and gave me the determination to run.

Sadly, few boys have a coach prepared to use his influence in the nonsporting arena. Sports are too often seen as an alternative to work rather than an adjunct to it. Kunjufu is deeply concerned that more than half the black boys he has spoken to state an ambition to become a famous athlete. He points out to them that there are ten thousand athletes chasing approximately twenty places per year in professional basketball and that they have a better chance, even in difficult economic times, of becoming a doctor or an engineer.

Without a means of translating excellence in one arena into effort in another, these categories can be almost as limiting to those who do find their way as it is to those who do not. In the

United States and Great Britain, commentators have observed that black boys gravitate toward sports or music and feel that academic work is not for them. Working-class white boys may have similar difficulties, because academic success is associated not only with being white but also with being middle-class and, in some schools, with being a sissy.

GETTING AHEAD OF THE GIRLS

For those boys who have learned to float, secondary school has some distinct advantages. For the first time (at least in British schools) the curriculum is divided into subjects. Girls may have been happy working across the curriculum because they are working from the inside out. Boys blossom when they can concentrate on one thing at a time, often showing no interest at all in the things that don't grab their attention.

The other advantage is that, often for the first time, they will be working with male teachers. Of course, there are some male teachers in elementary schools but the vast majority gravitate toward the secondary system and, once in it, they move toward the top, where greater responsibility brings bigger rewards. According to one study (Merrett and Wheldall, 1992), male teachers in secondary schools give significantly more encouragement to boys, whereas no such difference was found in elementary schools.

Suddenly boys find that they have male authority figures to look up to and male role models to learn from. For many it will be the first experience of a direct and sustained relationship with a man. The potential for hero worship is enormous, and one or two of the young men I have talked with spoke very warmly of teachers who steered them toward a particular interest or provided them with a steadying hand when things got rough.

Sadly, the boys who, arguably, are most in need of a benign male influence are those least likely to strike up good and sustaining relationships with male teachers. Henry Biller (in Lamb,

1981), looking at the effect of father absence on boys, found that while younger boys without fathers gravitate toward male authority figures, adolescents may well reject them. Biller speculates that these boys could be expressing disillusionment with male adults.

Clearly a large number of these boys have had pretty rough treatment at the hands of the men in their lives. Most have already experienced the desertion of their father, and many will experience extremely difficult relationships with stepfathers. Too often the men in their mothers' lives set themselves up as authority figures before they have made any attempt at friendship and without any respect or sensitivity to the boy's feelings. They may also engage in a power struggle with adolescent stepsons for supremacy in the mother's affections. In a sense these boys are acting out the Oedipal struggle with men who have no compensating love for them. Rivalry for the mother's love may well turn to surly rage, not only at the man who has taken Mother away but, by extension, at all adult men.

Boys who are willing to accept male authority figures will be rewarded. In elementary school good work is encouraged, but it does not enhance a child's sense of masculinity. It is just like being good for Mommy, part of what a boy has to do in order to escape the wrath of the women in charge, but it doesn't necessarily have much to do with self-expression. That happens somewhere else: on the playground, with Dad, with an older brother or friends. Now there are men around who do things that he can learn from. He has been longing to learn about being male and at last he can see that it has to do with science, math, technology (all areas in which male teachers predominate and the few remaining areas where boys do better than girls).

Of course, some of these teachers will be found to have feet of clay. They may turn out to be authoritarian, or weak, and the boys will turn against them with extra wrath because, having found male figures at last, they are so disappointed by them. A few will embody everything a particular boy feels he has been looking for. A male teacher who can help a boy find the thing that really interests him, and give him the support he needs to become skilled, will not only be teaching a subject; he will be providing a larger-than-life, detailed role model of what it is to be male. If he recognizes the responsibility of this role, he can provide a lifeline. If he abuses his position, he can do enormous damage.

These male teachers have also been through the experience of school. They remember what it felt like to emerge from the nursery world with its female domination into the heady world of men. These teachers will themselves have experienced the search for heroes that boys go through as they try to piece together a sense of their own identity. They must know that, in a school, they will be putting themselves forward for that role. It is perhaps not surprising, then, that these men, recognizing their potential power over their male charges, go out of their way to encourage them. They know how important they are.

Some no doubt feel a sense of mission: they must turn these hag-ridden milksops into real boys, show them that men are made of sterner stuff. They are the phys. ed. teachers who shout and bark instructions and humiliate the boys who cannot keep up; the technology teachers who expose to ridicule those class members (often girls) who don't know how to use a saw; the science teachers who crack jokes and, when the girls don't laugh, "tease" them for being humorless.

No doubt these male teachers believe that what they are doing is making up for the loss of confidence that boys have already experienced in their female-dominated world. Coming at this moment, the interest of male adults serves to speed up a process that was already under way. The little boy who said that boys are better than girls didn't really believe it. The adolescent, now in greater control of his world, thinks it might be true. He has noticed by now that most jobs of note in the world belong to men and, closer to home, the father who showed little interest in him may suddenly start to notice his existence.

Eleven-year-old boys asked about the good things about being a boy were starting to see some advantages: "I help my dad to do stuff like fixing"; "I feel that it is good being a boy because I can help my dad to fix the car and our dad takes boys out the most." For those with higher aspirations, a father can provide an important example. Billy says: "I was going to do civil engineering. I was consulting Dad all the time. I was going to do exactly what he did." After years of watching his father leave for work and return at the end of the day, the boy may now discover that he can enter that world and start to find out what it is made of.

Just as the three-year-old girl felt a pride and power inhabiting the borrowed role of mother, these boys are at last discovering the power of men and enjoying the borrowed air of self-importance. They are not yet men, but men are what they are going to be and, in the world out there, it is still men who rule. Now, more than ever, it is necessary for a boy to show that he belongs to the world of men, and that means an even clearer rejection of the power and influence of women. Boys who have learned to like and respect women find that they are pressured to conform to a group denigration of the female sex. A thoughtful fifteen-year-old wrote:

There is a lot of pressure on me to start making crude comments when women walk past. I think the thing that makes men leer at women (etc.) is whether they are with their buddies or not. I mean, if a man was walking on his own and passed a nice-looking woman, he wouldn't say, "Hey, baby!" He would if he was with his friends. So I think this whole masculinity thing is whether a man or boy is with his friends.

Teachers may not realize that they are enforcing the group behavior they may purport to reject. In one secondary school, which prides itself on its progressive policies, the principal, address-

ing a class of first-year children, said: "We know that it can be difficult at times for you girls. The boys are noisy and rough and you
are more quiet and gentle." The ebullient, self-confident girls were
immediately disempowered. The boys (who at this point were sitting just as quietly as the girls) enjoyed this affirmation of their
masculinity and immediately started to brighten up.

A young female teacher made the same mistake. The class had
been very disruptive, so she kept in all the boys for detention and
allowed all the girls to leave. One boy told me angrily: "She went
through the register saying who could leave. She just read out all
the girls' names. Even one girl who wasn't there." Once again, the
boys were being told, negatively in this case, that they are male
first and everything else is secondary.

UP AGAINST THE SYSTEMS

Inside any school there will be two systems at work: the official
system, in which boys who do well academically are rewarded, and
the unofficial system, in which boys who are seen to be creating an
alternative power structure are rewarded by the adulation of their
peers. In a school in which working-class children predominate,
and at a time when jobs are scarce, many children will see little
chance of winning via the official route, and it is hardly surprising
that the alternative system holds enormous attraction. In these circumstances, working hard may be seen as a sign of snobbery or
arrogance, or as evidence of capitulation to authority.

Boys have to decide where their interests lie. Is it better to try
your best even though you may not succeed, or to avoid failure by
refusing to try? Letters from fourteen-year-olds showed that for
many of them, fear of the outside world was a major factor. Take
this one:

One of my fears is that I won't get good enough results to be
a car mechanic. I need good marks in science, math, technol-

ogy, and English. Another fear is if I don't have enough
money I will be living on the streets and begging for money.

Some decide early on that the legitimate route, through exams
and work, will never get them what they want. Others are less certain. They know perfectly well that their future depends on being
able to do well on tests, but any suggestion that they are worried
about the future could be construed as a sign of weakness. If they
feel particularly uncertain about the approval of their peers, they
will have to operate on a knife edge to retain their credibility with
the chosen peer group while doing enough work to get by.

Harry, at seventeen, has dropped out of school because the
group of young people he hangs around with do not see further
education as relevant to them. Harry's parents are disappointed.
They feel that his opportunities were blighted very early on when
he had difficulty learning to read and write and joined up with
boys who would rather fool around than work. With his parents'
help he did catch up academically and he certainly has the ability
to go to college, but in the war between the school system and the
peer system, his peers won.

He spends most mornings in bed because there is no reason to
get up. He is desperate to get work and has spent days combing
the town for a job but, with no qualifications, there is very little
available. Youth and strength are not considered useful attributes
these days. He feels that anyone is to blame but him for the situation he finds himself in. At seventeen he sounds like a six-year-old
still saying, in an indignant voice, "But, Miss, it's not fair, Miss." It
is the protest of a small boy who, having no internalized sense of
how the world works or how he fits into it, feels that all authority
is arbitrary.

When he was nine he ran away from school because "the
teacher hit me and I hated her." He adds, however, that he used to
fight with the teacher and throw things at her. At secondary school,

he says: "We had good fun. We did no work at all, just had a good laugh. We would do booby traps for the teachers, smoke in class, everything." Then he left because: "Someone accused me of stealing a computer. So I threw a chair at him and walked out." Harry blames the school for depriving him of an enjoyable experience.

At his new school, without the support of those children who had been cheering his misdeeds since elementary school, he was unhappy. Perhaps at this point someone could have reached through the mist in his head and pointed out to him that he had a responsibility for his own future. Busy teachers don't necessarily have the time to put a child's feet on the road. A child who is clearly capable of working, but refuses to do so, is a nuisance, a disruption, and teachers are more likely to respond with punishment (as one of his did) than discussion, continuing the pattern in which the Harrys keep on fighting against external control rather than taking over the reins of their own destiny.

Roger Graef noted in his book *Living Dangerously* that: "Many of the young offenders shared an acute sense of fair play as they saw it. Johnnie's concern for the rules that he chose to respect was an obsessive way of trying to make sense of the world."

Harry also wants everyone else to stick to the rules that he has generated to make sense of his world. When they fail to oblige, he is enraged; but he clearly finds it hard to see how his behavior affects others and even harder to take responsibility for his own shortcomings. On the subject of school he has this to say: "School was boring. Everyone with half a brain knows all that stuff that they teach you. The teachers think that if you don't write things down you are not learning, but I bet I learned more than most people."

OUTWARD BOUND WITHOUT A MAP

Without clear internalized boundaries, both Harry and Tom tried latching on to external ones. Tom tried the conformity of uniform and, when that failed, lashed out against his tormentors with bursts of aggression, throwing chairs and yelling at other boys. Finally he retreated to the relative order of his own bed and an obsessive weight-training program. Harry has attached himself to the people who continue to reassure him that his rebellion is "cool." These days he joins them breaking into cars and stealing radios. He assures me that this is what everyone does where he lives in order to get the money they need for the weekend. He feels that if only he could have a job, with an income, everything would be all right. The fact that it is hard to get work he now blames on girls, because "it's much easier for a girl to get a job. A man would rather have a girl working for him than a man."

Harry talks tough but he comes over as a small, lost boy who is still waiting for some mythical mother figure to pick up his bowl and feed him. His vision of the future is utterly unrealistic, and he has no real sense of the fact that he is responsible for getting there. At no point in his seventeen years has he learned that part of growing up should be learning to feed yourself.

There is one weak spot in Harry's defenses, and it is what will almost certainly save him. He is very fond of his parents, particularly his mother, and he knows how far he has pushed her tolerance. His mother has supported him through everything so far, and he loves her for that, but hurting her makes him feel bad. When I spoke to him he had vowed to stop stealing—for her sake.

Boys (as I suggest in an earlier chapter) seem to be particularly in need of a clear external framework, while they sort out what is happening on the inside. Harry, the eldest in his family, seems to have had particular problems. Perhaps as he was the firstborn, his parents had not yet worked out sufficiently consistent boundaries to make him feel safe. His educational difficulties undoubtedly compounded his feeling of insecurity, and the aggression of his teacher might have been enough to shake his faith in the wisdom of adults, so that part of the external framework collapsed before the internal one was in place.

For Samuel, who described school as "a kind of male hell—the end of civilization," the problem lay in the gulf between his working-class parents and the middle-class ethos of his secondary school:

> For the first two years I was a genius, for the next two years I was depressed, then I got into drugs. I never told my parents about anything. They didn't know what was going on. I was a long way from them. They were fooled by the system into believing that, if your son was at a selective school, it must be good. They trusted the school and, when I went off the rails, they didn't want to see what was going on.

Harry and Samuel both have the advantage of knowing that they are loved. Samuel's parents didn't understand him, and couldn't help him, but they didn't reject him. In fact, he says, "The only thing that got me through all this was a sense of my father being a happy man at peace with himself. He was the only important thing in my life, and after he died I gradually became more and more like him." It was the sense that life could be good that gave Samuel the incentive to save himself. He lives quietly, has little ambition, but is content.

When parents are fighting each other, children are particularly vulnerable. The framework is shaking around them. Mavis Hetherington, in a presidential address to the Society for Research in Child Development (1989), talked about the "winners, losers, and survivors" of family transitions. She pointed out that children, and particularly boys, could be protected during this process by "schools with explicitly defined schedules, rules and regulations, and with consistent, warm discipline and expectations for mature behavior. This protective effect of authoritative schools is most marked for boys, for children with difficult temperaments, and for children exposed to multiple, stressful life events."

The other protective factor is authoritative parenting. *Authoritative* is very different from *authoritarian*. Authoritarian parents undermine their children's security by living their lives for them, so that they never develop independently. An authoritative parent provides a clear framework within which the child can grow. Davy, who got through school successfully, has no doubt about who provided his framework:

> There was just Mom and me at the beginning, and she made it very clear what was expected of me. I would come home and get shouted at to wash the kitchen floor, but when I didn't understand Arthur Miller she could talk about it. I resented being harassed about homework. It was our biggest source of fights and I learned to get away with doing as little as possible, but she made sure I didn't drop out.

FLYING SOLO

Growing up means leaving behind the external rules, which have provided the boundaries, and discovering whether the ones built on the inside will work on their own. Graham, a black student, explained how this feels:

> At school you just follow the rules; you become institutionalized. Then you leave and you have to start making your own decisions, rely on yourself, and you are scared and shocked that everything you have learned isn't true. You have to learn what's true for yourself. I went through a real adolescent crisis. I started having arguments with my mother. I felt she didn't love me anymore. I suppose I just wasn't getting any attention from anyone. When you are down and depressed, you look around and see that the others are doing all right. It's so easy to join everyone else and make a quick buck. I tried for a while, selling smoke, but then I realized I wanted more than that, so I started to read and talk to people.

Graham is in the process of making a life for himself, free from the peer-group pressure that nearly engulfed him in its demands for him to conform, wear the right sneakers, be seen at the right parties. He feels that it's a journey he could not have taken if he hadn't been prepared to "listen to myself." For some young men, the only opportunity to listen to themselves will come through convictions and referral to the probation or social services. Intermediate treatment programs (an alternative to prison for young offenders) provide many young men with the only opportunity they will ever have to start the process of self-knowledge. For many of them it will be too little and too late.

Once the support from his mother and the familiarity of his home territory had disappeared, Davy, like Graham, hit a crisis:

> You don't appreciate how much you are influenced by where you grow up. I've grown up with black people, and I take it for granted that people are nonracist and nonsexist. It was a shock to find that they aren't. At college it was very white, very middle-class, and very regional, the music was very straight, the people were homophobic, and I just wasn't into it. I felt as though I was floating around in free space. There was no underlying structure, no sense of security, and no shared interests to keep us together. I had thousands of acquaintances who could leave me at any moment.

After a semester he dropped out and ran away to the country, working for a while in a factory, and doing a great deal of thinking. Perhaps the most important realization for him was that unskilled work is not much fun:

> I did two weeks' work in a factory. It was hard physical work and I was completely incompetent. There were lots of nice people there, but I couldn't understand why anyone was nice

to each other. I was miserable all day and then I went home: eight hours a day of misery for three hours of pleasure can't be right.

He is fortunate enough to have other options and, now that he has arrived at his decision himself, he will undoubtedly use them. He has started learning how to manage without the external framework he relied on to get him through school. He will manage the rest himself.

13

Taking Power

It isn't just boys who see the move to secondary school as the time to put away the world of women and move away from the protection of Mother. Girls, at this point, are also starting to turn away from the narrow confines of the home and reassess their view of men. A girl may well have been aware for some time of men looking at her. As a child the flirtatious interest of adult men made her feel confused and self-conscious but also powerful (unless, of course, interest became abuse). Now she is trying to test out her own feelings and, if she is beginning to take an interest in boys and men on her own account, she will feel less certain of her power because now she cares about what they think of her.

Twenty years ago, sexual etiquette ensured that girls kept quiet about their dawning sexual interest. No self-respecting twelve-year-old would have telephoned a boy, let alone initiated a relationship. She would have been forced to wait to be chosen. The changing climate of sexual behavior means that there is little to prevent girls from acting more directly on their impulses—except that the reaction of boys and biology have arranged things to make reciprocation unlikely. Boys of twelve are rarely ready for this sexual interest.

On the positive side, the more assertive behavior of the girls means that, for some teenagers at least, the long rift between girls and boys can start to be healed. Girls who have been positively affected by the more egalitarian atmosphere of the last decade have a great deal more than their femininity to bring into relationships with boys. There is a real opportunity for friendship that is not sexual, as well as the basis of more equal relationships that do include sexual experimentation.

In an earlier section I mentioned a boy who had found elementary school hard to cope with because his broad expectations of what it is to be male came up against the narrow definitions of a school ethos in which boys were not expected to show emotion. This child, once he reached secondary school, was very relieved to find that he could now socialize with girls again without being laughed at. His friends rather admired him for having a "girlfriend" and he was relieved that, after years of being forced into the unexpressive mold of elementary-school masculinity, he had a friend with whom he could share feelings.

Where adolescents socialize in mixed groups there will be far less pressure on boys to conform to male behavioral norms and far less likelihood that girls will see boys only in terms of sexual conquest. If girls are part of a boy's peer group he is far less likely to treat them as objects to be leered at, or sneered at, and he will almost certainly find that these friendships open up the closed doors of the place in which he stowed his feelings.

However, for the majority of boys, security among boys takes priority over socializing with girls. They simply don't feel sure enough of themselves to risk stepping out of line with their pals. For these boys any approach by a girl will just arouse suspicion. Boys are used to suspecting the motives of the people they call friends. A girl who wants to "go out" may just be trying to humiliate him. This is the comment of a thirteen-year-old boy:

When I first started at this school I had girls calling me up who I didn't even know. I wouldn't mind if I liked them but they were the most disgusting girls in the school. My sister keeps trying to persuade me to go out with girls, but why would I want to go out with a complete stranger?

This boy was clearly panic-stricken and, in his fear, he could see girls only as disgusting. The members of his family were very amused that he had suddenly become the object of female attention (they were unaware that the same thing was happening to most other boys of his age) and made it clear that they were proud of what they took to be his maturity. He felt that if he didn't act up to their expectation they would despise him. So he visited one or two of the girls (though never more than once) and boasted about the things they had done together (in fact, they watched TV), but he felt trapped and humiliated by it all.

It is common for boys to cover their confusion by indulging in group denigration of girls. Surveys of boys' sex talk find that girls and women are, at least publicly, held in general contempt, at the same time as being objects of lust. The boy quoted above was the one who said he would rather go out with a girl nobody knows, so people can't talk about it and say anything nasty. Every time he showed any interest in a girl, the others would dig up some scandal about her.

For girls, used to a world in which people talk about their feelings with some level of honesty, the behavior of these boys is both hurtful and baffling. Why would a boy come to your house and then never speak to you again? Is it because there is something wrong with the way you look, smell, talk? This may well be the first time in her life that a girl, brought up in an era of feminism, has had cause to doubt the superiority of her sex, the first time she has felt vulnerable, because it is the first time she has cared whether or not men are interested in her.

She may well never have experienced close and physical affection from a person of the opposite sex, whereas a boy of her age knows what it feels like to be loved by a woman. In fact, in early adolescence he is probably working hard to shake off that passionate interest, to break free. The girl has always had to work hard at attracting the real attention of her father. Now she has to work hard again. The additional disinterest of the male teachers in her academic performance simply confirms what she already suspected: she is not woman enough to get a man. No wonder she starts to lose confidence in herself.

It will take several years, for most boys, before the desire for sexual experience overcomes their fear of it. One boy of fourteen listed "having sex for the first time," along with unemployment, destitution, and the death of his parents, as his major fears of growing up. Ironically, by the time he is ready for such an experience, the girls in his peer group may well have moved on to experiment with older boys, whose sexual development more closely chimes with their own. They will probably regard his dawning interest with disdain. For teenage boys and young men, romantic relationships may seem a pretty unattainable dream. Few sixteen-year-old boys are involved in a "steady" relationship, whereas many sixteen-year-old girls are.

Looking back, Liam says rather regretfully:

> At the beginning of secondary school I felt very threatened by all those girls who liked me. A couple of years later I thought of all those could-have-beens when girls were coming to me. Now I was interested but I couldn't go out and get them.

The girls, on the other hand, will have learned by now that the eager assertiveness of their early efforts did not have the desired effect. They will probably have become more restrained, and learned how to make themselves available, rather than issuing direct invitations and risking rejection. Those young men who have learned to socialize within the clear structures of male groups may find it very hard indeed to decode the subtler signals that the girls use.

Liam found:

> I didn't know how to get from being a friend to sex. I felt
> that the more separate I could be, the more attractive it
> would make me, but in fact the girls thought I was a wanker.
> I had got it completely wrong.

This young man solved his own problem via a relationship with a
girl he, fundamentally, rather despised. It allowed him to explore
his own feelings while ignoring hers. It was a solution to his fear of
rejection but at her expense. Many of the boys he envied for their
apparent lack of confusion were almost certainly having similarly
soulless encounters with girls, out of panic rather than pleasure,
knowing that this is ultimately the way in which a boy proves he is
a man. Psychoanalyst Christiane Olivier (1989) quotes a male
client who said to her: "I've got to sleep with a woman so that I
can say I have done it, I'm a man, I've got the upper hand. That is
all the proof I want."

By the time this man (and others like him) does find a woman
to "sleep with," she will also certainly be younger than he is.
Girls look to older boys in the hope of finding greater maturity.
For boys, the advantage of a younger girl is that her inexperience
will allow him to feel more powerful, more of a man. By dominating one woman he can prove that he has finally moved away
from the domination of "that woman": his mother. For some
young men, the acquisition of a younger, less experienced, and
more passive girlfriend is the final act in the long struggle for
separation.

For a man who feels uncertain of his own power, a younger
woman provides proof. He may have a hard time at school, or be
bullied at college, left out of the job market, treated like dirt at
work, or ordered around at home, but with his woman he can be
king. He has found the place where the power he was promised
can come true.

The need for a man to be older than a woman is not just a personal matter. Individual men may feel perfectly happy to have a relationship with a woman who is older, but the social sanctions against such behavior are severe. Newspapers go out of their way to comment on any woman who has a younger boyfriend. There is always an implied sneer, the suggestion that she must be paying him, that he must be a man without honor or substance. Indeed, so deeply ingrained is this male fear of the older woman that, in reports of an IRA bombing trial, in January 1993, tabloid newspapers gave more emphasis to the age difference between the man and his female companion than they did to the crime he was supposed to have committed.

In recent years, as women have become more financially independent and more able to make their own choices about relationships, pairings between older women and young men have become more common but, if anything, the reaction against them is getting more strident. If the age gap is more than a couple of years he will be derided and dismissed as a "toy-boy." Interestingly this is one of the very few derogatory expressions exclusively used to describe a man (there are many used to describe women), and its sting lies in the assumption that a man who goes with an older woman has given up power. He has become a plaything, a child again.

Power through sex is the last resort of the man who feels insecure about his role. It manifests itself in the whole range of behavior that is now described as sexual harassment and, at the far end of the spectrum, in assault and rape. Boys who jeer, whistle, and catcall are not showing admiration or affection; they are demonstrating their greater strength and their intention is to intimidate. In the same way, a man who makes sexual innuendoes to a woman at work, or denigrates her sexually, is not being amusing; he is attempting to humiliate her and so reduce her power.

GETTING ON TOP

By the time they emerge from school, the boys who have floated to the top will have begun to see that girls no longer hold the power. Those who have fallen by the wayside academically will be finding other ways of showing that they are on top. If they cannot find work that pays enough, they are the boys who will look for illegal methods of getting their hands on the money they need to prove that they have power. As a young man in an earlier chapter put it: "It looked as though I would need a BMW with big speakers if I wanted a girl."

In the world of work, all the lessons that men have learned at such cost while they are at school start to serve them well. The girls who ruled in preschool may still be bursting into tears when things go wrong, but the boys have learned to ignore their feelings and push on regardless. While girls divide their lives up according to the things that concern them—people as well as work, love as well as success—boys are more likely to concentrate on one thing at a time, using the single-minded dedication they developed as a way of cutting out the pain and pressure of their peer group.

Girls have been used to determining their own lives on the basis of an internal map of what seems appropriate, what makes them feel comfortable. Boys who have adapted to the school system are used to working inside rail lines of other people's making or their own. A job may, initially, be boring but they see it as a means to an end, a way of getting money or getting ahead. Girls find that the necessary formality of the workplace hierarchy cuts across the intimate social behavior they grew used to at school. Boys may find the clearly ordered relationships and manners of the workplace a welcome relief after the social anarchy of school, and they will already be equipped with that common language that binds together men with widely differing interests.

Perhaps the most important advantage lies in the way in which men have learned to operate in teams rather than as individuals. In the last chapter I referred to a young man who said that he had learned "the rules of interpersonal relationships" via sports. In a team game players are not thinking about how their teammates are feeling; they are working out a joint strategy that will allow them both to win. These are not intimate relationships; they are strategic relationships. Strategic relationships allow men to do each other favors in later life, keep an eye out for the advancement of their friends, help each other up the ladder.

Women often feel that to use a friend for personal advancement is a betrayal of friendship rather than a natural consequence of it, and as a result they fail to build the strategic networks that men do. Women see friendship as stuff for the soul rather than rungs for the feet, but intimate friendships can be a curse as well as a blessing. Little girls control each other's behavior by the withdrawal of love: "If you talk to her, I won't be your friend anymore." The fear of that emotional blackmail doesn't disappear; it is transferred into the workplace. Most boys, on the other hand, have grown used to emotional cutoff among their peers. They can take or leave each other according to the need of the moment.

Women's monitoring of each other's behavior means that they may actually be holding each other back with that old unspoken taunt: "If you move up and leave me, I won't be your friend anymore." So instead of helping each other to get ahead, women too often use subtle blackmail to block each other's progress. Boys' lack of close male role models means that they are much more inclined to hero worship than girls are. Boys admire those who get ahead. They seek to emulate them, not to drag them down.

Women who can free themselves of these jealous bonds find that their ability to understand (and manipulate) the behavior of others will stand them in very good stead. Women, as many companies are beginning to discover, are brought up to be self-motivated, and those verbal and interpersonal skills that have always been denigrated as less important than mathematical ability can be very useful indeed. However, in spite of their obvious abilities, women are held back by the very things that make it easier for men to get ahead.

Most career structures are built on the assumption of continuous employment. Women are sometimes accused of sleeping their way to the top (in fact, sex usually operates the other way—to keep women down). Men sleepwalk their way to the top. The world is full of men who rose through the ranks just because they hung in there. Women are less likely to have continuous employment patterns, because when babies arrive, even the most super of superwomen will have to take some time out. A man need not. Indeed, men have a great deal invested in a social system that refuses to allow women time off. The point at which a woman goes on maternity leave (even if she intends to return) is often the point at which her less lumbered colleagues will pass her by.

A fair number of those men, who have made it most easily through these carefully placed rail lines by way of strategically positioned relationships, will not only be making use of the team spirit that they learned at school; they will never, quite, get over the fear of being trapped in the world of women. They are the men who are still desperate to prove their masculinity by keeping women at bay. If equal-opportunity laws insist that women must be employed, they will follow those laws, but the women they employ will be young women who can be sexually dominated (in the mind, if not in practice). Experienced women will be sidelined into areas where they cannot threaten the status quo. When it comes to important jobs, employers will go for the guy, the one who shares the same language, understands the importance of cheerful camaraderie, but never tries to go below the surface.

For those men who do not operate within a career structure, these rules of engagement will be moved into other fields. They will operate in trade unions, in clubs, in sports, and in the search for work—in all the structures that men build for themselves to give them security. Some of these men will still not feel safe enough in these man-made structures and will use other means of keeping women at bay. Topless waitresses and soft porn magazines provide those men who cannot dominate women in practice with a means of keeping women out by demeaning them.

As the men at the top consolidate their power, those at the bottom find that the emotional stripping of those years at school has left them with little that they can use to effect, except anger. There have been many times when the men at the top have made use of that anger, whipped it up, and turned it against some imagined foe: Hitler turned it against the Jews and then against most of the rest of Europe; the U.S. government turned it against the North Vietnamese; and now in Europe, small-time hard men are harnessing the anger, and the greed for power, against new enemies: Serbs against Croats, both against Moslems. At the end of this bloodletting a few men will have more power and everyone else will have lost.

Without the external discipline of an army and a "cause," some men, as we saw earlier, will use that anger to establish an alternative power on the back of illegal activity such as drug dealing or burglary. But there will be others who have only one place in which they can be angry: their homes. Anger is not useful in a home. It will not bring love or warmth or friendship.

THE ROUNDABOUT SOCIETY

In the late 1960s, for a brief moment, some men stopped trying to show how hard they were. Shaved heads gave way to flowing locks, it was cool to wear flowery shirts, and adult men talked about love and peace. It was a blip, a bubble. It didn't last, it didn't bring freedom; but it did happen. It was possible to "turn on, tune in, and drop out" because, for a split second, between the era of postwar regeneration and the coming slump, there was full employment.

For a little while it was possible for young people to stop worrying and dream. In the mid-1960s the postwar baby boom began to pour out of schools and colleges. It was the largest cohort of teenagers ever. Young people talked of a world in which people would live collectively, share their money, and support one another. The crime rate in England stood at three offenses per hundred people. By 1991, after years of boom and bust, collective living had become a joke, cooperation an idea for the trash can of history; it was each man for himself and the devil take the hindmost. In spite of a massive decline in the number of high school dropouts, the crime rate has risen more than threefold.

The British government blamed the rise in crime on lack of discipline, inadequate parenting, and, most recently, socialism (though there hasn't been much in the past fifteen years). But the ideals of socialism, far from being a reason for lawlessness, have always been a focus of hope. In the interwar years, in spite of recession and depression, they gave people a reason to work together for a future in which they would have a place.

Today in Britain even the Labour Party seeks only emancipation of the individual. The only way to a place in society is through individual effort. The only success is individual success. In this "I'm all right, Jack" society, there is no room for change and experimentation in human relationships. Indeed, the very values that militate against the involvement of men in the lives of children are extolled as virtues.

Competition has become the motor of our economy. In every competition there must, by definition, be losers. As unemployment climbs, the losers increase in number and the competition becomes fiercer. In order to win, it is necessary to become a little leaner, a little nastier, and a little harder than your competitors. The winners are richer than ever. They have more things to flaunt, bigger cars, more electronic equipment. The losers have their noses rubbed daily in their failure as they sit trapped in their homes, watching as the world they can never be part of is fed onto their television screens.

In this fairground society there is no time for cooperation. It takes time to work cooperatively, far more time than it takes to pass orders through a rigid hierarchy. People don't have time to help each other; they would rather pay for what help they need and keep running so that they can be sure to be the first on the merry-go-round. Those who stop to help a friend may never get on at all.

It is the worst possible atmosphere in which to suggest to men that they reorder their priorities. A man who takes time out to share the care of his child knows that he may never get in again. He will rationalize his decision by saying it's what his wife prefers, but he won't fight for the right to stay home. Why tie your legs together when you have a race to win?

Young men learn that money and power are the only passports to a place in society. The cult of the individual is busy creating an ever bigger army of men who have no place. If these men don't belong to society, why should they recognize its laws? Why should men believe that they have a vested interest in being caring, more thoughtful, more open, when everything they learn tells them that, on the contrary, winning is all—and the only way to win is through, as one man I spoke to put it, "kicking the other man when he is down just to make sure you stay up."

In the barren housing projects of deindustrialized Britain, few men have power for anything other than destruction. In my experience it is nearly always a group of women who are using their interpersonal skills, their ability to work cooperatively and without hierarchies, to make and mend, keep each other together, campaign to keep their communities afloat, and occasionally perform real miracles to ensure that life doesn't keep getting worse.

POWER SHARING

What women have is also a power of a kind. It is a way of working that builds on mutual concern. It will create few stars because it is not designed to promote the few but to sustain the many. It is the power of intimacy, which women have passed down in just the same way as men have passed down to each other the power that comes from distance. I suspect that this kind of power also does the women of these communities far more good than the power of the bottle and the fist does for the young men who roam its streets.

The power that women have lies in their collective ability to weave the carpet of life. Each time the carpet is destroyed, women will set about patiently rebuilding it again. Fire, famine, war, and disease destroy their work. The children they bear and raise may be killed or sent to kill others or may turn on their communities, but there will always be more women, having more babies, and continuing that work of making and mending and nurturing without which there can be nothing.

I am not sentimental about this job. It is often boring, depressing, and exhausting, and the women who spend their days weaving the carpet are often beaten down and undervalued. Nevertheless, given the option, few women would be without it. A woman may be a big-shot manager but, if she has children, part of her mind will always be engaged in that other world. She will care where her children are, what they have for lunch, who their friends are, whether they are happy or sad. The alternative attraction of the family is often seen as a woman's Achilles' heel—the reason why she cannot give her all to work, why she cannot fly around the world at the drop of a hat, why she is "unreliable." I believe it is her greatest strength. It is the thing that allows a woman to stay plugged into the real world. It emotionally attaches her to values far more important than the shape and color of next year's cars.

However much they want power in the world, few women voluntarily relinquish their part in the other power structure, the invisible one that holds everything up. Perhaps they feel that power in the world is empty if it is not complemented by the

everyday intimacy of caring. Work may be interesting and stimulating, but women also want to connect at a deeper level. There is
no deeper level than the bond that women feel with their children.

Even women who, worn down by poverty, self-loathing, and
isolation, abuse their children physically and mentally still cling to
them. They dread the idea that someone might take them away.
Women who have had children taken from them because they
have beaten and neglected them still beg and plead for their
return, even though they know the cycle will probably start again.
They know that this emotional connection is vital, even though
they don't know how to tap into it in a constructive way. When
women leave their children they rarely disappear completely, as
many fathers do, and the trauma so often described by women
who have had babies adopted is a testament to the almost uncanny
sense of connection that women feel with their children.

Emotional connection is the bane of a woman's life and the
golden thread that runs through it, and it is also the thing so many
men give up in the search for the key to masculine power. The
division robs both sexes of the possibility of being whole. It stops
women from operating in the world on equal terms with men, and
it cuts too many men off from the possibility of experiencing real
emotional involvement. While women's loss of power is more
obvious, what men lose is just as important.

The trouble is that, at the moment, few men are aware of their
loss. Just as women in the 1950s accepted passivity and powerlessness as the price to be paid for being female, so men today see
toughness as the price they have to pay for being male. However,
just as women then felt uneasy, so some men now sense that something is wrong with their side of the bargain.

Many men have reacted to the sense of unease by redoubling
their efforts to be "real men." They protect the bastions of male
power with bluster. They use ridicule and contempt to keep
women at bay. Others see that they have an interest in buying into
the power base that women have held for so long. They see that

emotional connection is not only about pain; it is also about pleasure that goes far deeper than the buzz of excitement from fast
cars, the rush of adrenaline when their team scores a goal, the
surge of power when a big deal goes through, the rush of blood to
the head that precedes a good fight.

As more women move into the world of work and up the power
structures within it, they are themselves breeding a new kind of
woman. Their daughters are less tightly connected. The distance
may mean that they lose some of the need for intimacy that makes
it so much harder for women to succeed. A world in which
women are more like men is unlikely to be a better place unless it
is complemented by men who are brought up with a correspond-
ingly greater investment in close and nurturing relationships.

The hard thing for both men and women to cope with is the
realization that sharing means that both sides need to give something up in order to take on something new. Men are being
pushed to relinquish the structures that keep them in power at the
top, but so far no one has really put much pressure on women to
let men in at the bottom. Women believe that they are already
doing this. They are convinced that men stay away from home and
children because they are fundamentally selfish. The difficulty
with this explanation is that it makes no sense. However selfish a
woman might be, she very rarely abandons her children because to
do so would simply hurt too much. Women don't stay with their
children because they are more altruistic, but because they are too
closely tied. Men don't leave their children just because they are
selfish, but because they were never tied closely enough.

If boys are to give up the dream of power in the world, what
will they get in exchange? Are women really willing to give up
their preeminent position in the home? To share the job of taking
care of children? Are women ready for custody arrangements in
which both parents really do share the care of their children after
divorce? These are not questions that many women now have to
consider. Few fathers ask to share what they have been taught to

see as a burden, but if we want boys and men to grow up more emotionally open and connected, that is what they will ask for.

Once we accept that boys, as much as girls, have a right to a place in the family by virtue of their connection with their children, not only their ability to provide money, all the questions of access to power in the world will start to change. If men have an equal right to the care of children and an equal desire to use that right, then women will no longer be structurally disadvantaged in the workplace. If men were as closely connected to their children as women are, far fewer boys would grow up without a real sense of what it means to be a whole human being. Boys who really care about other people will not grow up to abandon their children and destroy their communities.

We are a very long way away from this picture. Many women today refuse to share the care of their children because they fear for their safety. They have experienced men as brutal and unfeeling and have no desire to expose their children to risk. In many cases they are right. But women alone cannot bring up boys to be different kinds of men. There will be little change until more men see the need for it themselves.

The trouble with boys is that they must become men and, if the only picture of men available is that of a brute, then in order to become male they must be brutish. If we care about the way our boys will grow up, we have to try to change that picture. But we will only be able to make very small alterations unless, at the same time, we are prepared to try changing the society that painted it.

REFERENCES

Anderson, Sherwood. 1942. "Memoirs." In *A Book of Men*. Edited by Ross Firestone. New York: Stonehill, 1978.

Archer, John, and Barbara Lloyd. 1985. *Sex and Gender*. Cambridge: Cambridge University Press.

Atwood, Margaret. 1989. *Cat's Eye*. London: Virago.

Balint, Michael. 1935. "Critical Notes on the Theory of the Pregenital Organizations of the Libido." In *Primary Love and Psycho-Analytic Technique*.

Biller, Henry. "Father Absence." In Lamb (1981).

Blackwell, Christina. 1989. *A Guide to Encopresis*. Northumberland Health Authority.

Bly, Robert. 1991. *Iron John*. London: Element.

Brannen, Julia, and Peter Moss. 1991. *Managing Mothers: Dual Earner Families After Maternity Leave*. London: Unwin Hyman.

Brown, Michael. 1976. *Image of a Man*. New York: East Publications.

Buchanan, Christy, Eleanor Maccoby, and Sanford Doenbusch. "Adolescents and Their Families After Divorce: Three Residential Arrangements Compared." *Journal of Research on Adolescence* 3: 261–91.

Chodorow, Nancy. 1978. *The Reproduction of Mothering*. Berkeley/London: University of California Press.

Chodorow, Nancy, ed. 1989. *Feminism and Psychoanalytic Theory*. New Haven/London: Yale University Press.

Corneau, Guy. 1991. *Absent Fathers, Lost Sons.* Boston/London: Shambala.

Coward, Ros. 1992. *Our Treacherous Hearts.* London: Faber.

Croll. 1985. "Teacher Interactions with Male and Female Pupils in Junior Classrooms." *Educational Research* 27: 220–23.

Dennis, Norman, and George Erdos. 1992. *Families Without Fatherhood.* Institute of Economic Affairs Health and Welfare Unit, Institute of Health Economics.

Erikson, Erik. 1950. *Childhood and Society.* London: Pelican.

Glendinning, Caroline, and Jane Millar, eds. 1987. *Women and Poverty in Britain.* London: Wheatsheaf.

Goldberg, Herb. 1976. *Hazards of Being a Male.* New York: Signet Books.

Grabrucker, Marianne. 1988. *There's a Good Girl.* London: Women's Press.

Graef, Roger. 1992. *Living Dangerously.* London: HarperCollins.

Graham, Hilary. "Women's Poverty and Caring." In Glendinning and Millar (1987).

Green, R. 1987. *The Sissy Boy Syndrome.*

Hargraves, Jane, and Ann Colley. 1986. *The Psychology of Sex Roles.* New York: Harper & Row.

Hetherington, Mavis. 1989. "Coping with Family Transitions: Winners, Losers and Survivors." Presidential address to the Society for Research in Child Development.

Hetherington, Mavis. 1991. "Families, Lies and Videotape." *Journal of Research on Adolescence* 1 (4): 323–46.

Hetherington, Mavis. 1992. *Coping with Marital Transition.* Monographs of the Society for Research in Child Development.

Hetherington, Mavis, Martha Cox, and Roger Cox. 1982. "Effects of Divorce on Parents and Children." In *Non-Traditional Families.* Edited by M. Lamb. Hillsdale, N.J.: Erlbaum.

Hetherington, Mavis, Martha Cox, and Roger Cox. 1985. "Long-term Effects of Divorce and Remarriage on the Adjustment of Children." *Journal of the American Academy of Child Psychiatry* 24: 518–30.

Hillman, Mayer, John Adams, and John Whitelegg. 1992. *One False Move.* London: Policy Studies Institute.

Hornby, Nick. 1992. *Fever Pitch: A Fan's Life.* London: Gollancz.

Hoyland, John. 1992. *Fathers and Sons.* London: Serpent's Tail.

Keir, Cheryl. University of East London, research in progress.

Kelly, A. 1988. "Gender Differences in Teacher-Pupil Interactions: A Meta-analytic Review." *Research in Education* 39: 127–36.

Kesey, Ken. 1962. *One Flew over the Cuckoo's Nest.* London: Picador.

Kinsey, Richard. 1992. *Survey of Young People.* University of Edinburgh.

Kitzinger, Sheila. 1989. *The Crying Baby.* London: Viking.

Kolvin, I., F. J. W. Miller, D. M. Scott, S. R. M. Gatzanis, and M. Fleeting. 1990. *Continuities in Deprivation?* The Newcastle 1000 Family Study. Aldershot: Avebury.

Kujawski. 1984. "Origins of Gender Identity." In Hargraves and Colley (1986).

Kunjufu, Jawanza. 1985. *Countering the Conspiracy to Destroy Black Boys.* Chicago: African American Images.

Lamb, Michael, ed. 1979 and 1981. *The Role of the Father in Child Development,* 2 vols. Wiley Interscience.

Leach, Penelope. 1979. *Who Cares?* London: Penguin.

Lewis, Charlie. 1986. *Becoming a Father.* Open University Press.

Lewis, Charlie. "Early Sex Role Socialization." In Hargraves and Colley (1986).

Lim, M. H., and V. Bottomley. 1983. "Combined Approach to the Treatment of Effeminate Behaviour in a Boy: A Case Study." *Journal of Child Psychology and Psychiatry* 24 (3): 469–79.

Lowenstein, L. F. 1978. "Who Is the Bully?" In Munthe and Roland (1989).

Maccoby, Eleanor. 1992. "Adolescents and Their Families After Divorce." *Journal of Research on Adolescence* 2 (3): 261–91.

Merrett, Frank, and Kevin Wheldall. 1992. "Teachers' Use of Praise and Reprimands to Boys and Girls." *Educational Review* 44 (1).

Mooney, Jayne. 1993. Survey at Middlesex University Centre for Criminology.

Munthe, Elaine, and Erling Roland, eds. 1989. *Bullying: An International Perspective.* London: David Fulton/Professional Development Foundation.

National Children's Bureau. 1977. *Highlight on Violence, Disruption and Vandalism in Schools.*

Olivier, Christiane. 1989. *Jocasta's Children.* London: Routledge.

Panter, David C. 1988. "Child Social Relations and Gender," unpublished. Open University.

Perkins, Eugene. 1975. *Home Is a Dirty Street.* Chicago: Third World Press.

Pruett, Kyle. 1983. In *The Psychoanalytic Study of the Child,* vol. 37. New Haven: Yale University Press Resources, p. 257.

Radin, Norma, in Lamb (1981).

Samuels, Andrew, ed. 1985. *The Father: Contemporary Jungian Perspectives.* London: Free Association Books.

Santrock, J. W. 1972. In Lamb (1979).

Slater, Philip. 1968. "The Glory of Hera." In Chodorow (1978).

Snow, M. E., C. N. Jacklin, and E. E. Maccoby. 1983. "Sex-of-Child Differences in Father-Child Interaction at One Year of Age." *Child Development* 54.

Spender, Dale. 1980. *Learning to Lose.* London: Women's Press.

Spender, Dale. 1982. *Invisible Women.* London: Women's Press.

Warshak, Richard. 1992. *The Custody Revolution.* New York: Poseidon.

Wilson, William Julius. 1987. *The Truly Disadvantaged.* Chicago/London: University of Chicago Press.

INDEX

verbal skills, 226, 262–63

violence: acceptable, 73; of
fathers, 62, 64, 186–88; as
form of manliness, 25–33; and
hard men, 29–33; as out-
growth of failure, 23–30;
toward women, 5, 8, 72, 187,
226–27

vulnerability: of boys versus girls,
72–73; fear of admitting, 76.
See also bullying

Walter, Martin, 31–32

Warshak, Richard, 107, 178

welfare system, 14, 22–23

Westmeads, Zelda, 97

Wheldall, Kevin, 243

Whitelegg, John, 56

Whiting, 120

Whitty, Joe, 200

Who Cares (Leach), 150, 153

Wild Men, 141

William, Prince, 59–60

Wilson, William Julius, 6

women: education of, 17–19;

men's attitudes toward, 5, 8,
128–29; and misogyny,
128–29, 141, 143; power of,
13–14, 266–70; unemploy-
ment of, 14; violence toward,
5, 8, 72, 187, 226–27; working, 3, 106, 125–27, 135, 136,
153–54, 261–64. *See also* femininity; girls; mothers

work, 261–70; emotional
restraint at, 261; hours spent
by men at, 106, 154, 172–73;
male attitudes toward,
261–64; of men, changes in,
4–5; power sharing in,
266–70; sexism at, 17, 18–19;
teamwork at, 262

working. *See also* unemployment

working class, 251; absent fathers
in, 196; apprenticeships in, 4,
17; education of, 17; job
opportunities in, 4–5, 6–7,
243

working mothers, 3, 106, 125–27,
135, 136, 153–54

writing skills, 223–25, 228